Cuca, Richard &
Ricky —
Please accept this with
all my gratitude, love,
and friendship.
Your friend, always!
Sydney Forsyth
2/2/87

HISPANIC AMERICAN VOLUNTARY ORGANIZATIONS

HISPANIC AMERICAN VOLUNTARY ORGANIZATIONS

Sylvia Alicia Gonzales

Ethnic American Voluntary Organizations

GREENWOOD PRESS

Westport, Connecticut • London, England

Library of Congress Cataloging in Publication Data

Gonzales, Sylvia Alicia.
  Hispanic American voluntary organizations.

  Bibliography: p.
  Includes index.
  1. Hispanic Americans—Societies, etc.
2. Voluntarism—United States. I. title.
E184.S75G65 1985   362.8′468073   84–19317
ISBN 0–313–20949-9 (lib. bdg.)

Library of Congress Catalog Card Number: 84–19317
ISBN: 0–313–20949-9

First published in 1985

Greenwood Press
A division of Congressional Information Service, Inc.
88 Post Road West
Westport, Connecticut 06881

Printed in the United States of America

10 9 8 7 6 5 4 3 2 1

For those special people who made this work possible. For my family. For my cousins Felix and Maria Dolores Cerda for their loyalty and companionship during the difficult times. And for my friend, Rosa Emma de Ruiz, for her faithful friendship when I needed it most.

Para las personas que hicieron este trabajo realidad. Para mi familia. Para mis primos Felix y Maria Dolores Cerda por su lealtad y companía en los momentos defíciles. Y para mi amiga, Rosa Emma de Ruiz, por su amistad fiel cuando mas la necesité.

Board of Advisors

Contents

Acknowledgments

This volume is a project that has been completed with the support and encouragement of a number of individuals and organizations. Every major work has its acknowledgments. The efforts that went into this work, however, are special because of the nature of the project.

Hispanic American Voluntary Organizations (HAVO) represents the first major attempt to compile a historical dictionary of Hispanic organizations. These are historically based entries with details on the founders, leaders, structure, mergers, and activities, where information was available. The majority of the entries are based on original research.

This was a difficult work to complete. Hispanic American populations in the United States have not had the historical origins of their associations systematically documented. And when they have, there has been a lack of interest on the part of the majority population to collect and preserve them. Thus, until very recently there have been few library collections dedicated to recording this information. For this reason, this author is especially grateful to those individuals and organizations that facilitated the collection of data.

The Board of Advisors merits much gratitude for their assistance in helping this author identify individuals and associations in the Hispanic community. Especially helpful were Polly Baca Barragan, Silvia Unzueta, William Velasquez, and Linda Armas who extended lodging, personal time, and even meals to this author and my research assistant while we were on field investigation. This project would not have been possible without their guidance and personal commitment.

A major contribution to this project was the financial assistance provided to this author by the Robert Kennedy Memorial and the encouragement of its executive director, David Hackett, who gave support throughout the project. Also, RFK administrative assistant Bunny Ronecevic was extraordinary in her visionary support and practical follow-through with Memorial administrative functions concerning this project. The Memorial provided an RFK intern, Carmen Davila, as research assistant to the project for a period of two years. David Hackett continuously emphasized the importance of this work for inculcating the needs, understanding, and aspirations of the Hispanic population into the national consciousness. To David Hackett and the Robert Kennedy Memorial I am grateful.

Carmen Davila assisted in identifying organizations, writing and mailing questionnaires, and compiling working files. She was committed to the project and demonstrated dedication and perseverance, traveling to Washington, D.C., Albuquerque, and San Antonio and throughout the state of California. Carmen deserves special gratitude.

This investigation was also made possible through the support of an Affirmative Action Grant from the state of California and San Jose State University, which provided release time and financial remuneration so that this work could be completed. Instrumental in this support were Dean Gerald Wheeler and Associate Dean Lela Noble of the School of Social Sciences at San Jose State University.

Gratitude is owed University of California at Los Angeles anthropology students Bradford Bagasao and Rosa Colorado for their assistance to the research and compilation of data for the entries. Bradford Bagasao diligently tracked research data during the important mid-stages of this project as well as assisted in the writing of the first draft entries. For his participation, I am profoundly grateful.

Special acknowledgments are expressed to Dr. Andre Simic, Professor of Anthropology, University of Southern California; Dr. Armando Migueles, Professor of Spanish, University of Arizona; and the Robert Kennedy Memorial for their unselfish sharing of archival materials. I humbly thank them.

And finally, I would like to thank my niece, Carolina Lopez, for assisting in the final tasks of alphabetizing index cards, notes, and other organizational details. All of these individuals helped to make this work a reality.

Preface

The Introduction of this work presents the rationale for this first attempt to document historically a significant number of Hispanic American voluntary organizations in the United States. The investigative research and resultant product have determined the immediacy of this work. The introduction discusses the organization, research methodology, and other pertinent information for understanding this volume.

Compilation of resources was a most difficult task since Hispanic populations have tended not to document formally or store relevant historical information. Hispanics are a literary people and there exists an abundance of leaflets, newspapers, and other printed material describing major and minor events in the lives of these people, but there is no single resource or storehouse of information that an investigator can turn to for this information. Only recently have major universities sought to include Hispanic collections in their libraries. The most notable are those stored at the Universities of California at Berkeley and Los Angeles. The University of Miami and the Center for Puerto Rican Studies at City University of New York contain records and files on voluntary organizations, albeit limited.

The task, then, of identifying and documenting the histories, purposes, goals, and organizational structure of these associations, with analysis, requires ingenuity and diligence. It is expected that this initial attempt will facilitate further and more complete documentation. It is also hoped that the publication of this work will encourage organizations to come forward with information to be included in future works.

This volume focuses on the three major Hispanic groups, Mexican American, Puerto Rican, and Cuban. But it also includes information on other Latin American organizations. There is, of historical necessity, a greater inclusion of Mexican American associations. Mexican Americans comprise the largest proportion of Hispanics and have longer and deeper roots in this country. So naturally they have been more active in forming voluntary associations. But a serious attempt was made to document as many Puerto Rican, Cuban, and other Hispanic organizations as possible. When there was no response to the questionnaire described later in this section, special efforts were made to secure the information. These included investigative field trips to New York, Miami, Albuquerque, San Antonio, and Denver. A board of advisors was assembled to assist in identifying organizations and included representatives from the Mexican American, Puerto Rican, and Cuban groups. Individuals were selected on the basis of their accessibility to the required information through their professional or voluntary activities in the respective communities. Telephone contact was also utilized.

This work begins with a historical introduction. That is followed by the body of the work, which contains the organizational profiles. Appendixes include a listing by state of the organizations that were mailed questionnaires and a listing by type of organizations in the book. The latter listing will assist those interested in a particular type of group. There is also a historical chronology for the three major groups and the organizations included in the text to provide the reader with a connection between the establishment of a particular organization and its historical context.

The primary vehicle for securing information on the organizations was a mailed questionnaire. A cover letter also requested articles of incorporation, bylaws, and other printed material. Various archives were consulted, in particular those of the Robert Kennedy Memorial, Professor Andre Simic, and Professor Armando Migueles, as well as directories which have appeared in recent years. The most useful of these was *A Guide to Hispanic Organizations* (1979), compiled under the auspices of the Department of Public Relations of Phillip Morris, Inc. From these sources, addresses were extracted, and the Hispanic American Voluntary Organization's (HAVO) questionnaire and cover letter were mailed out. Appendix 1 lists all of the organizations sent the questionnaire. If an organization failed to respond to the first mailing, it was sent a second and third mailing. Three mailings were sent, totaling over a thousand mailings.

Because the collection and storing of written documentation of Hispanic organizations has been localized at best, it was difficult to include analysis in the writing of these profiles. Only recently have works appeared that present background information on Hispanic voluntary organizations. Most of these recent works have been done as master's and doctoral theses. The source data for the individual entries include these references. Where additional references were available, analysis was included. But in many cases, sources only provided for basic information on the goals, purposes, and organizational structure of the group. Where an organization failed to provide printed material on the association such as newsletters and quarterlies, this material was generally not available, since the compilation of these resource materials is a recent occurrence. So, although organizational publications would provide further study of a particular group, these materials are not readily available to the general public unless one is a member of the organization or the group provides them.

Many of the organizations included in this volume have Spanish names. It was decided that all of the entries should be listed by their official names, whether that name is in Spanish or English. When the official name of an organization is in Spanish, an English translation is provided in parentheses after the entry heading. Thus, the bilingual integrity of this community remains intact. When an organization is known more commonly by a name other than the official name, the text includes an entry providing a cross-reference to the name under which it is discussed. Then, too, an organization may have experienced a name change, in which case cross-references are again provided.

Finally, this author has chosen to use the term *Mexican American* throughout this volume instead of *Chicano*. Chicano is used only when it is part of an official organization name, event, or reference. This decision was based on the novelty of the term, as indicated in the literature. It is evidently recorded that Chicano is not a term instinctive to this population. Yet for many, especially the younger generation, it carries an important and profound significance. Chicano became symbolic of the Mexican American *zeitgeist* of the late 1960s and 1970s. It represented a period and a process, more political in nature, that too often resulted in further polarizations of communities.

This work makes abundantly clear the fact that Mexican Americans are on a course of transcending that period and process. The terminology used in defining personal and group identity is in transition. This work seeks to establish the historical precedent as well as to reflect this transition.

Introduction

The Hispanic population of the United States, despite its rapid increase in size, represents one of the communities least identified as an object for scholarly research. Most of the works currently circulating on this vital group have been written by Hispanics themselves, and oftentimes these studies have been viewed by the scholarly and academic communities as a less than worthy focus of study. Yet, the question of whether the study of Hispanics constitutes an academic discipline meriting investigative pursuit would be moot were the academic community to apply the same critical criteria to the historical and contemporary geopolitical realities of the neighboring hemispheres as it does to other areas of proposed research.

There has been a substantial body of research conducted on the impact of the various ethnic groups on the development of this "melting pot" nation. In the 1950s, studies such as Daniel Patrick Moynihan's work on ethnic isolation directed attention to the investigation of racial and ethnic minorities in the United States. Still, the emphasis was on black Americans.

No other country can claim the masses of immigrants representing such a variety of nations as those that were to sweep across the United States. At the same time, unique among nations has been the broad-based introspection and nervous search for identity that has accompanied the evolution of these populations of immigrants. Perhaps this was the result of the deliberate attempt by the young nation to establish an identity through the forced assimilation of its people. The result, however, was to produce a society fragmented and confused by the tensions borne of the forced fusion of many groups into one.

It can be justifiably argued, within this context, that no group is more deserving of intense study than Hispanics. Other racial and ethnic groups traditionally have come to this country, voluntarily or involuntarily, in large waves and within a limited time period. Their infusion into the larger population already in place was essentially a static one. Not so with Hispanics. Influx over the United States–Mexico borders and from the Puerto Rican commonwealth has been constant and will probably continue to be so regardless of improvement in the economic conditions of the two nations. Bonds are too strong. Family lines cut across these borders with ease and continuity. In addition, the southwestern United States, as well as parts of other areas such as Florida and Louisiana, are deeply rooted in the Hispanic historical past. Because of this, representatives of other Latin American nations are quickly drawn to the culturally active and vibrant Hispanic communities now located throughout the United States. One is just as likely to discover a culturally relevant experience in Chicago, Illinois; Racine, Wisconsin; Lorrain, Ohio; Springfield, Massachusetts; Tucson, Arizona; Miami, Florida; or El Paso, Texas, as one would experience in the cities and towns of Latin America. So it is not economics alone that decides continued Latin American immigration.

The organizations presented in this volume illustrate the expanded demographics of this population. There are nearly 200 national and local voluntary organizations and associations detailed in this work. In addition, there is a listing of organizations with information on these where available but not substantial enough to include in the body of the work. The diversity of the subgroups, as well as the cities and states represented, indicates the increasing importance of this community.

It can no longer be said that Hispanics are concentrated in five southwestern states. Granted, Mexican Americans make up the bulk of Hispanics. But there have been two significant waves of Cuban immigration to the United States. The first occurred immediately following the Cuban revolution in 1952, and the second, the Mariel boatlift, in 1980. The Carter Administration, with Mariel, actively encouraged American patriotism and opened a floodgate of massive Cuban defection from Castro's Cuba, thereby discrediting Marxist communism. Representatives of the first Cuban wave consisted mainly of educated, sophisticated Cubans. These prospered and increased their numbers within the tropical, geographically familiar ambience of Florida, while smaller numbers spread across the United States, contributing substantially to the communities where they settled. The second wave was comprised of products of two decades of Castro policies. They were poorer and less educated. Also, they were made up of a greater racial mix, including whites, blacks, and Indians, as opposed to the first group, which was in the majority white. This made it more difficult for this second wave to be accepted into this race-conscious nation.

The first real movement between Puerto Rico and the United States occurred following World War II in 1945, although the policy for recruiting Puerto Rican workers for United States industries had begun as early as 1943. New York's teeming job market increased a mainland population of only 70,000 in 1940 to 301,000 in 1950. By the 1970 census, there were nearly 1.5 million Puerto Ricans on the mainland, with 650,000 of these second-generation United States born. This group continues to increase rapidly in population, geographical dispersion, and political and professional influence.

Mexican Americans, the largest of the three main Hispanic groups, have deep roots in the history of the United States. Many of those considered part of this group actually date back to the original Spanish settlers. Especially in New Mexico, Arizona, and southern Colorado, there are families whose ancestors have lived under the flags of Spain, Mexico, and the United States. This group has undergone such a startling transformation in the 200 years since the Spaniards first stepped onto southwestern soil that their cultural survival, and even more so stability, is remarkable. Hispanic cultural tradition permeates the southwestern landscape.

This cultural transmission between generations might be explained by the continued penetration of Mexicans into the border states and beyond. But this would hardly account for the permanence of the traditions, music, and even seventeenth-century language forms of the mother country of Spain still remaining in the many towns and villages of New Mexico, for instance. This is highlighted in this work in discussion of the Brothers of Our Father Jesus of Nazareth* (BFJN), more commonly called Los Penitentes. If the history of the Spanish conquest with the persistence of the Indian character through the mestizo personality fails to establish Hispanic peoples as masters of survival, then this documentation of the Hispanic Southwest through voluntary organizations should more than suffice to confirm this.

This introduction to the three major Hispanic groups in the United States is necessarily brief. It is not the intention of this presentation to give a history of these groups, which would each require a major work of its own. But it is important to understand the historical foundations of the Hispanic peoples in relation to the types of organizations that emerged. Of course, the oldest and largest voluntary organizations existed within the Mexican American communities of the southwestern and western United States. There is, too, a sharp contrast in the types of organizations and goals and purposes of the early associations as contrasted to those that formed in the 1950s and later. The early Mexican American groups of the 1800s largely reflected an altruistic, educated, flourishing Hispanic community engaged in discussion meetings surrounding such topics as music, literature, and the predominant intellectual movements of the period. Club Unión* (CU) is an example of this.

That is not to say that all Mexican Americans enjoyed this prosperous and enlightened existence. But a good many did, and as such, it was indicative of a personal growth and intellectual expansion that was abruptly and brutally interrupted. As early as the late 1800s, mass Anglo immigration into the Hispanic Southwest was taking its toll. The devastating effects of discrimination provided the impetus for voluntary associations. Such older organizations as the Alianza

*An asterisk (*) after a title indicates there is an entry on that organization in this book.

Hispano Americana* (AHA) were formed for the specific purpose of counter-acting discrimination and, at the same time, to encourage continuance of the nobility of spirit and behavioral integrity characteristic of early Hispanic communities. Other groups increasingly formed to combat Anglo discrimination and included among them the League of United Latin American Citizens* (LULAC).

After decades of discriminatory practices, diminishing influence of Mexico across the U.S. border, and the advent of two world wars, in particular World War II, in which Mexican American soldiers traveled beyond their Hispanic communities to the European and Pacific theaters, voluntary organizations underwent radical change. No longer were Mexican Americans privileged in the art of intellectual and artistic pursuits. What little remnants of this former existence remained provoked hostility among the majority of Mexican Americans as an example of privilege they had never experienced. Younger Mexican Americans, in particular, had not experienced "*esos tiempos*," those times. Discrimination had relegated "*mexicanos*" to the bottom rungs of the economic, educational, and social ladders.

Confrontation with the harsh realities of ethnic prejudice by returning Mexican American servicemen after World War II caused the formation of such organizations as the American G.I. Forum* (AGIF). But the 1950s brought on a still more radical realization characterized by a growing need for assimilation into American society and culture. The impetus was to anglicize. The Eisenhower decade brought urban flight, an illusion of prosperity, and an extreme push for conformity. Within this climate of a heightened sense of suburbia and middle American social values, Mexican Americans sought increased acceptance by the standards of the predominant group. The Spanish language was forgotten and Hispanic traditions shunned. However, as the French anthropologist Roger Bastide has articulated in his book *Applied Anthropology* (1973), when a group has sacrificed its language and culture, in essence its personal and social identity, and is still not allowed into the decision-making processes of society, they will rebel. U.S. majority society did not readily accept Hispanic mainstreaming. So first, Mexican Americans rebelled. Calling themselves Chicanos, they ushered in a generation of "roots" seekers, or what is scientifically called "a return to nativism."

Puerto Ricans experienced immediate discrimination upon their arrival on the mainland. The groups that formed in the early years after their mass arrival in the 1940s were largely social. However, John Burma in *Spanish-Speaking Groups in the United States* (1954) and Steven Martin Cohen and Robert E. Kapsis in "Participation of Blacks, Puerto Ricans, and Whites in Voluntary Associations" (*Social Forces* 54:4 [June 1978]) contend that Puerto Ricans tended not to form voluntary associations. Particularly Cohen and Kapsis claim that Puerto Rican culture tends to discourage formal affiliation. But this can be argued against in light of the tendency of Hispanics in general to form voluntary associations.

A more probable reason for lack of formal voluntary associations in this early period of Puerto Rican immigration to the mainland was the very poverty and harsh material conditions that met them upon their arrival. These realities did not facilitate formal organizations. But like most other immigrant groups, informal networks surely existed in large numbers. And most likely, limited forms of unrecorded social clubs provided consolation and cultural security for the population.

In the 1960s Latinos joined the civil rights push. Especially Mexican Americans and Puerto Ricans cried for a bigger piece of the American economic pie. Once again this movement determined the kinds of associations that were formed. During this period, formal associations largely concentrated around publicly funded agencies formed to respond to the economic, health and welfare, and educational needs of these communities. In a sense, institutions such as Interstate Research Associates* (IRA) and the Puerto Rican Family Institute* (PRFI) were not true voluntary membership organizations. But they did perform many of the functions of the same and therefore make up a substantial part of this work. In fact, if poverty handicapped Hispanics in their ability to organize, formally, then public funding facilitated it.

Because of the social background of the Cubans that constituted the first major wave of immigration that ended in October 1962, this group did not aggressively join the movement activities of the mid- and late 1960s. Their organizations—such as the Cuban Dental Association in Exile* (CDA) and the Cuban Medical Association in Exile* (CMAE)—reflected the professional makeup of their community. They also tended to despair of the tactics of these other Mexican American and Puerto Rican communities, which smacked too much of revolutionary Cuba. Also, Cubans received massive economic and educational aid upon their arrival in the United States by a nation determined to shelter and provide for the victims of Marxist communism, certainly the fiercest of American patriotic causes. Decidedly more conservative, better educated, and with greater economic support, Cuban Americans tended not to join forces with the other Hispanics in their pursuit of participatory democracy via federal funding but instead championed the virtues of free enterprise and individual initiative as vehicles for upward mobility.

By the mid-1970s, after Mexican Americans, Puerto Ricans, and some other Hispanics had experienced tremendous social gains because of the New Society programs of the Kennedy and Johnson administrations, a new conservatism swept the country, and much of the funding for community-based organizations decreased dramatically. Even with the election of Jimmy Carter to the presidency in 1976, neoconservatives dominated the political landscape. At the same time, Hispanic organizations responded to the climate of the times and adopted a different character and tone. Considerably more sophisticated, albeit not in the erudite fashion of the Mexican American organizations of the 1800s, they sought a politic of unity. Yet unity stubbornly eluded them. This may have been because these organizations became exceedingly more political, backing candidates for office and participating in presidential politics. Politics inherently tends to be divisive. On the local level, Hispanic groups competed with each other for political influence. Political power and community leadership became the spoils while fear of political exclusion was the primary motivation. For the first time real mainstreaming seemed within reach of these groups. So while rhetorically decrying Anglo values and economic materialism, individuals and organizations turned on each other in their scramble to claim a "piece of the action." Gaining a piece of the American pie became synonymous with political action, and Hispanic voluntary organizations reflected this.

The second generation of the first wave of Cubans are definitely more activists than their parents. They too had been introduced to Anglo discrimination, although hardly to the extent imposed upon Mexican Americans and Puerto Ricans. Even more importantly, they had learned the advantages of federal funding for the purposes of community organizing.

During this period, what once was the only vehicle for expanded opportunities for a seriously neglected sector of U.S. society became an instrument of opportunistic self-advancement for the few, with continued exclusion of the many. Typical of many organizations during the 1970s was the claim by the leadership that their organizations, and their organizations alone, were representative of the entire community. These leaders argued that they should, therefore, act as the intermediaries between the Anglo power elite and dispossessed Hispanic communities. In local, state, and national elections they promised to "deliver the Hispanic vote" and, thusly, bargained away their own communities for political gain. Elected officials chose to believe them in lieu of giving attention to the real situation of the majority of Hispanic peoples. In this context, organizations were short-lived. One of the organizations presented in this work easily runs the gamut of changes described here: the Alianza Hispano Americana* (AHA). In its history, the reader witnesses the transformation from altruistic concern to political self-interest of not only an organization but also an entire community.

The 1980s have signaled greater real unity and organizational activity based on coalitions. The universal term *Hispanic* is used to describe the entire community as an extended family of Latinos, a "familia de la raza." An increased educational consciousness and self-confidence have already moved many organizations and individuals away from the self-conscious tactics of the 1970s. It is interesting here to note that these groups seem to have come full circle. In the 1800s even Mexican Americans described themselves as Hispanics because of an enlightened Pan-American vision. They rejected the term in the 1960s in one mammoth act of rebellion that resulted in a clash between generations. For this group, "Chicano" was the battle cry. "Chicanismo," this rebellious quest for identity, had little meaning to an older generation who were raised on shattered hopes for noble dreams but for whom cultural pride was beyond questioning. Perhaps the return to the use of the term *Hispanic* for all the groups signals a healed identity and, as such, a renewed potential for nobility.

Sylvia Gonzales

HISPANIC AMERICAN VOLUNTARY ORGANIZATIONS

A

ACCIÓN '80's (A's) In 1982 United Way (UW) of Tucson became very aware of the poverty in the city's Mexican American community and of the wage differentials between Anglos and Hispanics. Rather than provide funding for expanded human services, this organization considered serving as a catalyst for communitywide change. The UW staff conceived bringing together business, governmental, religious, and educational leaders in an effort to deal with the disparities confronting the Mexican American community. UW may not have been conscious of deeper lines of disparity within the Mexican American community, disparity between an older class of Hispanic elites and more recent working-class immigrants. However, they did call together representatives from the emerging professional Mexican American group, including Jose Gabriel Loyola, Octavio Molera, Dr. Macario Saldate, and Dr. Nelba Chavez. Together, these representatives formed a larger committee to plan for a forum to discuss the needs of Hispanics in Tucson and to recommend specific action for meeting those needs. Gerald Garcia, a newcomer to Tucson and editor and publisher of a local newspaper, was selected to chair the committee. Garcia added a critical, outsider's perspective. However, as a product of Kansas City and originally Beeville, Texas, cities made up primarily of Mexican working immigrants, he may have been handicapped in discerning the political and social nature of the differences within the Mexican American community and thus in following a politic of detachment to group allegiances.

A committee of forty members held its first meeting in April 1982. A result of this and follow-up meetings was a two-day workshop in May. Such topics as health, mental health, education, transportation, housing, employment, media, and the judicial system were discussed. The workshop was successful in paving the way for further discussion. Additional funding was granted from United Way

in the form of staff time and from the Gannett Foundation, which awarded a
$25,000 grant to the group.

On October 7 and 8, Acción '80's hosted 500 participants at a forum held in
Tucson's Doubletree Hotel. Once again, workshops and discussion sessions
addressed the needs of Tucson's Hispanic community. From this civic forum
emerged the organization. Acción '80's appears to be an ad hoc committee
charged with sponsoring annual forums. There is an ambiguity reflected in their
literature regarding organizational structure. A report entitled "Acción '80's
Purpose, Structure, and Process" presents an elaborate organizational chart including the role of an executive committee, planning committee, topic areas,
and process. But it is still unclear how the organization functions. The leadership
seems to be undecided as to whether it envisions a voluntary organization or a
community-based agency. It proposes providing for a speakers bureau, a request
and contact file, a phone tree, and a quarterly bulletin as well as an organizational
brochure. There is also included provisions for media inclusion. Membership
consists of the categories of regular, sustaining, honorary, corporate, and
institutional.

Acción '80's has received considerable coverage from both the *Arizona Daily
Star* and the *Tucson Daily Citizen*. The organization issues a press packet containing individual newspaper articles upon request. However, the packet presents
clippings without dates of publication. The group has also published information
on the organization's goals and objectives as well as its brief history. Several
of the forum speeches are also available upon request. Most of this information
is available from the organization's spokesperson, Gerald Garcia, at the *Tucson
Daily Citizen*.

**AGRUPACIÓN PROTECTIVA MEXICANA (MEXICAN PROTECTIVE
ASSOCIATION) (APM)** Most Hispanic organizations of the early 1900s were
divided into moderate and radical factions. One of the more moderate groups to
form was the Agrupación Protectiva Mexicana, which was organized in 1911 in
San Antonio, Texas. At another time, however, the activities of the APM would
hardly be considered moderate. APM's goals were to protect Mexicans from
increasing discrimination and violence and to organize farmworkers. But in 1911
there were considerable political stirrings on the Mexican–American border.
Mexico was engaging in its violent struggle for political reform and the border
state of Texas was greatly affected by this revolutionary movement and its militant
response to social injustice.

At the Primer Congreso Mexicanista* (PCM) in San Antonio in 1911, the
Agrupación received criticism from the partisans of Ricardo Flores Magón, a
labor organizer in the Southwest. Magón accused the Agrupación of misappro-
priation of funds and of not being fit to carry the fight against the "bourgeoisie."
This attack was apparently in response to the organization's refusal to help the
Magonistas when they were being prosecuted in Marfa, Texas, for violating the
neutrality laws.

This organization also functioned as a mutual aid society. Its membership included property owners, shopkeepers, and tenants. Internal dissension split the organization in 1914.

The Agrupación appears in discussions of the Primer Congreso Mexicanista* (PCM), which include Rodolfo Acuña, *Occupied America* (1981), and Jose E. Limon, "El Primer Congreso Mexicanista de 1911: A Precursor to Contemporary Chicanismo," *Aztlan* (Spring and Fall 1974).

ALIANZA FEDERAL DE MERCEDES (FEDERAL ALLIANCE OF MERCEDES) See ALIANZA FEDERAL DE PUEBLOS LIBRES.

ALIANZA FEDERAL DE PUEBLOS LIBRES (FEDERAL ALLIANCE OF FREE COMMUNITIES) (AFPL) In the early 1960s an organizational nucleus concerned with the problems of the dispossessed and impoverished Hispanics of New Mexico began to stir new hope throughout the Southwest. Social forces had worked to destroy the autonomy of the rural Hispanic way of life. One way to challenge these forces was to initiate a movement to reclaim original Spanish land grants.

Originally called the Alianza Federal de Mercedes (Federal Alliance of Mercedes),* the Alianza focused its efforts toward the restitution of lands to the heirs of Spanish land grants through constitutional means. The organization planned to achieve these goals by forcing the U.S. government to honor the Treaty of Guadalupe Hidalgo, which ended the two-year war between the United States and Mexico in 1848. The treaty had committed the U.S. government to protect the rights of the Mexican people who remained in the newly acquired territory of the United States. In addition to the question of acres lost and their cash value, the Alianza wanted to draw attention to the effects of Anglo internal colonialism. The organization attributed the depopulation and destruction of their communities, inaccessibility to the resources of their ancestral lands, and dire conditions of poverty to this colonialism.

The founder and president of the Alianza was Reies Lopez Tijerina. Tijerina was the son of poor Texas farm laborers and a descendant of dispossessed Texas land grantees. He had had little formal schooling but possessed obvious talents, the most formidable of these being his charismatic public speaking ability. He further developed this talent as a minister of the Assembly of God sect, preaching his faith as he and his family traveled the migrant labor stream.

In the 1950s Tijerina settled a cooperative village on cheap desert lands in Arizona with nineteen farmworker families. In 1957, after business interests decided the property was valuable real estate, the village was burned down. The Tijerinas then moved to northern New Mexico, where they became acquainted with the various groups attempting to assert their rights around the issue of land grants. These people faced a futile struggle against government indifference and oppressive dependence on welfare. Under these circumstances, the idea to unite all land grant heirs was born.

Earlier, Tijerina's evangelical work had taken him to Mexico, where he interested himself in the Mexican revolution and its land reforms. In the 1960s he returned to Mexico and managed to spend three winters there studying land grant law and history in the national archives and consulting with scholars in the field. He personally visited with then President Miguel Aleman, to whom he suggested the possibility of some kind of recognition by Mexico of the land grant demands. As a result of his intensive research, he was convinced that the National Forest in Tierra Amarilla belonged to the Pueblo de San Joaquin de Chama. He also learned that there were a total of 1,715 land grants in the United States and that most had not been honored by the U.S. government.

He returned to New Mexico with extensive facts and information and began to meet with the land grant heirs. After weighing the advantages of uniting into an organization, the Alianza was formally incorporated in October 1963. One of its first acts was to demand a congressional investigation into the circumstances under which the grants had been handled since 1846.

San Joaquin de Chama was *ejido* (communal or village) land that, according to Hispano-Mexican law, could not be sold but was to be held in common by all people. Villagers had the right to graze their animals and cut and gather timber in these forest lands. The Treaty of Guadalupe, according to Tijerina, committed the U.S. government to protecting the rights of the people, but instead it participated in frauds that deprived the people of the *ejido* lands. Tijerina also became involved with the Albiquiu Corporation, the forerunner of the AFPL, an organization committed to the return of the lands to Hispanos in an effort to unite the people.

On July 2–4, 1966, the Alianza led a march to the state capitol from Albuquerque, where they petitioned the state authorities for the return of the lands.

On October 15, 1966, Tijerina and the AFPL physically occupied the national forest campgrounds known as the Echo Amphitheater in an attempt to "revive" the land grant community of San Joaquin de Chama, whose 1,400 acres lie mainly within the confines of the Kit Carson National Forest. The group remained there. Accompanying them was Francisco Salazar, a direct descendant of the founder of the pueblo. In less than a week, state police, the sheriff's deputies, and rangers began to move in. On November 6, 1967, Tijerina stood trial for the Amphitheater affair. The original charges included conspiracy but the jury dismissed it. It did, however, convict him of two counts of assault. He was sentenced to two years in the state penitentiary, with five years' probation. Tijerina protested that the court had convicted him for a political crime and that the court had no jurisdiction. He appealed the conviction and was released on bond.

Before the trial of November 6, 1967, Tijerina made national news by leading the so-called raid on the Tierra Amarilla Courthouse on June 5, 1967. The main reason for entering the courthouse was to make a citizen's arrest of Alfonso Sanchez, district attorney. They could not find the district attorney. They met resistance and a fight broke out. Several people were wounded. The Tijerina group then left the area with two lawmen as hostages. The Tierra Amarilla Courthouse raid touched off a massive manhunt that involved New Mexico National Guard planes, helicopters, and tanks. Relatives and suspects were rounded up and kept prisoners in an open yard with minimum conveniences. Tijerina decided to surrender. But as soon as he was out on bail he was active again.

In October 1967, Tijerina took part in opposition activities to the El Paso Cabinet Committee Hearings. The hearings were organized by President Johnson's Cabinet Committee on Mexican American Affairs. Tijerina also appeared on numerous college and university campuses and attended numerous rallies called by black militants. In May and June 1968, Tijerina participated in the Poor People's Campaign. In the fall of 1968, he ran for governor of New Mexico on the People's Constitutional Party ticket.

On November 12, 1968, Tijerina stood trial for the courthouse raid. Much of the trial centered around the right to make a citizen's arrest. Tijerina proved his points, and the jury ultimately entered a verdict of not guilty. On June 5, 1969, Tijerina again attempted to occupy the Kit Carson National Forest at the Coyote campsite. He allegedly resisted arrest and pointed a carbine at one of the rangers and subsequently was charged with aiding and abetting the destruction of U.S. Forest Service signs and assaulting and threatening a federal agent. For this incident he was sentenced on January 5, 1970, to three years in federal prison. He spent seven months in solitary and was released in the summer of 1971. During the time he spent in prison, the disparity grew between Tijerina's direction and the Mexican American movement. While in prison he made the announcement that he was resigning from the Alianza because he disagreed with AFPL strategy as approved by the membership during his incarceration. That strategy mainly consisted of a petition to President Nixon demanding the return of the bulk of the Southwest to the Chicano people. From that point on the Alianza's activities declined.

The Alianza as a structural organization consisted of a president, vice-president, and secretary-treasurer. Membership within the organization was comprised mainly of poor Hispanics in New Mexico. There is no accurate membership count because Reies Tijerina did not disclose rosters. Membership dues were one dollar per family per month.

During the height of the Alianza's activities, there was much media coverage, including articles in major magazines such as *Time*, and there was even a film produced on the raid. However, much of the writings on the Alianza and Reies Tijerina have been sensational and distorted by ethnocentric bias. One of the most fair and accurate chronicles of New Mexico history has been Frances Leon Swadesh, *Los Primeros Pobladores: Hispanic Americans of the Ute Frontier* (1974). Also useful are Swadesh, "The Alianza Movement: Catalyst for Social Change in New Mexico," *Proceedings of the 1968 Annual Spring Meeting of the American Ethnological Society* (1968):162–77; and Swadesh, "The Alianza Movement: The Interplay of Social Change and Public Commentary," in *Minorities and Politics* (1969), Henry J. Tobias and Charles Woodhouse, eds.

Other sources on the Alianza include Peter Nabokov, *Tijerina and the Courthouse Raid* (1969); and Richard Gardner, *Grito Reies Tijerina and the New Mexico Land Grant War of 1967* (1970). Among the more recent Mexican American works is Rodolfo Acuña, *Occupied America* (1981).

ALIANZA HISPANA (HISPANIC ALLIANCE) (AH) Located in Roxbury, Massachusetts, this organization was created in 1969 to help the Hispanic community of Boston achieve better living conditions and equality as well as socioeconomic and political independence.

The Alianza Hispana offers education services, employment counseling, youth services, senior citizen groups, home ownership and rehabilitation services, consumer mediation, general advocacy, and information referrals.

This brief description of the Alianza Hispana is contained in the archives of the Robert Kennedy Memorial in Washington, D.C. There is little other material available on this organization. The organization must have unpublished materials, however, such as meeting minutes for its members.

ALIANZA HISPANO AMERICANA (HISPANIC AMERICAN ALLIANCE) (AHA) The history and purpose of this organization was documented in 1928 by Tomas Serrano Cabo in *Las Crónicas (The History) of the Alianza Hispano Americana.* According to Cabo, Hispanic residents of Arizona found it necessary to unite in order to become strong and to defend their rights. Because of the "bad will" that existed against Hispanics at the time, it was decided that an organization was necessary to generate respect and to protect Hispanics.

Cabo elaborates extensively on the choice of the name *Hispanic American.* In abundantly baroque Spanish, so typical of early Hispanic writings, he explains that the Hispanics of the southwestern United States felt a strong spiritual and cultural connection with all of Latin America. The theme of Pan-Americanism is so strong and eruditely described throughout this historical document that the reader is rewarded with a portrait of an educated, intellectual, and culturally refined Hispanic community. In florid language, Cabo describes the cultural heritage of the "mother country," a heritage of outstanding literature, music, and language which is shared with Hispanos of the Southwest.

The Alianza was founded, according to *Las Crónicas*, with a noble spirit of fraternity and to embark on a path of practical solutions designed to create a better society for all. Most important, it was an organization founded by Hispanics for Hispanics and with the distinction of being the first of its kind to expand its membership beyond the United States and to enlist thousands of members.

The beginnings of the Alianza were superficially political. On January 14, 1894, Carlos I. Velasco invited Hispanos to a political meeting which resulted in the idea for a mutual aid society. The actual founders of this organization, Carlos I. Velasco, Pedro C. Pellón, and Mariano G. Samaniego, had long been laying the mental groundwork for such an association. And the choice of a mutual aid society hinted at the deeper purpose of the organization.

The bylaws for the new organization gave its official name as "Sociedad de Alianza Hispano-Americana" (Society of the Hispanic American Alliance), but it was always known simply as the Alianza Hispano Americana. The new board of directors was unanimously elected and included Carlos I. Velasco, president; Pedro C. Pellón, first vice-president; Hilario Urquides, second vice-president; Enrique Meyer, first secretary; Manuel Montijo, second secretary; and Mariano G. Samaniego, treasurer. It was also unanimously agreed that meetings would be held twice a month. Carlos I. Velasco, Carlos Tully, and Pedro C. Pellón were charged with writing the bylaws. The founding members of the Alianza were Pedro P. López, B. Brichta, Carlos H. Tully, Manuel Caballero, Carlos Jácome, Filiberto Aguirre, Fernando Aguilar, Pablo Soto, Lucas Estrella, Ramón Gallegos, J. M. Valdenegro, Carlos Castelum, R. Gurrola, Ignacio Terrazas, Max Zuñiga, Santiago Ward, Carlos I. Velasco, Pedro C. Pellón, Hilario Urquides, Enrique Meyer, Manuel Montijo, Mariano G. Samaniego, J. M. Martínez, Ignacio Calvillo, and Miguel Riesgo, and others who are not listed.

The original officers served throughout 1894–95. Elections were held in 1896, and Pedro C. Pellón was elected president to serve for another two years. During the presidency of Pellón, six chapters were established, taking on numerical designations such as Chapter 1 (Florence), Chapter 2 (Clifton), Chapter 3 (Bisbee), Chapter 4 (Globe), Chapter 5 (Tempe), and Chapter 6 (Nogales), all of these in Arizona. Each of these chapters were autonomous until 1897, when the Supreme Chapter was created with its new president, Mariano G. Samaniego. Samaniego resigned shortly afterward, however, and Samuel Brown was named as his replacement. The Tucson headquarters was known as Chapter 0 until the seventh convention of the organization held in El Paso, Texas, when it was designated Founding Chapter.

Since its inception, the Alianza had been an association of persons dedicated to moral and altruistic goals. In 1902, the Alianza decided to incorporate the organization under the laws of the state of Arizona. It is not known whether it was through lack of information or negligence that the AHA followed incorrect filing procedures and remained in legal limbo until 1913.

The first convention of the AHA was held in Tucson, Arizona, in 1897. A committee composed of F. A. Ordematt, Samuel Brown, Ignacio W. Covarrubias, Carlos Tully, and Pedro Salazar was charged with writing the organizational bylaws. They consulted with many prominent individuals and finally decided to borrow almost verbatim from the bylaws of the Antigua Orden de Trabajadores Unidos de America (Traditional Order of United Workers of America), one of the oldest North American institutions, founded by John Jordan Upchurch, a distinguished and celebrated Mason.

The various chapters of the Alianza were called lodges, as was common with other esoteric and fraternal societies. *Las Crónicas* spells out the kind of members the Alianza desired. Most important were individuals of sound moral and noble character. Its founding principles were based on the teachings of Christ, which encouraged charity, virtue, and brotherhood and actively discouraged hate, scandal, jealousy, and violence. Because it was basically a mutual aid society offering life insurance, the AHA stressed the importance of work. The Alianza did not admit exconvicts or individuals not comitted to hard work, according to its bylaws. It also did not admit "persons of African heritage or of the yellow race." Historian Cabo takes pains to explain this latter policy as stemming from the organization's being made up of Hispanics and for Hispanics. It is interesting to note that Cabo's deliberate attempt to explain the exclusion of these groups acknowledges early on a shared social plight while advocating an autonomous response.

Because of its Masonic modeling, it was decided that the AHA should establish an official ritual. Ritual symbolisms were designed and executed. In 1910 a commission was assigned the task of revising the ritual. It was left intact. But six years later Antonio A. Sedillo was again commissioned to revise the ritual. His contribution was to assure that the ritual in no way excluded the "feminine application." In other words, he made sure the ritual was nonsexist.

The emblem of the Alianza was a triangle and a circle. The colors were red, white, and purple, symbolizing protection, morality, and education. The selection of these colors as described in *Las Crónicas* was based on the highest knowledge of mystical principles. In discussing the use of purple, for instance, Cabo speaks of the association of purple with the human spirit's noblest aspirations to understand and analyze the universe. The color purple to the Alianza signified peace, meditation, and critical thinking. The colors were used on stamps, insignias, jewelry, and other articles made available to members. Different shades of gold were also included on Alianza articles to symbolize both the United States and Spain, the dual heritage of Hispanic Americans.

In terms of Alianza allegory, two crossed hands in salutation symbolized the intimate and fraternal union of Spain with Latin America, again, the Alianza's strong theme of Pan-Americanism. The laurel branch stood for peace and glory, the shield for protection, the flower for purity, the book for education, and the triangle for protection, morality, and education as well as for *alianza* (alliance). And finally, and of greatest significance, a skull on the emblem stood for protest. It was customary for initiates to put the hand over the emblem, a ritual to continue for as long as there was a need to protest.

The first bylaws of the Alianza Hispano Americana were signed on January 28, 1894, by Carlos I. Velasco and Enrique Meyer. They specify the following: all members shall have a vote; members shall be obligated to attend all meetings of the association including special meetings and general sessions; members shall live an honest and exemplary life; members shall pay monthly dues of twenty-five cents and one dollar in the case of death of a member for contribution to the member's family; members shall carry out assignments of the executive board; prospective members shall be nominated by two members and approved by the majority of members at the nominating meeting; meetings shall be held every fifteen days with a majority of the members present. The bylaws also clarified the manner and reasons for which members could be expelled as follows:

five members petition for expulsion; nonpayment of dues for three months; absence from meetings for three consecutive months without legitimate cause; less than exemplary behavior. The expulsion was to be decided at the general sessions and with a two-thirds vote of those present.

Fifteen members were required to be present for general sessions, and the executive board met the second and last Sundays of each month. Members of the executive board were elected the first Sunday of each year for a one-year term. Membership was open to those between the ages of twenty-one and fifty. All members were urged to advise the executive board of the arrest and incarceration of any Hispanic and to provide, in detail, facts and circumstances in the case so that the board could determine whether the Alianza should provide protection. And finally, seven individuals were necessary to constitute an Alianza chapter. Chapters were to contribute one dollar of their dues to headquarters.

In order to provide insight into the organization's inspirational foundation and its relative success throughout a long history of activity, it is important to discuss the backgrounds of its founders. The "father," founder, and first president of the Alianza was Carlos I. Velasco, who was born in Hermosillo, Sonora, Mexico, in 1837. Velasco completed a law degree there and went on to serve in key positions with the Mexican government. He moved to the Arizona territory, where in 1878 he organized the first Spanish-language newspaper in Tucson, *El Fronterizo*, and subsequently dedicated his life and career to journalism.

The second president of the Alianza, Pedro C. Pellón, was born in Spain in 1852 and moved to Tucson at the age of twenty-three. Pellón, together with Carlos Tully, the first secretary of the Alianza, was largely responsible for the expansion of the association. They were the Alianza's organizers, Pellón mainly in California and Tully in Arizona. Pellón, Tully, and Velasco were called the "apostles of the society" by *The Alianza*, the official publication of the AHA. Once again note the tendency toward Christian/spiritual terminology.

Mariano Samaniego, another of the AHA founders, was an 1862 graduate of the University of St. Louis in Missouri, where he received high honors. He also served with the Confederate Army of Texas during the Civil War. Active in Democratic politics, he served Arizona for three years as a delegate from Pima County to the territorial legislature. He was a county supervisor for ten years and Pima County's first assessor. He served on the Tucson City Council and University of Arizona Board of Regents. Samaniego was also a businessman who owned and operated Tucson's largest freight company, which he sold in 1880. In 1897, Samaniego was installed as the first supreme president of the Alianza.

Samuel Brown was born in San Francisco, California, to a Mexican mother and Anglo father. His father died when he was fourteen. After attending schools in Los Angeles, Brown was forced to leave that city at an early age for Tucson, where he sought the means to support his family. Brown became the second supreme president of the Alianza in 1902 and served until 1927. A Republican, he was elected to represent that party in the state legislature, where he advanced the cause of education. He also served as mayor of Tucson, as well as a city council member.

Another prominent founder of the Alianza was Carlos Jácome. Jácome founded a general store in Tucson that subsequently became a highly regarded department store and fine example of Hispanic business leadership. It continued to operate into the 1970s, when a changing central district forced it to close its doors. A Republican representative to the Arizona Constitutional Convention in 1910, Jácome assisted in writing the state constitution.

A source of great pride for the Alianza was the participation of the Honorable Antonio A. Sedillo of New Mexico. Sedillo was also a founder and supreme president from 1927 to 1933. Educated in law in New Mexico, he practiced in New Mexico, Texas, California, and Arizona. He represented his district as a delegate to the New Mexico Constitutional Convention of 1912. He held various state and federal posts and defended cases before the U.S. Supreme Court. He served as solicitor for the Second and Fifth Judicial Districts. Sedillo was most responsible for formulating the rituals and symbols of the AHA.

In spite of the fact that these founders were educated and prosperous individuals, the organization appealed to and encouraged membership of persons of humble origins. As long as the individual members were honest and hard-working and persons of integrity, they were welcomed into the Alianza. As a matter of fact, the majority of the organization's members were poor and working-class, and the Alianza was dedicated to solving their problems. These more successful founders saw a moral imperative in raising the political, educational, economic, and spiritual consciousness of the entire Hispanic community.

The united thrust and sound organizational strategy demonstrated at the first 1897 convention allowed for expansion of the Alianza to 320 southwestern cities and also to Illinois and Pennsylvania. In addition to the U.S. chapters, fifteen lodges were established in Mexico City and four Mexican states.

It is interesting to note here that at the time of this expansion there was considerable debate as to whether Californios (Hispanic Californians) should be looked upon as part of the "Hispanic family." The reasoning for not including Californios centered around their tendency to be more Anglo and English-language oriented than Hispanic and Spanish-language oriented. There was greater "dependency" in California on the North American government than in the southwestern states. Chronicler Cabo refers, however, to the works of Californio Jorge Santayana as an example of the permanence of the Hispanic cultural heritage within an articulate English-language literary world. He also points to the city of Los Angeles with its Spanish architecture, fiestas, municipal coat-of-arms, and other artifacts of Hispanic origin to dispute any quarrel with the inclusion of Californios in the Alianza's extended family.

For purposes of incorporation in the state of Arizona, the Alianza Hispano Americana wrote its constitution, dated December 21, 1902. Although basically the AHA proclaimed the same goals and purposes as originally proposed, the organization began to take on a new and different tone. In just eight years, the reference to the spiritual, quasi-Masonic vision of the founders was being superseded by other concerns. The constitution's language no longer referred to the dignity of the human spirit or the moral obligations of fraternity. In fact, the streamlined and sophisticated document concentrated solely on the business and administrative functions of a voluntary association. This change in theme seemed to reflect a far deeper socio-historical transition that was occurring throughout the Hispanic Southwest.

In 1903 the Alianza's attention focused on labor rights as a result of the Clifton-Morenci district mining strike. Also, the organization supported the 1915 copper strikes, which sought equal pay for Mexicans. The interests of the Alianza at this time were further diversified when it fought for the rights of Mexican children within the school system, especially through the Tolleson and West-minister civil rights desegregation cases.

In the early 1920s, the Alianza began to focus its attention positively on civil rights and fair treatment of Mexicans who had problems with the law. The organization's leadership believed that legal and civil rights paved the way for all other rights. According to some recent historians, this moved the organization toward a search for political power based on full political participation. But it should also be noted that the more recent accounts of the Alianza ignore the fact that there was full political participation by most of the founders of the Alianza. These accounts are written from the perspective of the 1960s Chicano political movement, in which the experience of ethnic isolation and discrimination predominated.

Acting as a legal aid society, the Alianza and its chapters established a legal defense fund. It provided legal assistance to Mexicans who could not afford a lawyer and sought to assure that legal procedures would afford the poor a fair trial. Alianza legal aid was centered around the issues of civil rights, opposition to capital punishment, educational inequalities, and aid for the alien worker.

In 1921 the AHA valiantly fought against the injustice of capital punishment. The reasons for the Alianza's stance were much the same as contemporary arguments against capital punishment—the execution of a possibly innocent person. The Alianza's concerns were heightened, however, by the denial of due process to defenseless Mexican Americans. The case that drew the attention of the Alianza was that of Aurelio Pompa. The AHA asked the governor of California to intercede on behalf of Pompa so that he could be tried fairly in a court of law.

The Tolleson school case occurred in 1951, when the AHA stepped in to assure the end of legal segregation in Arizona. Alianza attorneys Gregorio Garcia and Ralph Estrada argued in federal court that the Tolleson schools were not equal in that Mexican children were assigned to inferior schools solely on the basis of their ethnicity. The federal court ruled in favor of the AHA attorneys.

In Winslow, Arizona, the local AHA chapter challenged an ordinance that designated Wednesday as Mexican American swim day. City policy specified that Wednesday was the only day that Mexican Americans could use the municipal pool. Thursday the pool was emptied and disinfected. AHA pressure and publicity persuaded the city officials to change their policy.

As is common during periods of severe economic distress, the government and the press during the post–Korean War period initiated a propaganda campaign against alien labor. Similar to the Immigration and Naturalization Service (INS) raids organized around the recession and high unemployment during the Reagan Administration, Mexican nationals became the target of irrational and discriminatory behavior by government officials. The INS, however, went even further during this period and engaged in a massive, military-style deportation campaign. Families were separated, and people were exposed to mass arrests. Not only Mexican nationals were affected but also Mexican Americans.

Alianza attorneys intervened on behalf of Mexicans, especially in the case of Daniel C. Gonzalez, a U.S. citizen, who was accused of evading the draft by going to Mexico during the Korean War. Gonzalez was deported and deprived of his U.S. citizenship. The Alianza lawyers' reasonable and just arguments against the arbitrary use of immigration law to deport and revoke Gonzalez's citizenship won the favorable ruling of the Supreme Court. These successful legal efforts by the AHA persuaded the organization to establish a sub-group, the American Council on Spanish Speaking People (ACSSP), dedicated to the pursuit of legal and social justice for Mexican Americans as guaranteed by the U.S. Constitution.

In 1955 the Alianza civil rights division was established to coordinate the activities of its legal aid society and the ACSSP. The first head of the civil rights division was Ralph Guzman, an East Los Angeles community activist. This division joined with the National Association for the Advancement of Colored People (NAACP) and the American Civil Liberties Union (ACLU) in championing the civil rights of minorities.

The Alianza's prestige was further enhanced with World War II and the world's fight against fascism. The organization was uncompromising in its condemnation of Hitler's forces in Europe. A large number of the Alianza's members joined the armed forces, winning war commendations for their heroic efforts in Europe and the Pacific. Raul Morín, a war correspondent and member of the AHA, documented the participation of Mexican Americans in the war in his book, *Among the Valiant, Mexican Americans in World War II and Korea* (1966). The Alianza worked diligently to promote national patriotism during the war. It held parades celebrating "human liberty." It collected millions of dollars for the war effort through its campaign to sell U.S. war bonds. It initiated a letter-writing campaign for the soldiers. And it ran Red Cross centers serving the non-English-speaking.

The year 1960 was another turning point for the AHA. The new Supreme Council leadership, perhaps possessed of a different and contrary vision to that of the association's founders, joined the Kennedy presidential campaign through the establishment of Viva Kennedy Clubs. These "Chicanos," armed with a new name and a political rather than spiritual purpose, sought to install under the auspices of the Alianza a power-brokering system reminiscent of that which they witnessed among Anglo political bosses. They offered the large AHA membership as bargaining chips for negotiating this contract for greater political gains. And with this they ushered in a new cycle of Hispanic/Chicano activity that predominated in Mexican American communities during the 1960s and 1970s and continued somewhat into the 1980s. The noble intent of the AHA founders to encourage the wealthier, more educated Hispanics to assist in the advancement of the less fortunate and, thus, the advancement of the entire Hispanic family gave way to bitter rivalries within this community. The Chicano-identified were pitted against Hispanic-identified, the less educated against the better educated, the grass roots against the more established professionals. And a few politicians reaped the benefits of this dissension. The cultural unity of the past was replaced with arguments as to who best represented the "grass-roots" community. This resulted in a policy of exclusion of, often, the better educated and prepared of Hispanics, including descendants of the original founders. This eventually led to the decline of the organization.

More recent Mexican American writers have referred to this as a time of political accommodation. It could better be described as a period of ambition and indiscriminate power seeking on the part of Mexican Americans anxious to get a "piece of the American pie." They modeled themselves after Anglo power figures with whom they associated. They chastized these same for their discriminatory practices while emulating their political tactics. This was in great contrast to the early Hispanic heritage of the Velascos, Sedillos, and Tullys, and it caused much dissension within the Tucson-based fraternal lodge. Many of the old-timers wondered whether this organizational decline paralleled a decline in the organization's purpose, that which had propelled the AHA from its early organizational efforts to the most numerous and prosperous of Hispanic organizations in the United States.

Following the successful election of John F. Kennedy to the presidency of the United States, AHA Supreme President Ralph Estrada was appointed director of operations of the Agency for International Development in Latin America. Civil rights division head, Ralph Guzman, was appointed Peace Corps country director in Venezuela. And finally, James C. McCormick, son-in-law of Estrada, ascended to the position of president of the Alianza. This last transition, a not uncommon instance of Estrada family mobility within the hierarchy of the Alianza, provoked charges of nepotism within the organizational ranks.

This once highly respected, high-purposed organization began its final decline in the late 1960s. Its membership, which once numbered over 20,000, now stood at 6,100. The leadership unsuccessfully called for increased membership among younger Mexican Americans. But the younger generation just wasn't interested. The Alianza leadership reasoned that increased educational opportunities for Mexican American youth had protected them from the harsh realities of past discriminatory practices and that this younger generation therefore saw little need for an organized body of action.

The Alianza had been a powerful political machine, especially in the state of Arizona. Anglo American and Hispanic politicians joined as active members. These included Representatives Stewart and Morris Udall, Senator Barry Goldwater, and Mayor Don Hummal of Tucson. The editor of a September 1961 issue of the *Alianza Magazine* went as far as to write, "Fraternalism, as it is practiced today, is neither brotherly nor spiritually enlightening, . . . political aspirants have joined the society with the mistaken intention that they will receive the 'Mexican vote.' "

And finally, in 1959 allegations began to surface that the Alianza was being mismanaged. On May 23, 1966, the Alianza Supreme Council filed a $68,465 lawsuit against the Valley National Bank of Tucson. The suit alleged that the bank had paid out that amount on forged signatures. The transactions covered the period from November 1, 1962, to August 8, 1963: the period during which James C. McCormick served as supreme president. The following year, on January 27, McCormick was convicted of eleven counts of embezzlement. Also, the Arizona Appeals Court had discovered that McCormick had exercised a promissory note of $164,096 payable at the rate of $100 per month and interest-free allowing 136 years and nine months to pay the loan. The Superior Court set a bond of $15,000, which McCormick was unable to raise. He was imprisoned February 2, 1967, and was later sentenced to a six-to-eight-year prison term after a conviction of stealing funds from the Alianza.

Alianza finances were audited by Richard W. Bean, an insurance actuary from Los Angeles, who reported to the insurance commissioner of California that $281,426 had been spent illegally in air travel by the fraternal president and that a mortgage loan of $101,355 had been made to the Pan American Corporation, for which McCormick also served as president. In June 1965, the Pan American Corporation went into bankruptcy and the Alianza was forced to assume control of the defunct radio stations. There were several other unauthorized loans, which included: $75,000 to Arizona Newspapers, Inc., in 1962; a mortgage loan to Mr. Emilio V. Carrillo and wife for a property purchased in a sheriff's sale on June 5, 1958, and for an amount larger than the actual purchase price; and other mortgage loans to Carlos R. Estrada made in 1959 and 1962, when his father, Ralph Estrada, was president. Bean's appraisal showed Alianza assets at $924,013 and liabilities at $1,487,422, with a deficit of $563,408. The Maricopa County Superior Court stepped in to supervise the finances of the Alianza while the organization underwent management and financial reorganization.

Eventually McCormick's lawyers managed to have all twenty-one counts of embezzlement leveled against him dismissed. McCormick pleaded guilty to grand theft of $150 and on December of 1969 was sentenced to five years' probation by the Pima County Superior Court. The Alianza entered into receivership with the same Emilio C. Carrillo, one of three individuals charged with this function.

Jose Amaro Hernandez, in his doctoral dissertation, attributes the decline of the Alianza to a lack on the part of the executive officers of management and business skills, especially in dealing with large sums of money. This political scientist even goes so far as to say that, although the men and women in the Supreme Council were devoted to the principles and goals set by the founders of the order, they simply lacked financial expertise and efficiency. The historical record refutes this analysis. The original founders of the Alianza were extremely successful and prosperous businessmen. Even more so, those individuals most intimately involved in the leadership during the Alianza's decline were astute politicians, some of them charged with managing large federal budgets as Kennedy Administration appointees.

The Alianza, then, is a remarkable story of the Hispanic Southwest, but its historical lessons are universal. The comprehensive record clearly indicates that the Alianza's decline and eventual extinction was due not to a lack of skills or expertise but to a decline in purpose.

There are two important sources on the Alianza Hispano Americana. First is *Alianza*, the official publication of the organization, the entire series of which is housed in the Special Collection of the University of Arizona, Tucson. Also, *Las Crónicas*, published by the AHA in 1928, is the official history of the organization. This author was able to secure a copy of *Las Crónicas* from an original member, but it is not certain how many have survived and where they are held. Newspaper accounts from the *Arizona Daily Star* on Alianza activities over much of the organization's existence are preserved on microfilm at the Arizona Heritage Center in Tucson. Although many contemporary writers on Mexican American studies have discussed the Alianza, perhaps the most comprehensive studies are Kaye L. Briegel, "Alianza Hispano Americana, 1894–1965: A Mexican American Fraternal Insurance Society" (Ph.D. dissertation, University of Southern California, 1974); and Jose Amaro Hernandez, "The Political Development of Mutual Aid Societies in the Mexican American Communities: Ideals and Principles" (Ph.D. dissertation, University of California, Riverside, 1979).

AMERICAN ASSOCIATION OF SPANISH-SPEAKING CERTIFIED PUBLIC ACCOUNTANTS (AASSCPA) In 1970 Hispanic Americans represented 5.2 percent of the total U.S. population. At the same time only 0.3 percent of certified public accountants in the country were of Hispanic descent. In June 1972 a group of Hispanic accountants, concerned with narrowing this gap, founded AASSCPA in Los Angeles, California, as a national nonprofit organization. Among the founders and leaders of this organization were Joe Acosta, Andrew J. Alderete, Michael Cardenas, Ralph A. Cordova, Gustavo L. Garcia, Seferino Hernandez, Robert S. Marquez, Ramon Navarro, Joe B. Pacheco, Felipe L. Quezada, Benjamin Ramirez, and Ray Salazar. All of these charter members had private CPA practices or were in partnership with one another.

The main goals of AASSCPA are threefold. The organization seeks to improve opportunities for Hispanic CPAs, to promote and maintain professionalism among Hispanic CPAs, and to encourage Hispanic youth to consider careers in accounting.

AASSCPA is a hierarchically structured organization headed by a board of directors, which sets administrative and operations policy. Board members are elected by the membership at the annual AASSCPA meeting. Under board scrutiny are a number of standing committees, including nominations, finances, professional ethics, legislation, and advisory committees. The association's membership is mostly Hispanic and male. Approximately 40 percent of Hispanic CPAs in the United States are members of AASSCPA. While the organization's headquarters are in Los Angeles, the membership is located throughout the United States, Mexico, Saudi Arabia, and Spain. The national organization holds an annual meeting, and periodic meetings are held in the organization's four regional districts in the United States.

The association has implemented a number of programs and services which reflect AASSCPA goals. Representatives of the organization appear before public and private bodies to speak on the need for increased opportunities for Hispanics in accounting. The organization conducts classes and seminars providing continued professional education required by members' state societies and licensing boards. In addition, the association maintains a data bank on Hispanic CPAs seeking employment and advancement opportunites and researches and communicates information on available positions to its members.

As part of the organization's commitment to the wider Hispanic community, AASSCPA offers seminars for minority small business owners to better acquaint them with their reporting responsibilities and effective management and accounting techniques. AASSCPA also provides financial aid and career counseling to Hispanic youth considering accounting as a profession.

AASSCPA publishes a newsletter, *La Cuenta*, which carries articles on general business and economic trends and on developments in the accounting profession. The organization's operating expenses are derived under a contract with the Office of Minority Business Enterprise of the U.S. Department of Commerce. These funds are supplemented by membership dues and contributions.

Information on this organization was obtained from their completed HAVO questionnaire and other materials submitted by the organization, which included the AASSCPA bylaws, its informational handbook, and its *National Directory of Members*, sections 1 and 2 (1980).

AMERICAN G.I. FORUM (AGIF) After World War II, Mexican American veterans were being subjected to certain discriminatory practices in the areas of education, employment, health care services, and housing. Although government legislation provided a new G.I. Bill of Rights, the Veterans Administration, a governmental agency, was improperly distributing benefits to Mexican Americans in Texas.

The American G.I. Forum was created on March 26, 1948, in Corpus Christi, Texas, as a nonpartisan, nonsectarian, nonprofit service organization to improve the social, economic, and political conditions of Mexican Americans in general. Chapters of the American G.I. Forum quickly spread throughout Texas and the Southwest to educate Mexican Americans about their rights under the GI bills of the postwar era. It expanded to educate Mexican American communities about service agencies and civic affairs.

Formation of the American G.I. Forum was led by Dr. Hector P. Garcia, who served in the armed forces in combat as a major in the Medical Corps. Through his dynamic leadership, a group of interested persons formed the first chapter of the American G.I. Forum as a vehicle to end discriminatory practices against Mexican American veterans. Other important figures involved with the formation of the American G.I. Forum were Gus Garcia, an attorney who had been fighting school desegregation cases in Texas and who was a member of the League of United Latin American Citizens* (LULAC); Vicente Ximenes, who formed chapters of the American G.I. Forum in New Mexico and created the mechanisms for the organization; and Dr. George I. Sanchez, a noted educator at the University of Texas.

The constitution of the American G.I. Forum states that its purpose is "to secure the blessings of American democracy at every level of local, state, and national life for all citizens. To this end, the organization, its officers and members, pledge to further the aims of all persons of Spanish-speaking or Mexican ancestry or descent and according to their bylaws:

1. Uphold and defend the Constitution of the United States of America and the American flag.

2. Foster and perpetuate the principles of American democracy based on religious and political freedom for the individual and equal opportunity for all.

3. Foster and enlarge the opportunities for training and education of all citizens.

4. Secure adequate participation and representation by the organization at policy-making and administrative levels of local, state, and national government in all departments, agencies, bureaus, or other governmental units.

5. Combat all practices of a prejudicial or discriminatory nature in local, state, or national life which curtail, hinder, or deny to any citizen an equal opportunity to develop his full potential as an individual.

6. Foster and promote the broader knowledge and appreciation by all citizens of the cultural heritage and language of the Mexican American and other Spanish-speaking minorities in the United States of America.

7. Use only nonviolent and lawful methods in pursuing the objectives of the organization as above set forth.

The organization adopted as its motto "Education Is Our Freedom and Freedom Should Be Everybody's Business." It also has an official prayer to St. Francis of Assisi and an official seal. The Pledge of Allegiance to the Flag of the United States is binding to all members and is given at every meeting of the organization immediately after the official prayer.

The American G.I. Forum quickly gained victory in the area of veteran's rights. The organization had pledged to work within the following written goals and objectives:

1. To develop leadership by creating interest in the Mexican American population to participate intelligently and wholeheartedly in community, civic, and political affairs.

2. To advance understanding between citizens of various national origins and religious beliefs in order to develop a *more enlightened* citizenry and a *greater America*.

3. To preserve and advance the basic principles of democracy and equal social and economic opportunities for all citizens.

4. To secure and protect for all veterans and their families, regardless of race, color, religion, sex, or national origin, the *privileges vested to them* by the Constitution and laws of our country.

5. To combat juvenile delinquency through the youth G.I. Forum program, which teaches respect for law and order, discipline, good sportsmanship, and the value of teamwork.

6. To award scholarships to deserving students.

7. To uphold and maintain loyalty to the Constitution and flag of the United States.

8. To preserve and defend the United States from all enemies.

9. To aid needy and disabled veterans.

The American G.I. Forum is essentially a Mexican American family organization. Membership is open to all persons, male or female, who are U.S. citizens and who served in the armed forces of the United States or who at time of applying for membership are serving in the National Guard, reserves, or other component of the armed forces of the United States. The organization is open to all females (G.I. Forum Auxiliaries) who are U.S. citizens, twenty-one years of age or older, and related through blood or marriage in the third degree to a veteran or member of the armed forces. Junior G.I. Forums consist of all young persons who are American citizens, between the ages of fourteen and twenty-one, single, and related through blood or marriage in the third degree to a veteran or member of the armed forces. Nonmembers of the armed forces consist of any adult male person who does not fulfill the aforementioned requirements but is of good moral character and whose general reputation as to character in the community in which he resides is good. These people must be recommended by an active member and must be approved by a simple majority vote.

In 1976, the American G.I. Forum existed in Arizona, California, Colorado, Idaho, Illinois, New Mexico, Ohio, Oregon, Texas, Utah, Wyoming, and Washington, D.C. In 1980, the organization consisted of 6,000 members in thirty-three states.

At the local level the organizational structure is as follows: chairman, vice-chairman, secretary, sergeant-at-arms, parliamentarian, public relations officer, chaplain, and historian. There are committees and subcommittees, which are the backbone of the organization. The local chapters extend to state and national structures which represent the entire body of the American G.I. Forum.

Major accomplishments of the organization involve veteran issues regarding not only discrimination but also segregation in education. The American G.I. Forum focused attention on equal education in the Texas school system, which deprived Mexican American children of the facilities and opportunities available to Anglos. In 1948, it joined the LULAC in the *Delgado v. Bastrop Independent School District (ISD)* case. It also was involved with court cases against the Del Rio, Sandia, Pecos, Hondo, Carrizo Springs, Kingsville, and Mathis independent school districts. The court cases culminated in 1957 with a decision in the Driscoll school case representing the final attempt of Texas school systems to obstruct overtly the legal establishment of Mexican American integration.

The American G.I. Forum has been in existence for over thirty-two years. It is the largest Mexican American veteran family organization in the country and is expanding in size and interests. The American G.I. Forum is an open voluntary association. Although membership appears to be limited, in practice, it is open practically to all. The organization is very patriotic, believes in the U.S. Constitution, and has respect for everything American. Members are required to take an oath of allegiance and be of good moral character.

The sources for AGIF are diverse. An important source is Carl Allsup, "Education Is Our Freedom: The American G.I. Forum and the Mexican American," *Aztlan* (1980):27–50; and numerous other publications. In fact, most recent works by Mexican American writers have included references to the G.I. Forum, for example, Rodolfo Acuña, *Occupied America* (1981), as well as several master's and Ph.D. theses. For purposes of this work, however, primary sources were used. These included the American G.I. Forum National Constitution; informational and recruitment pamphlets "Orientation for the New Forum," and "Join the American G.I. Forum"; and various issues of the organization's newspaper, *El Familiar*, reflecting a span of years.

AMERICAN PUERTO RICAN ACTION LEAGUE (APRAL) This is a national service organization founded in 1960 and based in New York. APRAL provides housing, educational, cultural, family, and recreational services to the Puerto Rican community. The organization claims 1,200 members of Puerto Rican descent. There are no membership dues, but donations are accepted.

There is little printed information on this organization available in the public record other than that which appeared in the *Directory of Spanish Speaking Organizations* (1970), a publication of the U.S. Cabinet Committee on Opportunity for the Spanish Speaking.

ARIZONA MEXICAN AMERICAN CHAMBER OF COMMERCE (AMACC) This profit-making organization was founded in 1968 to develop opportunities on both sides of the American–Mexican border for Hispanic businesses. AMACC is based in Phoenix, Arizona, a state which has a long tradition of border commerce. The state's Hispanic community has been unique in its perpetuation of cultural, educational, and economic exchanges between Arizona and its sister Mexican state of Sonora. This organization is reflective of this continuing commercial interaction between bordering nations.

The Chamber assists Hispanic entrepreneurs in establishing businesses in Arizona as well as providing help to existing firms for the purpose of locating satellite operations in Mexico. AMACC sponsors several promotional events to advertise its goals and objectives. Among these is the hosting of a beauty pageant. This traditional activity among Hispanics is gradually disappearing from more progressive Hispanic communities, where women are taking a more active role in the developmental and political life of the community. But Arizona Hispanics, perhaps because of proximity to Mexico or the predominant conservatism of the majority population, continue to promote beauty and femininity and the selection of queens as goals for Hispanic women. This is especially evident in their frequent fiestas. The beauty pageant is held on May 5, Mexico's Independence Day from Spain, and a bigger fiesta is held September 15–16, in celebration of Mexico's expulsion of the French. The AMACC is a membership organization, with dues ranging from $50 to $200 annually. The Chamber publishes a quarterly newsletter, *The Fiesta*.

Sources on this organization are limited. The most widely circulated reference is *A Directory of Hispanic Organizations* (1979), a public relations document funded by Phillip Morris Inc. However, treatment of organizations in this widely circulated pamphlet is cursory at best. Still, it serves as an important directory for quick reference. The organization failed to respond to requests for primary resources such as issues of their newsletter and bylaws or articles of incorporation. These are generally not available in the public record or housed in accessible library collections.

ASOCIACIÓN DE JORNALEROS (ASSOCIATION OF DAY LABORERS)

(AJ) The Association was formed in 1933 in Laredo, Texas, as an independent labor union. Like so many others, it was founded in response to the National Recovery Administration.

Asociación membership included hatmakers, painters, carpenters, construction workers, miners, and farm laborers. In 1934 union activity was disrupted by *agents provocateurs*. By the spring of 1935, however, new life was breathed into the union as it assumed leadership over 1,200 union workers on strike. That strike failed because of the inexperience of the organizers and harassment by the Texas Rangers, who arrested fifty-six strikers.

In the spring of 1936, the Jornaleros Union was revived. Relief was a major problem for farmworkers throughout the Depression. Federal relief agencies excluded migrants, and a residence of one year was often required by state agencies. The AJ tried to organize workers on relief. Local authorities, immigration officials, Texas Rangers, and the U.S. Army harassed the Jornaleros, its sympathizers, and members of the relief organizations. The Jornaleros were chartered by the American Federation of Labor and became the Agriculture Workers Labor Union Local 20212.

There is little documentation on the majority of these early organizations. The AJ is mentioned in George O. Coalson, *The Development of the Migratory Farm*

Labor System in Texas: 1900–1954 (1977); and Rodolfo Acuña, *Occupied America* (1981).

ASOCIACIÓN LOS VIEJOS ÚTILES (ASSOCIATION OF THE USEFUL AGED) (AVU) In the early 1970s there was a large and growing community of Spanish-speaking elderly in Miami, Florida, yet there were few organizations responding to the unique needs of this population. Justo G. Regalado, a Cuban attorney in exile and instructor of human relations at the Dale Carnegie Institute, founded the Asociación Los Viejos Utiles in May 1971, to address the needs of senior Cubans in Miami. The primary goals of this new organization were to promote the moral and physical well-being of aging Hispanics.

Asociación Los Viejos Utiles is a hierarchically structured organization. The board of directors is responsible for setting organizational policy and overseeing the program operations. The board is assisted by an executive director, administrative secretary, administrative clerk, and three general clerks. The organization has a membership of 8,000 senior citizens, the majority of whom are of Cuban descent. Qualifications for membership include a minimum age requirement of fifty years and committed opposition to Marxist ideology. This latter eligibility requirement, albeit foreign to organization discussions in most social service organizations, is reflective of Cuban Americans' sensitivity to recent revolutionary history and forced immigration to the United States.

The AVU offers a number of programs and activities for its members. In the main, the organization's activities center around subsistence requirements. In the area of employment, AVU offers English as a second language instruction, office machine training, woodcarving and painting classes, and job placement services. Bilingual social workers are trained by the Association to assist members in filling out applications for residence, reentry permits, citizenship, and food stamps. The organization also provides other services, such as a notary public.

Another area of focus for the AVU is budget management assistance for the elderly. In 1979 the organization established a federal credit union chartered by Florida state law. The credit union's savings and loan services are available to members and their families. An initial five-dollar deposit and a one-dollar passbook fee are required. Loans secured through the credit union are commonly used by members to cover medical, self-employment, and transportation costs. Also, the Association has arranged for discounts for its members at over 100 business establishments, including medical and pharmaceutical concerns.

The AVU publishes a bilingual monthly bulletin, *UTIL, la Revista del Viejo*, informing members of upcoming activities and available discounts. The Association also broadcasts a short radio program on station WFAB Saturday evenings. Organizational operating funds are derived from its one-dollar monthly membership dues and private contributions.

The sources for this organization were provided by AVP and included the Asociación Los Viejos Utiles' Federal Credit Union information leaflet, the

Useful Aged leaflet, *UTIL, la Revista del Viejo* 7:72 (November 1979) and 7:77 (April 1980), the Asociación Los Viejos Útiles organization chart, and their completed HAVO questionnaire.

ASOCIACIÓN NACIONAL DE GRUPOS FOLKLORICOS (NATIONAL ASSOCIATION OF FOLKLORIC GROUPS) (ANGF) Founded in 1974 in Albuquerque, New Mexico, the basic objective of ANGF is to promote the dissemination of Mexican and Hispanic expressive arts. The Association also seeks to share the most salient artistic forms of music, dance, and other communicative forms with artists, members of the community, and institutions. Initially the Association was founded by four folklore groups, the Ballet Folklorico of the University of Colorado, Los Lupeños de San Jose (California), Ballet Folklorico de Albuquerque (New Mexico), and Semillas de la Tierra de Alamosa (Colorado). By 1979, numerous groups had formed and joined representing every southwestern state and including groups from Minnesota, Kansas, New Jersey, Washington, Utah, and Oregon. The founding members of ANGF were Gloria Falcon of Colorado, Kathy Gutierrez of Texas, Margie Hernandez of California, Frank Lucero of New Mexico, Herman Martinez of Colorado, Lorenzo Montoya of New Mexico, Virginia Muñoz of Texas, Milton Ortega of California, Aleta Ulibarri of Colorado, Ismael Valenzuela of New Mexico, and Lorenzo A. Trujillo, Susan Cashion, and Ramon Morones, directors of some of the newly formed groups. In 1979 there were 1,000 active members and 3,000 nonactive (non-dues-paying) members.

Organizationally, the ANGF is a national association with groups and individuals from each state and region making up the membership and presided over by a group of elected officials. Each state has two board members and increases that amount in proportion to the number of folklore groups that are members of the organization. In addition to these state officials, two board members are selected at large. In toto, these elected persons make up the board of directors of the Association, from which are elected the central administrative officers: chairperson of the board, vice-chairperson, treasurer, secretary, and parliamentarian. The appointments are for one year, but the chairperson of the board continues as past chair for one year following the election of the new board chair. In addition to these elected officers, the organization has two other important offices: first, the festival convention director, who is responsible for conducting the National Folklorico Conference held yearly in preselected sites; and second, the editor of the organization's journal, *ANGF*, which is published biannually.

While the organization seems to center most of its activities in universities and colleges, non-academic community groups also participate. For the most part, the membership is made up of persons of modest means. The members are mainly Mexican American but include Puerto Ricans, Mexican, and other Hispanics.

The chief activities of the organization involve the sponsorship of the annual

National Festival Folklorico, regional conferences, the publication of the *ANGF* Journal and a newsletter published every other month. In addition, members serve as consultants for community organizations and other bodies and are engaged in constant artistic exchanges between members regionally, nationally, and internationally.

The importance of this organization can only be evaluated with an understanding of the role of festive folklore in Hispanic communities. More than most other ethnic groups, Hispanics, and in particular Mexican Americans, have a long tradition of street fairs, musical fairs, and arts and crafts exhibits. Hispanic art is extrovert, and ANGF serves to promote this artistic tradition nationally.

Although there are a variety of sources available on this organization such as *ANGF* and the ANGF newsletters, these were not provided for this work. A request to the organization for reference material was graciously complied with through ANGF's submission of the completed HAVO questionnaire. This, then, served as the resource for this entry.

ASOCIACIÓN NACIONAL MÉXICO AMERICANA (MEXICAN AMERICAN NATIONAL ASSOCIATION) (ANMA) In May 1949, a trade union organizer with the Mine, Mill, and Smelters Union, Alfredo Montoya, organized the Asociación in Grant County, New Mexico. The ANMA national organization was founded in Albuquerque on August 14, 1949. ANMA strongly advocated human rights and encouraged Mexican Americans to join unions.

ANMA solicited memberships outside the Southwest, in cities such as Chicago, Detroit, and other industrial centers. It also sought to extend itself to Puerto Rico. The Catholic hierarchy, however, challenged the ANMA on the basis of its purported Communist leanings.

The Asociación was backed by the Independent Progressive Party (IPP) and shared both membership and issues. Virginia Ruiz, national secretary of ANMA, was a delegate to the 1950 IPP convention in Chicago. Mexican American candidates such as Arthur O. Casas for assembly and Richard Ibañez for superior court, were supported by the IPP. Both groups were harassed by the government.

In the summer of 1952, under the leadership of Alfredo Montoya, ANMA moved its national headquarters to Denver. The U.S. attorney general's office added ANMA to its subversive list in 1954, and its intense harassment of the organization successfully undermined its activities until it faded away.

There is little published information on this organization in spite of its activism. Rodolfo Acuña's *Occupied America* (1981) serves as a primary source of information on this organization. However, much of Acuña's work is based on articles which appeared in the Los Angeles-based *Eastside Sun* between the years 1947 and 1952.

ASOCIACIÓN NACIONAL PRO PERSONAS MAYORES (NATIONAL ASSOCIATION FOR THE ELDERLY) (ANPPM) The impetus for the formation of this organization in April 1975 in Los Angeles, California, was the recognition that the Hispanic elderly, as a minority within a minority, were subjected to social and economic discrimination and were without recourse to an organized, political voice. ANPPM was formed as a nonprofit agency by a group of Mexican American social service and public administration workers. The founders included Carmela G. Locayo and Manuel Ahuero.

ANPPM's goal is the attainment of social, economic, and civic opportunities and equal justice for all Hispanic American older persons. The organization engages in advocacy, direct services, research, and information dissemination. Structurally, the organization is hierarchically headed by a board of directors, which sets policy and oversees finances. Board members include Manuel Ahuero, Jack E. Christy, Gilbert Colon, the Most Reverend Patricio Flores, and Maria Ramirez. These individuals occupy prominent positions nationally and represent a cross-section of the Hispanic community. ANPPM's executive director also serves as president of the organization. Each of the regional offices is headed by a local director.

The national ANPPM office is located in Los Angeles, California. There are also three regional offices: the eastern regional office in New York; the southeastern office in Miami; and a liaison office in Washington, D.C. A fourth regional branch, the southwestern office in Albuquerque, New Mexico, was closed in December 1978 due to federal funding cutbacks.

The organization has 1,100 members, 75 percent of whom are low-income persons. The membership is well represented by American senior citizens of Mexican, Puerto Rican, Cuban, and other Hispanic ancestry. Membership is open to all persons who subscribe to the goals of the Asociación Nacional Pro Personas Mayores. Annual dues are assessed on a sliding scale and include the following categories: paraprofessional or student; professional; organizational; and senior citizen. Members receive a monthly newsletter and are entitled to attend local, state, and national ANPPM conferences.

ANPPM sponsors a number of programs and activities which reflect the organization's goals. It operates Project Personas Mayores (The Elderly Project), which is the primary vehicle for advocacy, research, information dissemination, and national and local conferences for the elderly. ANPPM provides technical assistance to local organizations concerned with the Hispanic elderly. In addition, the association administers the U.S. Department of Labor's Senior Community Service Employment Program in Texas, Louisiana, Oklahoma, Kansas, and California. Under contract with the Department of Labor, ANPPM is funded by the Administration on Aging through a Model Projects Grant and by membership dues. ANPPM has redistributed more than $3 million to community agencies serving the needs of the elderly.

The organization publishes a monthly newsletter containing reports on their activities and a legislative bulletin carrying news of proposed changes in state and federal laws affecting senior citizens. ANPPM publications are printed in both Spanish and English.

Information on ANPPM can be found in their various pamphlets and bulletins such as the ANPPM *Newsletter*, *Legislative Bulletin*, and the ANPPM brochure on its purpose and history. For this work, the May 1979 *Newsletter* and the August 1979 *Legislative Bulletin* were used as well as a completed HAVO questionnaire.

ASPIRA OF AMERICA, INC. (AA) Aspira is a national nonprofit social and education services organization founded in 1961 in New York City. At that time, as well as now, the vast majority of Puerto Ricans in the United States were residents of New York. The Puerto Rican community was characterized by high underemployment and student dropout rates. Also, there were few Puerto Ricans in policy-making positions in New York City's private and public institutions.

The founder and guiding spirit of Aspira was Antonia Pantoja, a Puerto Rican woman born on the island, raised and educated in New York, and trained in social work and education. This trailblazer was active with Puerto Rican youth groups in the 1950s and was one of the founders of the National Puerto Rican Forum* (NPRF). The former New York City Board of Education member and member of the Mayor's Committee on Human Rights joined together with other concerned Puerto Rican professionals to address the many problems facing Puerto Ricans, especially those relating to educational opportunities. In 1968 Pantoja returned to Puerto Rico to develop Aspira Clubs and to consult on other private and public projects. In 1971 she moved to Washington, D.C., to work as a consultant, and more recently, she relocated to California, where she established the Graduate School for Urban Resources and Social Policy in San Diego, an independent, alternative school. She has been a significant leader of Puerto Rican political, educational, and social change for over three decades.

Aspira's goals are to identify promising youth, motivate them to continue their education, provide educational guidance and leadership, and promote scholarships and financial aid to assist students in their education. Aspira also promotes the understanding of Puerto Rican cultural history and achievements for the purpose of developing a sense of self-confidence and identity among Puerto Rican youth.

Aspira is a hierarchically structured organization headed by a ten-member board of directors, which sets policy and goals. Each Aspira program is headed by its own executive director. Aspira employs program staff numbering more than seventy. Among the organization's leadership are Mario A. Anglada (executive director, 1970–79), Oscar Garcia-Rivera, Ramon Raimundi, Marina Mercado, Priscilla Ramos, and Anthony Santiago. There are five state branches of Aspira located in New York, New Jersey, Illinois, Pennsylvania, and Puerto Rico. The organization has a membership of over 700.

Aspira of America was originally an affiliate of Aspira of New York and was intended to serve as the educational research arm of the organization. Now, Aspira of America encompasses all the branches of Aspira, including its parent office in New York City. Too, the Association of Spanish Speaking People of America in Chicago is actually an Aspira of New York spinoff.

Aspira offers a number of activities and services which reflect its goals. The organization operates three eduational programs: the Career Educational Program (ACEP); the Youth Education Program; and the El Centro-Aspira Work Study Program funded by CETA (Comprehensive Employment Training Act). These programs provide educational counseling and career guidance and remedial skills classes to Puerto Rican college and precollege students. Aspira also offers grants-in-aid to its student clients. In 1966 Aspira provided grants to 331 college students. In addition, the organization schedules regular and varied social and cultural activities for students of Hispanic descent. Aspira also conducts a Leadership Development Program for potential community leaders from among parents active in the PTA. In an attempt to bridge the generation gap, Aspira counsels parents born in Puerto Rico on American attitudes toward the young and the habits of American teenagers. Because so many of these programs are dependent on federal funding, however, their existence is dependent on the political climate. Therefore, any documentation on the activities of Aspira must take into account that its many programs described here may be in a state of transformation or even winding down due to changes in federal funding priorities.

In 1961 Aspira sponsored a New York City conference on the educational needs of urban Puerto Rican youth, which was attended by educators, administrators, and school board members from several eastern and midwestern states. Along the same theme, in 1968 Aspira published "Hemos Trabajado Bien," a report on the First National Conference of Puerto Ricans, Mexican Americans and Educators on the special needs of Puerto Rican youth. And in 1974 Aspira filed a class action suit against the New York City Board of Education for its failure to provide adequate bilingual education for the more than 100,000 Spanish-speaking students in the public school system. In addition, Aspira published in 1972 a study, "Puerto Rican Employment in New York City," documenting the employment problems of Puerto Ricans.

Aspira maintains its headquarters and the Aspira Educational Opportunities Center at different sites in New York City. The organization publishes a quarterly newsletter. In addition to federal monies, Aspira's operating funds come from corporation and foundation contributions. These are supplemented by membership fees.

This organization sees education, professional training, and competence as the means for advancing Puerto Ricans in American society. This orientation has created some tension with other organizations that urge direct community action for problem solving. More militant groups have accused Aspira of being "too establishment." However, Aspira's gains have not been short-lived. The organization can claim much success and many tangible achievements over the years.

Aspira has been a most effective grass-roots organization. It is nationally known and has provided an important service to Puerto Rican youth. Aspira staff have acted as primary spokespersons on behalf of this community on educational issues. Aspira Clubs have been established in local high schools, and have sponsored group workshops and conferences throughout New York City. Aspira also publishes *Metas*, an educational research journal, three times a year.

Sources for this organization are varied but are rarely as detailed as Aspira merits. References to its activities can be found in *A Guide to Hispanic Organizations* (1979); *Directory of Spanish Speaking Community Organizations* (1970); and *Directory of Puerto Rican and Community Service Organizations Throughout the United States* (1979–80). Other somewhat more detailed sources include Edward Mapp, *Puerto Rican Perspectives* (1974); Francesco Cordasco, *The Puerto Rican Experience* (1973); Francesco Cordasco with Eugene Bucchioni, *The Puerto Ricans 1493–1973* (1973); and the archives of the Robert Kennedy Memorial in Washington, D.C.

ASSOCIATION FOR PUERTO RICAN-HISPANIC CULTURE, INC.

(APRHC) This is a regional cultural organization founded in 1965 and based in New York. The association attempts to promote and preserve "Spanish culture" in the United States by providing cultural activities and by supporting Hispanic artists and speakers. The organization's membership is open and is comprised of fifty members. Membership dues are ten dollars annually. General meetings are held annually.

The organization sponsors a Puerto Rican Library and Museum through which it conducts tours. It hosts exhibits and programs in the Museum of the City of New York, local schools, and institutions.

Reference to the activities of the APRHC can be found in the *Directory of Spanish Speaking Community Organizations* (1970). The organization failed to respond to the HAVO questionnaire and request for current materials. Therefore, it is possible that there may have been changes in number of members and membership dues and other more specific information on the organization.

ASSOCIATION FOR THE ADVANCEMENT OF MEXICAN AMERICANS

(AAMA) The Mexican American community of Houston, Texas, has historically experienced poverty, high unemployment, institutional discrimination, and low levels of adult education. Among Mexican American youth, school dropout rates and the incidence of drug abuse were especially high. Recreational facilities and other alternative resources for youth appeared to be lacking. AAMA was established as a response to these social ills.

Legally incorporated as a private, nonprofit organization in Houston, Texas, on November 23, 1970, the organization operates in the largely Mexican American northside district of Houston and has remained a local organization since its founding.

AAMA emphasizes education as the solution to the major social problems of the Mexican American community. Its goal is to develop future community leaders by instilling in youth a positive self-concept and a socio-political awareness and by motivating them to seek educational advancement. AAMA seeks to achieve this aim by providing a number of day care, educational, employment, and rehabilitative programs for Mexican American youths.

The founders of AAMA include Luis Cano, Yolanda Navarro, the organization's first chairperson, Froilan Hernandez, Nicolasa Cano, and Alejandro Guardiola. Many of the organization's founders are educators and businessmen from the Mexican American community.

AAMA is a hierarchically structured organization. At the top is an eleven-member board of directors, which sets policy and develops and evaluates programs. Next is an executive director, who oversees the implementation of board decisions by the project directors and staff. Also, there is an advisory board composed of community residents, which informs the board of directors of the specific needs of the Mexican American neighborhoods. Meetings of the organization are held quarterly. The membership is comprised mainly of low- and middle-class Mexican Americans. When the organization was founded in 1970, it had a membership of 14. By 1979, this had risen to 1,000.

AAMA began its organizational activities in the area of day care. In 1970 the Jovita I. Day Care Center was established to provide bilingual day care for preschool children. In 1971 a sister service, the Angelita Fraga Day Care Center, began operation.

In the educational field, the George I. Sanchez Junior and Senior High School was founded in 1973. This school was established as an alternative educational program for dropouts from the regular school system. The school eventually gained accreditation from the state of Texas. It provides similar courses to those offered by the Houston Independent School District, although individual instruction is utilized, and greater multicultural content is employed. In 1974 AAMA opened the Southwest Chicano Arts Center, which offers local youth instruction in film and fine arts.

In 1976 AAMA became active in drug abuse education and counseling with the establishment of a drug abuse program. Counselors are sent to the streets to administer individual treatment on a voluntary basis. They also counsel youth regarding available preventive programs and alternatives. In 1978 Casa de Esperanza was opened to provide a foster group home for males between the ages of ten and seventeen who have a problem with inhalant abuse. Other AAMA counseling programs include the Northside Family Center, which provides counseling to youth and parents and the Gustavo Garcia Youth Development Program, which employs therapeutic techniques such as transactional analysis, behavior modification, and reality therapy to engender leadership qualities in youth.

AAMA provides two manpower development programs. The School to Work Transition Program trains teenagers in practical skills. The Alternative Volunteer Program is concerned with career counseling and matches youths with trained volunteers. By 1979 more than 3,600 youths had participated in AAMA community programs.

In addition to the services AAMA provides, the organization publishes the *AAMA Journal*. Also, AAMA has developed several audio-visual presentations, such as the documentary, *Las Aztecas and Their Medicines: A Chicano Legacy*, which won the Seventh Annual Robert F. Kennedy Journalism Award.

This organization has provided the reference sources for this entry. In response to request for materials they have provided a completed HAVO questionnaire, AAMA membership brochures, and a pamphlet entitled "AAMA Model: An Educational Policy" (n.d.). Other reference sources may include the program and reports from the Seventh Annual Robert F. Kennedy Journalism Award ceremony.

ASSOCIATION OF CHICANA-LATINA NURSES (ACLN) Health care in the Hispanic community was an issue belatedly addressed, although of significant importance to the socially neglected, culturally different Hispanics. There was a lack of bilingual professional hospital staff in most areas of the United States as well as an insensitivity to the health belief systems and practices unique to Spanish-speaking peoples. And the impact of socio-economic conditions on the health status of Hispanics could not be ignored. So in San Jose, California, a group of Hispanic nurses organized in October 1977 for the purpose of addressing the general lack of awareness about the health needs of Hispanics among health and medical care professionals. They also sought to examine the reasons for and the solutions to the scarcity of Hispanic health care professionals. They called themselves the Chicana-Latina Nurses Association to reflect both their predominance of Mexican American membership and their commitment to the entire Latino community. The organization was founded, then, to explore these problems and to assist in the promotion of high-quality health care for the Hispanic community. ACLN also has the goals of promoting greater educational opportunity and upward mobility for Hispanic nurses and of encouraging Hispanic youths to enter the health professions.

ACLN is a hierarchically structured organization headed by a chairperson. Other ACLN leaders include a vice-chairperson and secretary-treasurer. The early leadership of ACLN included Alice Alvarez, Lina Carrillo-Fulk, and Connie Rodriguez. ACLN has a number of standing committees concerned with such issues as affirmative action, bilingual nursing education, and fund-raising. Most of the members of ACLN are professional or student nurses of Mexican American, Puerto Rican, or Cuban American descent.

ACLN is involved in a number of activities. The organization awards scholarships to Hispanas seeking undergraduate and graduate degrees in nursing. ACLN has successfully lobbied for and subsequently assisted with the expansion of the bilingual nursing program at Evergreen College in San Jose. Additionally, ACLN participates in affirmative action meetings at medical centers within the county, promoting affirmative action goals. And the organization conducts workshops for bilingual nursing programs' faculty.

The Association provides services for its members. ACLN holds monthly meetings where guest lecturers provide information on a variety of topics relating to health education. Annual retreats are held where members review, plan, and suggest organizational goals. Health-related job opportunities are circulated among members. Also, the Association sponsors several dances a year to raise operational and scholarship monies. Membership dues are assessed on the basis of a sliding scale, with twenty-five dollars for professionals, ten dollars for associate members, and five dollars for student nurses. The Association incorporates Aztec symbols into its logo. ACLN abides by its official motto, Enfermeras unidas para el progreso de la profesión y la comunidad (Nurses united for the progress of the profession and the community).

There is little printed information on this organization other than Association printed materials, although ACLN has contributed much to the social and physical well-being of the entire population of Santa Clara County. The primary sources of information utilized in this work were provided by ACLN and included the ACLN membership brochure and bulletins and ACLN meeting minutes.

ASSOCIATION OF HISPANIC ARTS, INC. (AHA) A number of local artists of Hispanic descent, recognizing the need for an organization to address the problems and concerns of the Hispanic arts community, founded the AHA in 1975 in New York City. The main purposes of AHA are to aid and promote Hispanic artists and to present to the general public of metropolitan New York the best in Hispanic creative arts.

AHA is a hierarchically structured organization headed by a board of directors, an executive board, an administrative staff, and an advisory board. Members of the board of directors have included individuals prominent in the Hispanic arts world such as Elsa Ortiz Pobles, an AHA executive director; Tina Ramirez of Ballet Hispanico of New York; Miguel Rosario of Chemical Bank and an AHA president; Jack Agueros of Museo del Barrio; Max Ferra of Intar, a New York City Hispanic cultural arts center; Gilberto Zaldivar of Repertorio Español; and Marta Moreno Vega of Visual Arts Research and Resource Center Relating to the Caribbean. Advisory board members include Miguel Algarin, of Nuyorican Poets Cafe; and Miriam Colon, of Puerto Rican Traveling Theatre.

AHA conducts a number of programs and activities. The organization's principal event is an annual Hispanic Arts Festival held throughout New York City's five boroughs. The organization also provides a number of services to sixty Hispanic art organizations representing the Puerto Rican, Dominican, Cuban, and other Hispanic communities. The Association conducts seminars and workshops on how to gain funds for arts organizations, and it maintains a Central office, which provides daily information to members of the art community and general public regarding local events.

An AHA, CETA (Comprehensive Employment Training Act) funded artist project provided free exhibits, performances, and art instruction to schools and community organizations. The Association's audience development project served to promote the activities of Hispanic art organizations with the Hispanic community. AHA also provides individual technical assistance to Hispanic art technicians.

Operating funds for the Association are derived from grants from the National Endowment for the Arts, the New York State Council on the Arts, and the New York City Department of Cultural Affairs. Funds are also secured from private corporations. AHA publishes two information organs, *Hispanic Arts*, a bimonthly newsletter, and a *Directory of Hispanic Art Organizations*.

Sources for AHA's history are not extensive, although this organization constitutes a vibrant, significantly productive contribution to New York's art world. The organizational brochure contains a useful summary on the goals and purposes of the AHA. Also, *A Guide to Hispanic Organizations* (1979) is helpful. The primary reference for this work was the completed HAVO questionnaire submitted by the Association.

ASSOCIATION OF MEXICAN AMERICAN EDUCATORS (AMAE) A nonprofit corporation founded in 1965, this organization provides information on educational programs and activities affecting the Hispanic community throughout the state of California. AMAE promotes bilingual education as an important response to the educational needs of Mexican American children. It conducts workshops on the special educational problems of these students.

Although its more than 1,200 members are concentrated in California, the organization has national scope and participation. It is supported solely by donations and annual membership dues. The dues structure includes professional membership forty dollars, associate membership ten dollars, and student membership five dollars.

The organization claims to publish a monthly newsletter for its members and to hold annual conventions, but several attempts to contact the current leadership of the organization based in Redwood City, California, were unsuccessful. It appears that AMAE may not be as active as in former years, particularly at the height in interest in bilingual, bicultural education and Mexican American studies. The most accessible source on this organization is *A Guide to Hispanic Organizations* (1979).

AZTECA CLUB (AC) A mutual aid society, this organization was founded in Toledo, Ohio, in 1955 by one Santiago C. and his brother Francisco. The two brothers, who worked in a plant with others of Mexican descent, formed the organization for the purposes of mutual benefit, particularly to provide money for health and hospital care.

Each member of the Club was allowed to bring in an additional member, including those from other plants. Nearly all of the members enlisted were consanguineal, affinal, or ritual kin. In fact, the original core of the members consisted of four brothers, their father, (an honorary member), two sons-in-law of one of the brothers, and two *compadres* (godparents). Eight of the twelve original members were related, and the other four shared ties of close friendship reinforced by the common work location. Monthly meetings were held in the homes of the various members.

Although the Azteca Club originally was organized as a mutual aid society, it was also a social club. It held dances as fund-raisers and sponsored a winter communitywide fiesta.

This organization illustrates the expanded presence of Hispanics in the United States. The little reference information that is available shows how Hispanics tended to form voluntary associations particularly for purposes of survival in a sometimes less than friendly environment. Even individual families were enough to provide the impetus for organizational activities. And Hispanics concerned themselves with mutual aid but also with maintaining the social and cultural life of the Spanish-speaking community.

References to the activities of the Azteca Club can be found in Barbara June Macklin, *Structural Stability and Cultural Change in a Mexican American Community* (1976).

B

BISHOPS COMMITTEE FOR THE SPANISH SPEAKING PEOPLES See SECRETARIAT FOR HISPANIC AFFAIRS.

BROTHERS OF OUR FATHER JESUS OF NAZARETH (BFJN) The Brothers of Our Father Jesus of Nazareth, commonly known as the Penitentes, are men of Hispanic descent who compose a lay and religious mutual aid society in New Mexico. Their history can be traced to about 500 years ago, when there was founded in Spain the lay order of Los Hermanos Penitentes (The Penitent Brothers), a fraternity of men of good morals who met for religious study. The Franciscan friars brought this order to Mexico during the sixteenth century and officially called them the Lay Third Order of the Franciscans. Within a century it was brought to what is now New Mexico and southern Colorado by the same and by some of the followers of the conquistadores, who were previous members.

The first recorded public penance in this area was performed by explorer Juan de Oñate and his men in 1594. The first recorded evidence of the Penitentes was reported in a letter written by Bishop Jose Antonio Zubiria, dated September 17, 1794, which was found in the archives of the Cathedral of St. Francis in Santa Fe. Zubiria mentions the existence of a Brotherhood of Penitentes in the area and expressed disapproval of the Penitentes due to their practice of flagellation. He stated that the Order had been in existence "since the beginning of the re-conquest of this province."

In 1833, Father Inigo Deanne, a Jesuit, witnessed a Penitente rite and proposed a medieval origin due to the similarities with the flagellation sects which emerged twice in the history of Europe. If there is a problem identifying its specific origins, it is clear that this is one of the first Hispanic voluntary associations in the Southwest. Whatever its origins, the Penitentes took root because it fulfilled vital needs for social integration and individual spiritual security.

The conditions prompting the formation of this organization were many. However, the Catholic Church was the major force promoting the development of this organization. No bishop had visited the area after 1760, and most of the Franciscan friars were expelled in 1828 by the Mexican Revolutionary Government. Even before the departure of the Franciscans, the isolated Spanish American villages had come to rely upon themselves and their brotherhoods for the performance of many religious rites.

In the late eighteenth century, church institutions were in an unsteady state. The few priests were charging exorbitant fees to perform rites of baptism, confirmation, matrimony, and burial. These conditions worsened with the population and territorial expansion under Mexican rule. It was during the so-called secular period (c. 1790–1850), that the Penitentes emerged strongest by fulfilling important needs for the spiritual solace and collective survival of the Hispanic populations in a semiarid environment and the hostile intrusions of the Anglo throughout the nineteenth century.

Control of the Penitentes quickly and definitely passed from the hands of church officials to local lodge masters. From 1800 to 1850 the Penitentes established a firm hold on the people, and when Bishop Lamy and the French priests arrived in the 1850s, the local brotherhoods did not care to relinquish their power, particularly to foreign priests who were not Franciscans. This did not please the priests, who tried to insist on supervision of Penitente rites, particularly to soften the savagery of the penances. No real objections were raised locally to any form of worship practiced by the Penitentes, and their worship took strange forms unauthorized by the original rules of the Order. The Penitentes had turned more and more toward a primitive worship of pain and death.

As a means of coercion, bishops and priests opposed the Order and threatened to deprive lodge members of the sacraments. The displeasure of church officials did somewhat weaken the Order, but it had the more important effect of driving it partly underground. Until this time the Penitentes had very open ceremonies, but now they became a secret order. As official anger increased, so did secrecy, and as late as 1900 far more Hispanics were Penitentes than were not.

Membership within this organization required sincere faith and commitment to Christian charity through mutual aid and unobstrusive good deeds for all neighbors and fellow citizens. Membership consisted mostly of men, but there were women who composed the Auxiliadoras de la Morada (auxiliary lodges), the female counterpart of the Brotherhood. The Auxiliadora was respected within the community and performed specific duties such as nursing of the ill, caring for their homes and families, tending to the elderly, as well as finding proper homes for children without parents. The actual number of members at any time can only be estimated since membership rosters remained secret.

The nature of mutual aid provided by the Penitentes centered around the care of each member of the society and their families in times of illness or distress. Upon the death of a brother, the *morada* (lodge) took charge of funeral arrangements. It collected funds, buried the deceased, and cared for the families and widows. The entire Penitente community cooperated in planting, tending, and harvesting the crops and formed types of economic cooperatives which loaned money to its members.

Although the strength of the Penitentes has been declining for seventy-five years, the Order is by no means dead. In the isolated villages of the Sangre de Cristo Mountains, many of the adult males are still members. And in the larger towns and villages the number of members is still significant. Their greatest strength is in the central mountain region of New Mexico, in San Miguel, Mora, Taos, Rio Arriba, Sandoval, Santa Fe, and Torrance counties. But these are areas of many cultural survivals. It is in these areas that sixteenth-century Spanish dances still thrive, as do ballads from the same period. And these, in fact, continue to influence contemporary dances and ballads. Corrupted forms of miracle plays and religious pageants, some dating from fifteenth-century Spain, are still performed.

To confront new developments, the Penitentes altered their objectives. Political involvement assumed increasing importance and eventually played a vital role in the continued existence of the Penitente organization. Penitente members resorted to active resistance from the early days of occupation by Anglos in New Mexico. Organized opposition occurred as early as 1847, when Penitente brothers joined the Taos Indian tribe in rebelling against the Anglo authority in what was later called the Taos rebellion.

Penitentes were astute politically, and many politicians and persons in high office were Penitentes. Their strength was in their willingness to remain united, bound by a common culture, and to adapt to the "new politics" of the Anglos. The *moradas*, composed mostly of Republicans, were unquestionably powerful. At the New Mexico State Constitutional Convention, their leaders demonstrated that they knew well how to protect their interests; 70 of the 100 member delegates were Republicans, and half of these were Hispanics. They sought and won protective clauses which they considered fundamental to their existence in the new society.

The Penitentes were influential in placing Article 7 into the 1910 New Mexico State Constitution. Article 7 states that no citizen shall be restricted from holding office or sitting on juries due to religion, race, language, color, or inability to speak, read, or write English or Spanish. Thus, this article made New Mexico a bilingual state. Article 7 was in direct opposition to the Enabling Act of 1910, which made the ability to read, write, and understand English a prerequisite to holding an office or sitting on juries. In 1911 the U.S. Supreme Court ruled the Enabling Act to be unconstitutional.

Bilingual education was officially recognized for the first time in this country as it became law in New Mexico. Section 8 of the New Mexico State Constitution, for example, states that the legislature shall provide for the training of teachers so that they may become proficient in both English and Spanish in order to qualify them to teach Spanish-speaking pupils. Finally, Section 10 deals with school integration. This section states that children of Spanish descent shall not be denied the right and privilege of admission and attendance in public schools and shall never be classed in separate schools.

Another example of this political influence is found in the first libel law enacted by the New Mexico State Legislature. The Fraternal Order of Penitentes had sued a Protestant missionary in the District Court of the County of Taos for making a mockery of their Lenten procession in a newspaper.

Members of the state legislature, sheriffs, county assessors, surveyors, and other elected and appointed officials belonged to a local Penitente society. Without support of the organization a person could not be elected to public office. Even Anglo politicians identified with this fraternity to secure political influence and backing.

After a hundred years of opposition, the church officially recognized the Penitente Brotherhood. In San Miguel County, of which Las Vegas is the county seat, two factions fell into serious dispute, threatening the unity of the parish and the peace of the community. To resolve this dispute, Archbishop Byrnes of Santa Fe, in 1946, recognized the Penitentes as part of the church.

The Penitentes are basically a religious order whose members are all Catholics. It performs useful but secular social, psychological, social welfare, and religious functions. The Order follows rather closely the pattern found in other secret societies based on mutual aid and brotherhood, patriotism, race or nationality, religion, sexual morality, temperance, and social reform. For about a century and a half, each lodge has run its own affairs as it saw fit, limited only by a broad, traditional constitution. Many minor variations exist between lodges, but there does emerge a general picture of the Order as a whole.

Each lodge is made up of adult males. It has a special meeting place called a *morada* (chapel or chapter or lodge) and sometimes has several. The *morada* is found in more mountain villages than not, its size determined by the financial capabilities of the local unit and its location dependent upon the desire for secrecy of the group. Usually it is built of adobe and consists of one large room (the chapel) and a small room in which the secret sessions are held and where the whips, chains, and other paraphernalia are kept. There are one or two small, high windows. The chapel has an altar or platform and a few benches. Some villages have one *morada* in the village and another back in the mountains near "Calvary." Women, children, and visitors are on occasion welcomed to the chapel but never into the inner room.

The officials of a typical Penitente lodge, all elected, include: (1) *hermano mayor* (older brother), who is the head of the organization and has general oversight; (2) *celador* (warden), who serves as the caretaker of the *morada* and as sergeant-at-arms; (3) *coadjutor* (helper), who cleanses the scourges and the bodies of the penitents after flagellation; (4) *infermero* (nurse), who looks after the sick members and does other works of mercy and charity; (5) *mandatario* (collector), who examines new members and instructs them in their obligations; (7) *secretario* (secretary), who is the custodian of the book of rules and explains the rules to the members; (8) *sangrador* (bloodletter), who inflicts the seal of the Penitentes, three horizontal and three vertical gashes across the back, cut with a flint or glass knife, and occasionally may whip members as punishment; (9) *resador* (prayer), who reads from the handwritten ritual book, praying for the flagellants during their penance and who also assumes a major role in some nonflagellation ceremonies; (10) *pitero* (flute player), who, during the ceremonies and marches, plays on a wooden flute furnishing all the music except that from the metracas, a ratchet type of rattle. As a whole, these officers are called Los Hermanos de Luz (Brothers of Light).

Much of the exotic reputation enjoyed by Penitentes surrounds their Holy Week ceremonies. The ceremonies begin on Holy Tuesday night. Each Penitente who participates goes to the door of the *morada*, is questioned by the officers, and responds with ritually proscribed answers. The Penitente then enters and receives the obligatory six gashes. He then ritually asks for and receives blows from the lash for the three meditations of the passion of the Lord, the five wounds of Christ, the Seven Last Words, and the forty days in the wilderness. Oftentimes he faints before he has received the forty strokes for the forty days in the wilderness. He is cared for by the *coadjutor* and may be taken to his home.

Ash Wednesday is occupied with confession, prayer, ceremonial processions to the cemetery cross, and in earlier days, additional ceremonies, and in some villages the procession of the *carreta del muerto*, a heavy, homemade cart. In the cart rides a hand-carved, skeletonlike effigy of death, holding a drawn bow and arrow. The cart is drawn by men harnessed by their necks or in other ways so as to make this penitential task extremely difficult. If not done previously, Christ is now chosen. There is honor attached to serving as the Cristo, and the same person is not chosen twice. Late Thursday night a formal procession is made to "Calvary." At the head of the procession is usually a statue of Christ and/or saints. The chosen Christ follows carrying his cross, and sometimes others also follow carrying crosses. All the officers are present, the *pitero* playing his flute, the *resador* praying, and all chanting in unison.

Those actively engaged in self-flagellation are accompanied by *compañeros* who carry lanterns, help those who fall, and lend moral and physical support to the ceremony. The flagellants occasionally wear black coverings over their heads to keep their identities secret. The whips are usually of a type of yucca locally called *amole* and Spanish dagger. The whips are about three feet long, four inches wide, and an inch thick, with the fibers pounded until they resemble hemp. Sometimes bits of glass or wire are tied on, and leather whips are used. It is common for the Penitente to take a few steps, swing the whip over one shoulder, take a few more, and swing it over the other shoulder. Before long, blood spills at every stroke and so stains the trousers that it appears that the legs are also bleeding.

This procession usually goes either to the mountain *morada* or to the "Calvary" and then before daylight returns to the *morada* near the village. On Friday morning further ceremonies and processions take place. That afternoon another march occurs, and it is this march that has been the source of the greatest critical attacks on the Penitentes. This march is either to "Calvary" again or to a neighboring *morada*. It was this march that in the old days ended with a crucifixion. But for many years this final ceremony has only occurred at night. This live Christ was nailed to the cross and his side slashed. A sermon on the Seven Last Words was read. The Christ stays on the cross until he faints, usually within a half-hour. He is immediately taken down and removed to the *morada*, where he is cared for by the *coadjutor*. Sometimes these Cristos died, as did flagellants. Today it is more common for an effigy of the Christ to be used.

The entire ceremony ends with the reenactment of the *tinieblas*, or earthquake. The people gather in the church or Penitente chapel late Friday or early Saturday for this ceremony. All candles are extinguished for five minutes, during which there is heard the clanking of chains, beating of tin, racket of metracas, shrieks of women, and slap of Penitente whips. Prayers are evoked for loved ones in Purgatory, and the *tinieblas* and lashing are repeated for each prayer. At the end, the Penitentes return to the *morada* to elect officers for the following year.

After World War II the Brotherhood affiliation was more prevalent in rural and poor urban areas. Hispanic village life grew more heterogeneous, and fewer males became brothers. Outsiders intruded more and more, resulting in the modification of Holy Week observances and severe rites, or else these services were conducted more covertly. In sum, the fraternal order of the Penitente Brothers, originally a lay and religious mutual benefit association, represented an attempt by Hispanics in the Southwest to meet their social and convivial needs. Although many lodges have long since ceased to exist, a large number still are found in small towns. These groups function very much as they did in the past. However, most are apolitical.

Sources for the Penitentes history are diverse. The most important references included John H. Burma, *Spanish Speaking Groups in the United States* (1954); Alice C. Henderson, *Brothers of Light* (1937); Harvey Ferguson, *Rio Grande* (1933); Marta Weigle, *The Penitentes of the Southwest* (1976); Frances Leon Swadesh, *Los Primeros Pobladores: Hispanic Americans of the Ute Frontier* (1974); and Alice Corbin, *Brothers of Light: The Penitentes of the Southwest* (1937).

C

CAFE DE CALIFORNIA, INC. (CAFE) In July 1975 a group of Hispanic California state employees met in Sacramento to discuss the participation of Hispanics in state government. The persons attending this meeting formally organized in response to the perceived underrepresentation and underemployment of Mexican Americans in California government and the inadequacy of bilingual services provided by the state to the Mexican American community.

According to the 1970 census, Mexican Americans comprised 13.7 percent of the total California labor force, yet constituted less than 7 percent of California state government employees. In the early 1970s the state adopted an affirmative action plan to increase minority hiring in government. Noting the number of Hispanic state employees in the 1970 census, and given the rate of achievement in minority hiring in the years 1974–75, it was determined that parity would not be reached until the year 2058.

CAFE's major goals eventually evolved to promote a greater voice for Hispanics in the social and political spheres. CAFE is an acronym for Chicano Advocates for Equality, a name which clearly reflects the organization's purpose. CAFE seeks to achieve its goals by assisting and encouraging the state of California in the recruitment, training, and employment of Hispanics, the advancement of Hispanics already within the civil service, and the provision of needed public services to the Hispanic community. CAFE also seeks to promote cultural and ethnic pride through the organization of regular social and recreational activities.

CAFE's organizers and leaders include Caroline Cabias, the first state president, Richard Perez, and Napthaly Aguilera. At the organization's outset, chapters were founded within individual state departments such as the Department of Motor Vehicles, the State Personnel Board, the Department of Food and Agriculture, and the Department of Health. By 1978 regional chapters were added in Sonoma, San Jose, Oakland, Fresno, Bakersfield, Orange County, Riverside, and San Diego, for a 1980 total of thirteen chapters.

CAFE is a hierarchically structured organization. At the head is a state board of directors composed of the state officers and elected chapter representatives. The board meets quadrenially to discuss issues of policy and action. Next, there is a staff of coordinators in charge of organizing ad hoc committees as needed. Following this are the regional chapters, organized on a geographical basis with a minimum of ten dues-paying members. These groups deal with matters affecting their local membership. CAFE holds annual conferences to elect state officers, act on proposed amendments to the bylaws, and discuss organizational objectives and strategy.

Though the majority of CAFE members are Hispanics, full membership is open to any state of California employee who supports the goals of the organization. A member in good standing is entitled to one vote in organizational elections, receive monthly issues of the organization newsletter and job referral information, participate in CAFE-sponsored training and state exam seminars, and receive an admission discount to all CAFE social and cultural activities. Dues are scaled according to salary. Members earning $986 a month or less pay $1 monthly. Those receiving salaries above $1,708 per month are assessed $5 monthly dues. Members with salaries between these two figures pay $3 monthly dues. These dues are shared by the statewide and local chapters at the rate of 40 and 60 percent, respectively.

CAFE has engaged in a number of activities in pursuing its goals. CAFE, at the request of the State Personnel Board Recruitment Unit, provides names and resumes of Hispanics interested in entering the civil service. CAFE holds periodic workshops providing management training to members seeking advancement within the civil service. Also, CAFE assisted in the 1980 census by distributing census promotion buttons and data-gathering materials and by providing workshops to help Hispanics achieve a higher score on the Census Bureau's enumerator test. In May and June 1980, CAFE de Sacramento sponsored a symposium on the legislative process. Capital legislators and staff were invited to speak to representatives from various Hispanic organizations on the topics of the legislative process and how to influence it.

CAFE de California is financed by organization fund-raising drives, membership dues, and contributions from private individuals and corporations. In turn, CAFE donates money to a number of political concerns affecting the Hispanic community. In 1980, CAFE contributed $100 to the NO-on-9 campaign, a statewide referendum on gay rights, and $500 to the Governor's Chicana Issues Conference held at the University of Southern California.

CAFE utilizes Aztec iconography to represent its activities. The organization publishes a monthly newsletter entitled *CAFE de California*. The chapters hold regular social gatherings and encourage members to participate in general Hispanic community festivities such as those held on May 5 and September 16.

CAFE cosponsors and participates in the Annual Raza Coed Softball Tournament in Sacramento.

The primary resource for information on this organization is CAFE headquarters. A request for materials and printed references for this work provided the following: the CAFE recruitment leaflet, the *CAFE de California* newsletter for June 1980, and the CAFE membership application. No further references were made available, and other reference sources were not readily identifiable.

CALIFORNIA COALITION OF HISPANIC ORGANIZATIONS (CCHO)

The California Coalition of Hispanic Organizations was established as a nonprofit organization in Sacramento, California, in 1977. The goals and objectives of the organization are to identity and address the needs of Hispanics in the state of California. Most important, the organization is committed to the development and maintenance of a communications network to include statewide and local organizations and coalitions. The communications network is intended to coordinate activities that positively affect the Hispanic community of California.

There are two types of membership in this organization, voting and nonvoting. Nonvoting members are either associate, honorary, or affiliate members. The associate has the right to participate in decisions relating to the business of the corporation but cannot vote or hold appointed or elected office. The associate can be any publicly funded organization of state or national scope that has a paid staff of five or more persons and whose goals and objectives are to provide services, training, or education to persons who are primarily Hispanic. An honorary member is one whose membership is conferred by the Coalition. Candidates for this category of membership may include organizations or individuals who have contributed significantly to the purpose and goals of the Coalition and to Hispanics in general. An affiliate membership must also be conferred by the Coalition. The affiliate can be an Hispanic or non-Hispanic organization whose goals and objectives complement those of the Coalition.

The second type of membership, voting members, includes those individuals and organizations eligible to vote in the organization and to hold elective or appointed office. A voting member is a regular member of the organization. A regular member can be any nonprofit Hispanic organization of state and or national scope or an organization that has a volunteer membership of twenty or more persons and whose goals and objectives complement the goals and objectives of the Coalition.

CCHO is a hierarchically structured organization. The structure includes a president, first vice-president, second vice-president, secretary, and treasurer.

There are few published references for this organization. Sources used for this entry include CCHO's bylaws and a personal interview with a former officer of the organization, Margaret Aragon.

CAMARA DE COMERCIO LATINA DE LOS ESTADOS UNIDOS (LATIN CHAMBER OF COMMERCE OF THE UNITED STATES) (CAMACOL)

This organization was established in 1965 to promote trade between the Hispanic and Anglo American communities. CAMACOL, located in Miami, Florida, is also a source of information on local tourism, economic development and cultural events.

CAMACOL is a nonprofit organization funded by annual dues of ninety dollars and by corporate donations. The organization also publishes a monthly newsletter, *The Bulletin*.

Because the organization failed to respond to a request for information and reference printed materials, it cannot be determined whether the organization is extant. The most recent and widely circulated reference to the organization's activities is *A Guide to Hispanic Organizations* (1979).

CANTO AL PUEBLO (SONG FOR THE PEOPLE) (CAP) Although literally translated as Song for the People, Canto al Pueblo should really be translated as Community Arts Festival, because that is what the name implies. This organization is truly reflective of the strong arts tradition in Hispanic culture. The CAP traces its origins to a meeting in January 1977 of a small group of Mexican American academics in Milwaukee, Wisconsin, which met to discuss alternative modes of promoting a sense of self-dignity and community consciousness among Mexican Americans in the face of continuing economic poverty and institutional discrimination. After identifying the arts as the most visible means of accomplishing this, they contacted artists in Milwaukee who had been active in community affairs and jointly organized the first National Mexican Arts Festival, Canto al Pueblo.

The founders of the organization include Reimundo "Tigre" Perez, Ricardo Sanchez, and Arnold Vento. The primary goal of Canto al Pueblo is to enhance individual and community pride and dignity through beauty and the expression of ideas in the visual and literary arts. Artists are brought together to share techniques, ideas, and criticism, and the community is provided with visual representation of themes related to their existence and aspirations. Wall murals are erected as a more permanent contribution to the community.

The organization is relatively loosely structured. There is a fifteen-member national board, comprised of representatives from midwestern and southwestern states, which establishes policy. A local steering committee is composed each year to execute the festival.

The organization's main activity is preparation for the annual week-long international Mexican American arts festival held in June at a different site each year. All events are free to the general public. The first Canto al Pueblo festival was held in Milwaukee, Wisconsin, and lasted for ten days in June 1977. Sixty artists and 6,000 community members participated, mostly Mexican Americans.

In 1978 Leonardo Carrillo coordinated Canto al Pueblo II, which was held in Corpus Christi, Texas, June 2–9. More than 100 Mexican American artists participated. Presentations during the eight days included film festivals, literary readings, and folkloric dance and drama performances. In addition, sculpture, painting, and photographic exhibits were situated at a number of community centers.

Under the leadership of the 1979 festival coordinator, Joaquin LeFebre of the University of Southern Colorado, a change in focus occurred. At the third Canto al Pueblo artists from a number of nations participated. Between June 8 and 15 over 200 artists from the United States, Mexico, Puerto Rico, and other countries of the Western Hemisphere came together in Pueblo, Colorado, to share their art and skills with each other and with the Hispanic community. The theme of this festival was the celebration of the artistic expression of all Spanish-speaking people of the world.

Canto al Pueblo annually publishes an anthology for educational purposes. In 1978 nine permanent murals were created in the *barrios* (Mexican neighborhoods) of Corpus Christi, and in 1979 a mural was painted on the Pueblo Dam.

The Canto al Pueblo board of directors and steering committees solicit taxdeductible donations from individuals, social organizations, and businesses to finance advertising, materials, publication and administrative costs for the festival and other activities.

The primary source of information on Canto al Pueblo used here was the HAVO questionnaire. Other references included *The Canto al Pueblo II* (1979) brochure and oral interviews with the office staff of Joaquin LeFebre regarding purpose, organizational history, and finances. References to its activities surely can be found in the festival anthologies.

CASA DE PUERTO RICO, INC. (PUERTO RICO HOUSE) (CPR) This local nonprofit corporation, established in Hartford, Connecticut, in 1967, was initially founded to offset the effects of discrimination against Hispanics in housing, education, and employment by providing social services. The organization has more recently redirected its focus to research and advocacy. The new goal is to provide a data base documenting the needs of the Hispanic community.

La Casa de Puerto Rico, Inc., is a hierarchically structured organization headed by a fifteen-member board of directors and task forces on employment, education, and housing. The task forces are composed of both community representatives and agency staff. CPR has a staff of fourteen full-time employees and is a United Way–funded agency.

La Casa de Puerto Rico engages in a number of programs and activities which reflect its goals. In 1974 and 1976 the organization published two studies on educational opportunities for Hispanic youth in Hartford. These later provided the basis for a successful class action suit against the city's Board of Education. As a result, a bilingual, bicultural education program was adopted for the city's public schools. In 1979 La Casa de Puerto Rico conducted an in-house study on "The Housing Crisis and the Community in Hartford, Connecticut." The reported findings led the organization to advocate for better housing programs for the poor. In 1974 the CPR entered a class action suit against the city's

Department of Personnel and the Fire Department alleging discriminatory hiring practices. In 1980, twenty-five Hispanics were employed as firemen.

In addition to these activities, La Casa de Puerto Rico maintains two major programs. Its Parent Training and Organization Program was instituted in November 1979 with a $25,000 grant from the Ford Foundation. Through this program ESL classes are taught and leadership training sessions are conducted. Parents are provided with the skills and information necessary to participate effectively in their childrens' education. La Casa de Puerto Rico began an Employment Monitoring Project in September 1979 with a grant from the National League of Cities and ACTION, an arm of the U.S. government. The staff of this program monitors federal contractors to ensure compliance with federal affirmative action regulations. La Casa de Puerto Rico has also supervised a multifamily homesteading project. Resulting from this was the construction of six low-cost family residential units, built with a $118,000 Federal Housing and Community Development Block Grant from the U.S. Department of Housing and Urban Development (HUD).

The organization's 1980 operating budget was $304,000. La Casa de Puerto Rico obtains the majority of its funds from state and federal governments and from private foundations. It also publishes a bilingual newsletter.

The primary reference sources on this organization were the HAVO questionnaire and the La Casa de Puerto Rico history and programs description paper (1980). Other sources on CPR activities would include copies of their newsletters.

CENTER FOR CUBAN STUDIES (CCS) The Center was founded in New York in 1972 to provide the American public and its educational and cultural institutions with resource material and information on revolutionary Cuba. According to the Center, this became necessary with the 1961 U.S. ban on trade with and travel to Cuba.

The Center distributes information on Cuba through its publications, films, forums, and exhibitions. It also provides speakers on Cuba to organizations and institutions. It makes its services available to the public through its reading room, subscriptions to Center publications, rental of materials, and memberships.

Center activities include film showings, lectures, seminars, discussions, concerts, exhibits, Spanish-language classes, and classes on revolutionary Cuba. On November 2–3, 1979, the Center sponsored a National Conference on Cuba held in New York City.

Annual memberships for individuals are $15 for regular, $25 for supporting, and $50 for sustaining members. Institutional memberships are $150 annually and include reduced rental fees on films and major exhibitions as well as multiple copies of all publications.

Information on the Center can be found in the *Center for Cuban Studies* brochure (1979) and in their *National Conference on Cuba* brochure (1980).

CENTER FOR PUERTO RICAN STUDIES (CPRS) The Center is located at the City University of New York. Instrumental in the creation and organization of the Center is its director, Frank Bonilla. The Center is concerned with high-quality research and teaching, especially at the graduate level. It has also cultivated a network of organizational relationships as a way to generate new research capabilities and opportunities in the Puerto Rican community.

The Center works with Puerto Rican community organizations as a way of combining theory with practice and to complement the informational needs of Puerto Ricans. The Center has conducted a number of studies and has been an important influence on information available by and about Puerto Ricans.

The CPRS has established a significant reputation in the Puerto Rican community. Therefore, references to the Center's activities are diverse, and certainly the most important of these must be their published studies. However, the CPRS failed to respond to the HAVO questionnaire and request for further information. Conversations via telephone were conducted with staff, which provided a minimum of current information. The primary source for this brief description of the Center's activities were the archives of the Robert Kennedy Memorial in Washington, D.C.

CENTRO CHILENO LAUTARO (LAUTARO CHILEAN CENTER) (CCL)
The Centro Chileno Lautaro was founded to maintain Chilean traditions and to encourage social, cultural, and sports activities among the members of the Chilean community in San Francisco. The organization claims a membership of 200 and a mailing list of 8,000. The Centro requires a registration donation of one dollar and monthly dues of one dollar. Magazines, bulletins, and newsletters are made available to members and friends of the Centro, although not necessarily originating from the organization.

This organization is typical of many such associations located throughout the United States which promote and provide social networking among particular segments of the Hispanic community. There are few printed references to these organizations other than in archives such as those of the Robert Kennedy Memorial in Washington, D.C. Most of the information contained on these organizations is available within the networking mechanisms and is usually unrecorded.

CENTRO DE INFORMACIÓN LATINO AMERICANO (LATIN AMERICAN INFORMATION CENTER) (CDILA)
In the mid-1970s many Mexican Americans in Nevada continued to face problems of inadequate housing, health care, education, and employment. Added to this, official government studies indicated that the Mexican American population of Nevada was rapidly increasing. Noting that demands on already inadequate available social services would also increase, local activists, including Remmey Brown, Julia Carlos, Carlos Romo, Sandra Fasquelle, and Josephine Gonzales, organized Centro de Información Latino Americano as a community services agency in Reno, Nevada, in 1975.

The organization's main goal is to aid northern Nevada in the integration of

Hispanics into the social and political institutions of the general Nevada community as quickly as possible. The Centro seeks to accomplish this by providing social services, thereby alleviating the pressure on other community programs.

CDILA is a hierarchically structured organization headed by a board of directors in charge of setting policy and program development. The board oversees the organization's finances. The executive director is in charge of coordinating the organization's various programs. Each of the several programs is overseen by its own director. In all, Centro de Información Latino Americano employs a permanent staff of twenty-six. Half of the staff are Mexican Americans, while the remainder are Anglos, blacks, Cubans, and South Americans.

CDILA activities are primarily to provide social services to the community. The organization operates Outreach for Senior Citizens, Substance Abuse, Manpower ESL (English as a Second Language), Title XX Information and Referral, and Family Health Outreach programs. Through these programs CDILA provides emergency food and shelter to indigents, plus family, housing, and health counseling and job placement and training. CDILA also provides bilingual interpreters for legal matters and conducts research on the needs and characteristics of the Hispanic population. CDILA formerly ran a Comprehensive Employment Training Act (CETA) Homebound Tutorial Project.

CDILA has a monthly client load of about 1,500 persons. Of the programs' participants the majority are Hispanic, of which 70 percent are Mexican Americans. Seventy-five percent of CDILA clients are considered poor according to state and federal guidelines. About 60 percent of the organization's clientele have limited ability to speak and write English.

CDILA works closely with other community organizations in pursuing common objectives. Among its other activities, CDILA translates important brochures such as the Department of Motor Vehicles manual. Also, CDILA airs a half-hour radio and television program and sponsors monthly neighborhood dances.

In 1978 CDILA became a member of the United Way family of agencies of northern Nevada and has since received annual funds from this charitable corporation. Other CDILA funding sources include the city of Reno, Washoe County, state of Nevada, CETA, and private contributions and fund-raising activities.

The organization provided primary reference sources for this entry, which included a completed HAVO questionnaire, a background information summary produced by CDILA, the CDILA bylaws, and an article from the *Reno Gazette* (April 22, 1979).

CENTRO DE SERVICIOS PARA HISPANOS (HISPANIC SERVICE CENTER) (CSPH) This organization was founded as an arm of the Catholic Archdiocese of Kansas City by Ruben and Gloria Corona, Manny Fierro, Mary Hernandez, and Father Ramon Gaitan, pastor of Our Lady of Guadalupe Church. El Centro was established in Topeka, Kansas, in 1972 as an instrument of advocacy for the fair treatment of Hispanic Americans in the areas of employment, education, housing, and recreation.

El Centro de Servicios Para Hispanos is a hierarchically structured organization headed by Archbishop Ignatius J. Strecher, the director of the Spanish-speaking apostolate, and by an advisory council. An executive administrator and staff are employed to operate the organization's programs. In 1976 a branch office was established in Kansas City. The organization has no membership per se, but has a mailing list for its newsletter *Adelante!* of 250 subscribers, the vast majority of whom are Mexican Americans.

El Centro de Servicios Para Hispanos (CSPH) engages in a number of charitable and educational programs and activities which reflect its goals. El Centro monitors city, county, and state legislation to assure fairness to Hispanics and serves as a lobbyist in the Kansas legislature. The organization maintains a community library and provides free income tax assistance. El Centro sponsors Mesa Redonda, a forum for Hispanic businesspersons. The organization also cooperates in combined efforts with other organizations and agencies. In addition, El Centro participates in the mayor's summer youth programs and joins the Christmas Bureau Program in providing poor families with food and clothing during the holidays. El Centro also coordinates a bilingual education program, which is funded by the Eastern Barrio Ministry. CSPH is, in part, staffed by Comprehensive Employment Training Act (CETA) trainees and migrant SER (Service, Employment, and Redevelopment) clients.

The source for this organization consisted of their completed HAVO questionnaire. Additional references may be available in the form of program reports, project evaluations, bylaws, and other printed materials and by provision of the organization.

CHICANA COALITION (CC) In 1979, San Jose, California, was quickly establishing its reputation as the feminist capitol of the country. It had a woman mayor, Janet Gray Hayes, and women majorities on both the City Council and County Board of Supervisors. That same year, Sylvia Gonzales, an associate professor of Mexican American graduate studies at San Jose State University, was awarded a grant from the Women's Educational Equity Program of the U.S. Office of Education to organize the first National Hispanic Feminist Conference (NHFC). Within this atmosphere of women's rights activities, a group of local Mexican American women met to discuss ways to achieve expanded educational, professional, and political opportunities for Hispanic women. They included Barbara Montaño, Delia Alvarez, Sylvia Gonzales, Esther Ono, Esther Medina Gonzalez, Bea Robinson, and others. Foremost on their list of concerns was the awareness of the rising political influence of women nationally and the exclusion of Mexican American women from political leadership and decision making in their own communities and, most likely, by their male counterparts.

The founders of the Coalition recognized that the NHFC would provide a platform for Hispanic women nationally, but it would also highlight Hispanas locally and could serve as further impetus for organizing. The Conference proposed to advance a national agenda for Hispanas, and the Coalition's founders anticipated an important role in the planning and coordination of this historical meeting. The Chicana Coalition was formally established that same year, and Bea Robinson, Anita Duarte, and Linda Jones were elected its first officers.

In its first year of existence, the CC was actively involved in preparation for the NHFC. The Conference planning committees were made up of Coalition members. The NHFC provided visibility to the organization, served as its primary recruitment vehicle, and assured its credibility in the larger community. Leading feminists visited the San Jose Conference headquarters, and the Coalition benefited from these visits. The organization hosted luncheons for such notables as the National Organization for Women (NOW) vice-president, Jane Wells Schooley, and the President's Commission on Women chair, Lynda Johnson Robb. Local newspapers covered these visits, and the coalition was advanced as a leading feminist and community organization in the city worthy of attention. Politicians took notice and clamored for CC support. Mexican American political leadership in San Jose began to pass over to women.

There was, however, a division within the organization over methods and strategies for meeting the CC's goals. Some members advocated a universal approach to civic issues by the Coalition, while other members considered this approach too moderate. The latter group espoused ethnic exclusivity.

Because the sentiments of the first group complemented those of the NHFC leadership, the moderate approach dominated actions of the CC during its first year. The original officers of the CC were voted out of office because of their advocacy of the hard-line approach. These original officers urged the exclusion of all but Mexican American women from the organization. They advanced political influence as the priority goal of the Coalition. But this influence was viewed as the prerogative of the leadership rather than the entire organization. When they were excluded from a singularly visible role in the NHFC program, they assisted in organizing a boycott of the Conference hotel on the premise that the hotel had been built on sacred Indian burial grounds. This action by CC members was done in defiance of the majority wishes of the membership, which stressed the importance of the Conference to Hispanic women as a whole as opposed to the individual needs of a few. Because of the boycott, CC officers were voted out of office after only one year of service.

After the original officers failed to win reelection, Cecilia Arroyo, a relatively unknown Hispana and an inactive member of the Coalition, was elected to the presidency. Her candidacy was advanced on the proposition that she, as a non-participant in the early history of the organization, would bring objectivity and independence to the Coalition leadership, and initially the CC continued to grow under Arroyo's presidency. But by the end of her term the organization had begun its decline.

The NHFC had attracted major press coverage, and as a spinoff the organization also grew in stature. But with the culmination of the NHFC and its activities, the CC was forced to create its own identity. It floundered in its inability to isolate its real purpose.

The Coalition has undergone a series of dramatic leadership changes since its founding, and it is currently in a state of decline. The universal, all-inclusive approach of the early CC to women's and civic issues gave way under Arroyo to a heightened distrust of the majority community. The leadership of the Coalition concentrated on the organization's political impact while ignoring the needs of the majority of Hispanas. The original founders of the CC left the organization and new members hesitated to join. Simultaneously, the city of San Jose was undergoing change. The feminist-sensitive Mayor Hayes was followed by a not-so-feminist Tom McEnery. Women continued to hold majorities on the County Board of Supervisors but not so on the City Council. And the one Hispanic council member, a woman, was decidely not a feminist. Most important, the County Commission on the Status of Women and its ardently vocal executive director, Rina Rosenberg, succumbed to the budgetary axe.

However general, the stated goals of the Coalition are commendable and stress four major areas of concern to Mexican American and Hispanic women. The first area emphasizes representation on affirmative action policy-making bodies and includes the evaluation of affirmative action programs. The CC recognizes affirmative action as an important vehicle for advancing institutional change. The organization is also committed to providing assistance to Mexican American women trying to group around a particular interest or issue. The CC sees this as a way of promoting Hispana leadership and, at the same time, a way of establishing a Hispana network. The Coalition seeks to serve as the primary advocate for Mexican American women in Santa Clara County. It especially has designated support services for economically disadvantaged women as a chief area of concern for the group. And finally, the CC pursues politicization of Mexican American women through organizational participation on political and policy-making bodies.

Although the above-stated goals and purposes begin to shape an identity for the group, they also reflect a certain ambiguity still to overcome. Perhaps the rapid success of the organization provided by the high visibility of the NHFC projected the organization into a leadership role beyond their immediate expectations. Regardless, the early organization in combination with the NHFC allowed for tremendous consciousness raising of Hispanic women, far beyond that of other communities.

Membership in the organization is open to all women. Open membership was one of the most hotly debated issues during the CC's first year. NOW vice-president, Wells Schooley, became the first non-Mexican American to join the organization. The dues are twenty-three dollars anually for regular members and five dollars for students. Each new member must be sponsored by an active member. The CC is hierarchically structured to include a president, vice-president, treasurer, secretary, and several committee heads. Each year the organization presents a fund-raising community awards event which is well attended.

The Coalition responds to a need in the Santa Clara County women's community. It is also evident from its early acceptance and prominence that this organization has a civic role and responsibility to fulfill. Perhaps its early success allowed little opportunity for real reflection on its goals. But at the same time, the Conference and the startling impact of the Coalition on the San Jose community served to highlight the drastic need for Hispana organization and leadership. Through a study of its history and a clarification of its goals, the CC may once again emerge to a position of organizational and civic leadership in San Jose.

There is mention of the Chicana Coalition in newspaper accounts of the NHFC in the *San Jose Mercury News* (March 30, 31, April 1, 2, 1980). Also, personal interviews as well as participation in the founding of the organization have provided firsthand knowledge of the early history of the CC. Other sources for this organization include the organization's bylaws, and meeting agendas and minutes. This work made use of meeting minutes for August 13, 1979, October 8, 1979, January 14, 1980, and February 11, 1980. The *San Jose Mercury News* has featured the Chicana Coalition in news reports on Hispana leadership in San Jose. Copies of these articles are in the archives of the Chicano Reading Room in the San Jose State University Library and compiled in a notebook devoted to Hispana feminists in Santa Clara County.

CHICANA FORUM (CF) The Chicana Forum was established in 1976 with the primary purposes of stimulating an increase in the number of businesses owned by Mexican American women while promoting simultaneously their involvement in community development. The CF was founded in Washington, D.C., as a nonprofit corporation. The organization relays information to the Hispanic community regarding the availability of government contracts.

The Forum is headed by a board of directors led by its founder, Sharleen Hemming. Other corporation leaders include an executive director and district director. As a national organization, Chicana Forum has advisory committees in operation in several locales in the Southwest, including El Paso, Texas; Albuquerque, New Mexico; and East Los Angeles and Orange County, California.

In the spring of 1980 CF representatives attended a conference on the economies of the United States-Mexico border areas. The Forum relies on a number of funding sources. Among these are government agencies such as the Department of Housing and Urban Development and the Department of Commerce.

There is only scant references to this group, and the organization failed to respond to requests for further information. It is, therefore, difficult to determine just how active the CF is and whether it is currently extant. The most recent reference source for this organization is *A Guide to Hispanic Organizations* (1979).

CHICANA SERVICE ACTION CENTER, INC. (CSAC) The CSAC was founded in Los Angeles in 1972 to assist unemployed Mexican American women secure employment counseling and training. It also strives to promote a positive image of the Hispanic woman. This organization originally developed from the

Comisión Femenil Mexicana Nacional* (CFMN), which was founded in 1970 by Francisca Flores, and in December 1974 the CSAC officially spun off as an independent organization. Those involved in the CSAC's transformation were Francisca Flores, Amelia Camacho, Frances Bojorquez, Connie Muñoz, Jo Valdez Banda, Anna Nieto Gomez, Irene Mendez, and most important, Lilia Aceves, CSAC's early director.

The organization's membership is 90 percent Mexican American women of lower economic status. It services approximately 500 women annually through its Women's Work Experience Program, Women's Comprehensive Employment Services and Women's Non-Traditional in Los Angeles, and Women's Job Training Program in Van Nuys. These programs are sponsored by the city and the county through Comprehensive Employment Training Act (CETA) funds. The CSAC also runs a women's shelter care facility and a child care center. However, these programs may have suffered from the cutbacks during the Reagan Administration. CETA was one of the most seriously affected funding sources. These cutbacks had a dramatic impact on poor communities, particularly for those seeking ways to reenter the job market such as reentry women.

The structure of the CSAC is hierarchically headed by a board of directors. Its members include a president, vice-president, secretary, and treasurer. The executive director is Francisca Flores, and it is generally believed that she is the chief decision maker for the organization. Other officers and personnel include the deputy director and a staff of forty, whose number is dependent upon public funding sources and so may fluctuate.

The CSAC has been featured in *Somos* (September 1979) and periodically in the *Los Angeles Times* and other local community newspapers such as the *Eastside Sun*, the *Eastside Journal*, and *La Opinión*. The best reference may be Octavio R. Costa's, "Instantaneas," featured in *La Opinion* (April 15, 1979). This work made use of the organization's completed HAVO questionnaire and the CSAC letterhead for current officers.

CHICANA WOMEN'S POLITICAL ACTION CAUCUS See MEXICAN AMERICAN WOMEN'S POLITICAL CAUCUS.

CHICANO ADVOCATES FOR EQUALITY See CAFE DE CALIFORNIA, INC.

CHICANO ALLIANCE OF DRUG ABUSE PROGRAMS (CADAP) The CADAP is a national umbrella organization chartered in 1972 and incorporated in the state of Texas on December 31, 1976. The corporation was formed out of concern for the high incidence of substance abuse, particularly among youths, in Mexican American communities. Among the organization's founders are Ramon "Manchi" Adame, a former convict and drug addict, Mario Obledo, former secretary of health and welfare for the state of California, and Henry Collins, executive director of a drug treatment program in California.

The organization's goals are twofold: to provide technical and community resource development support for Mexican American substance abuse, social services, and mental health programs; and to educate Mexican American communities regarding the dangers and consequences of substance abuse.

CADAP is a hierarchically structured organization headed by a board of directors, which sets corporation policy. There are two classes of CADAP membership, organizational and individual. Organizations are alloted two votes each at organizational meetings, and an additional one vote is alloted for every thirty individual members. The initial CADAP office was established in El Paso, Texas, in September 1975. Since then the Alliance has opened centers in New Mexico, Colorado, California, and Arizona. Until 1974 the Alliance maintained a branch, the Southwest Training Institute (SWTI), which was actively involved in the treatment of drug addicts. SWTI has since suspended operations.

CADAP sponsors a number of activities and programs which reflect its goals. In 1975 the National Institute on Drug Abuse (NIDA) awarded CADAP a $200,000 grant to establish a pilot training facility in El Paso, Texas. Since that time CADAP has been training "street-wise" drug counselors to help run various substance abuse programs in the Mexican American communities of the southwestern United States. Some of CADAP's trainees have subsequently been employed at the National Institute on Drug Abuse and at the National Institute on Mental Health (NIMH). CADAP participates in a joint task force with other organizations of the Multi-Cultural Drug Abuse Prevention Resource Center for strengthening combined training efforts. This task force has trained some 200 "front-line" counselors for employment in CADAP's various regional programs. CADAP also maintains close ties with drug programs in Mexico and allows other programs to utilize training manuals and other materials which it has developed.

CADAP obtains its operating expenses from a variety of sources, including its annual membership dues of $100 for organizations and $10 for individuals. The organization also receives grants from the Drug Abuse Council and the National Institute on Drug Abuse.

Reference sources on CADAP include the organization's bylaws and articles of incorporation (1976), various CADAP informational brochures (1976), and a summary background sheet on SWTI produced by CADAP and available from the organization.

CHICANOS POR LA CAUSA, INC. (CHICANOS FOR THE CAUSE) (CPLC) South Phoenix, Arizona, in 1969 was an economically depressed urban area lacking private industry, commerce, and employment opportunities. Concomitant social problems of inadequate housing, deteriorating physical environs, high rates of youth delinquency, high unemployment, and lack of social services characterized the area. That year a small group of young Mexican American community leaders formed Chicanos por la Causa to help meet the social needs of the impoverished south side of Phoenix.

The main goals of this community development corporation are to improve the south Phoenix community and to create more and better opportunities for the residents of its neighborhoods. CPLC seeks to achieve these goals by providing programs and services in the areas of education, housing, counseling, health and aging, and job training and development.

Chicanos por la Causa is a hierarchically structured organization. The general membership in the community informs the CPLC board of directors and officers of its felt needs and participates in the planning process of CPLC programs. The board considers the possibilities of implementing suggested undertakings and oversees the performance of the CPLC president. The board consists of fifteen persons, nine elected by members of designated districts in south Phoenix and six appointed by the board. There is an executive vice-president and three other vice-presidents in charge of economic development, finance, and community support. The Phoenix branch has 1,000 members, most of whom are Mexican American and of low to moderate income. CPLC has two additional branches established in Somerton, Arizona, in 1978 and in Tucson, Arizona, in 1979.

In pursuit of its goals of improving the south Phoenix community, CPLC provides a number of social services. In the area of housing CPLC provides counseling on such subjects as landlord–tenant rights, purchasing a home, and mortgage delinquency and default. More than 1,400 persons have taken advantage of this service. For the elderly, CPLC provides transportation, exercises, socializing, free lunches, and outreach services. There has been an average participation of thirty-five individuals in the daily program at the CPLC senior citizen center.

In the field of education CPLC is involved in the local High School Equivalency Certificate Program (HEP) in cooperation with Maricopa County education agencies. CPLC also conducts a supplemental reading program and a summer education program in which youths are employed in learning experiences. The organization also operates an evening adult education program.

In 1977 CPLC established the Westside Training Center. There are 791 youths enrolled in its programs, which include employment counseling, a manpower program, and skilled trades training for dropouts, according to the CPLC's most recent statistics. The Center has been recognized by the U.S. Department of Labor as a national model youth program. CPLC operates a credit union chartered by the Arizona State Banking Department and insured by the National Credit Union Administration, which provides inexpensive savings and loan services and financial management counseling to members. CPLC's services in the rural community of Somerton include information and referral, citizenship classes, immigration counseling, and notarial and interpretation services. More than 1,000 people have utilized these services. CPLC assisted the town of Somerton in obtaining a Housing and Urban Development (HUD) block grant of $250,000 to construct a water-filtering system.

In the late 1970s CPLC reoriented its goals toward long-term community revitalization by promotion of economic and business development. CPLC plans for the 1980s are to attract industrial parks and manufacturing plants to south Phoenix by combining federal dollars and private capital. The leadership hopes that this in turn will create jobs and bring about revitalization.

The corporation employs an outside accountancy firm to audit its finances. CPLC funds come from Comprehensive Employment Training Act (CETA), Ford Foundation, Housing and Urban Development (HUD), Community Services Administration (CSA), and Department of Health and Welfare grants. In addition, CPLC receives contributions from a number of local businesses, banks, and corporations. CPLC owns and operates International Spice and Foods, a Mexican food plant which manufactures and sells food products. The profits from this enterprise are fed into the CPLC operating budget.

The organization maintains a number of structures which house its youth training center, senior citizens center, manpower center, and administrative offices. CPLC has purchased land and has commissioned architectural plans for future offices. The organization publishes an annual report and utilizes Aztec symbols to represent its goals and purposes.

References for this organization include a completed HAVO questionnaire and the *Chicanos por la Causa Annual Report* (1978).

CÍRCULO DE CULTURA CUBANO, INC. (CUBAN CULTURAL CIRCLE) (CCC) The New York–based Círculo de Cultura Cubano was founded in 1979 to promote the exchange of cultural and educational events between Cubans in the United States and Cuba. The maintenance of ties with Cuba is stressed because Cuba is pivotal to Cuban culture and because there is a need to inform those residing in Cuba of the life style and unique development of U.S. Cuban communities. Mutual interest in Cuban cultural affairs has resulted in the establishment of ties between the Círculo and Latin American peoples in the Caribbean, Puerto Rico, and the United States.

In 1980 the Círculo was active in several areas. It cosponsored a Latin American art show at the Museo del Barrio in New York City with the Center for Cuban Studies; cosponsored with the Cuban Ministry of Culture a seminar, "On Culture, Literature, and Literary Criticism in Contemporary Cuba," held in Havana, Cuba; and participated in Cuba's First International Seminar on Psychology in the Community, sponsored by the National Psychology Group of the Cuban Ministry of Public Health and the InterAmerican Psychological Society. In 1981 the organization held the Cuban Cultural Congress in New York, involving participation from Cuba, Nicaragua, Puerto Rico, and the United States. The Círculo also coordinates and sponsors cultural and educational trips to Cuba. This organization is decidedly different from the majority of the anti-Marxist Cuban associations in the United States. They provide information on their activities in a newsletter, *Boletín*. Since this organization is only recently formed, perhaps it portends to a changing consciousness toward Cuba that is reflective of a new generation of United States-born Cuban Americans.

Reference sources include issues of the organization's newsletter, *Boletín*, and

Círculo informational materials. For this work the inaugural issue of the *Boletín*, no. 1, was utilized, as well as a Círculo subscription form.

CÍRCULO DE PUERTO RICO, INC. (PUERTO RICO CIRCLE) (CPR)

Established as a nonpartisan, nonprofit, fraternal organization in Washington, D.C., on July 25, 1957, the organization's purposes and activities are cultural, social, civic, and fraternal in nature. The Círculo de Puerto Rico seeks to maintain and promote intragroup interest in Puerto Rican culture and to effect a greater cultural interchange within the general metropolitan Washington, D.C., community. It further aims to stimulate an increased participation by Puerto Ricans in social and civic activities of that city. Also, Círculo de Puerto Rico seeks to facilitate the settlement of newly arrived Puerto Rican immigrants.

Círculo de Puerto Rico is a hierarchically structured organization. The board of directors is composed of the group's officers, who are elected by the general membership and serve one-year terms. The president, who is also chairman of the board, designates the heads of the permanent committees (programs, finances, cultural activities, rules and bylaws, membership, and public relations) and creates ad hoc committees at his own discretion. There are several classes of organizational membership, including active, nonresident, associate, juvenile, and honorary. To qualify for membership a person must either have been born in Puerto Rico or be of Puerto Rican parents and support the goals of the organization. The CPR conducts its meetings according to Robert's Rules of Order.

The organization raises funds from membership fees and annual dues and a variety of fund-raising activities. The CPR logo incorporates the U.S. and Puerto Rican flags. The organization's motto is "El fin corona los esfuerzos" (The outcome crowns the efforts).

Sources for the CPR consist mainly of the organization's constitution and bylaws and are available from the Círculo.

CLUB ARPA (HARP CLUB) (CA) The Club Arpa in Irvine, California, is a small organization of Paraguayans headed by the honorary consul of the Paraguayan Consulate. Each year the Club sponsors an Independence Day feast to celebrate Paraguayan Independence Days, which are the fourteenth and fifteenth of May. The feast is held in a member's home and is open to all members of the Paraguayan community, as well as all others interested in learning more about Paraguay.

The archives of Dr. Andre Simic, Department of Anthropology, University of Southern California, contain CA information.

CLUB HISPANO DE PRENSA (HISPANIC PRESS CLUB) (CHP) The Club Hispano de Prensa, established in 1979, develops media material for bilingual or Spanish-speaking audiences to ease the adjustment of Hispanic immigrants. With an office in Washington, D.C., the Club is a nonprofit corporation made up of media professionals and business people in greater Washington. The organization conducts workshops for community leaders on how to improve media coverage.

The CHP has a dues structure consisting of $50 annually for individual members and $100 for corporations. The Club also solicits funding from federal and foundation grants.

The primary reference source for this organization is *A Guide to Hispanic Organizations* (1979). The CHP failed to respond to further requests for materials and information.

CLUB MEXICANO INDEPENDENCIA (MEXICAN INDEPENDENCE CLUB) (CMI) The CMI was the first mutual aid society to be established by foreign-born Mexicans in Santa Barbara, California. It was initially formed on September 5, 1917, by a group of local Mexicans rather than as part of a larger regional organization.

CMI members appointed an eight-member legislative commission to draft a constitution. The constitution described the purpose of the organization in its ratified version as "to strive by all legal and just means to honor, to elevate, and protect this club and its members, so that in the future it may be the protection of our sons, brothers, and compatriots."

Membership in the CMI was restricted to citizens of Mexico by birth or naturalization. The founding members of the organization, by declaring themselves permanent residents of the United States, wanted to ensure that the society remained a nationalistic Mexican organization that would benefit only those who were actually Mexican citizens. It also served as a guarantee against U.S.-born and second-generation Mexicans introducing a diluted Mexican culture into the organization.

Although on the surface it may seem highly unlikely that a group would organize in one country around their loyalty or citizenship to another, it must be noted that at this time the borders were still psychologically invisible. Also, the CMI membership goals indicate an assimilation trend among the newer generation that was also of concern to other organizations such as the Alianza Hispano Americana* (AHA) in their discussions on the inclusion of California Mexican Americans.

The CMI offered a broad range of benefits to its working-class membership. Each member was entitled to weekly payments for sickness or in case of accident. If members were permanently injured and unable to work, they were entitled to a pension for an indefinite period. The CMI also offered death benefit insurance, providing burial costs and at least $250 for the family and an emergency fund for its members. The members also visited and cared for sick or needy members and their families.

The organization was guided by an elaborate set of rules concerning the responsibilities and qualifications of its members. It had a detailed organizational scheme, a formal initiation procedure, and a democratically elected or appointed officer hierarchy. The CMI was a nonsectarian and nonpolitical group. Although the organization was not involved in politics per se, it did assume responsibility as a politically oriented buffer group for the Mexican community in Santa Barbara against racist elements in Anglo society.

In 1925, women within the CMI formed their own chapter and called it the Club Mexicano Independencia Femenil (Women's Mexican Independence Club). Women had always attended meetings of the CMI, but through their own chapter they elected officers and conducted business in which men had no voting rights. CMI Femenil members were entitled to the same mutual benefits from the general fund of the organization.

During the 1920s the CMI and CMI Femenil were composed of between 70 and 100 male members and a smaller group of women. They held many exclusive functions where between 400 and 700 members and their families celebrated the social cohesiveness the organization provided for Mexicans in Santa Barbara.

The most important reference on the CMI is Albert Camarillo, *Chicanos in a Changing Society* (1979). Camarillo, who originally completed his study on early Mexican American life in Santa Barbara as a doctoral dissertation, used sources such as the Club Mexicano Independencia President's Notebook, 1914–17 and the 1924 CMI articles of incorporation contained in county and state records.

CLUB UNIÓN (UNION CLUB) (CU) This organization is an example of the many groups that existed circa 1880 in Tucson, Arizona, dedicated to literary and intellectual pursuits. The earliest recorded date for the Club Unión is 1877 and appears in a testimony to Mr. Ramon Soto, a member and community leader, and published in *El Tucsonense* (March 17, 1919). Professor Carlos H. Tully is described in the article as the Club president.

The group met regularly to discuss philosophy, art, and politics. Of primary importance to the members was a critical analysis of the positivist philosophy popular in Porfirio Diaz's Mexico. It should be noted that the Club Unión was comprised of the same individuals who founded the Alianza Hispano Americano* (AHA). Given these individuals' humanistic and spiritual guiding principles, it is appropriate that they would question the pragmatic focus of positivism. A debate held in Mexico City on the subject was reproduced in a local newspaper and stated that Comte, the father of positivism, "inspired only skepticism which thereby killed all impulses towards the ideal, all natural tendencies which flow towards God."

Reference materials on this organization are contained in the archival files of Armando Migueles, professor of Spanish at the University of Arizona. Dr. Migueles has done extensive research into the early cultural organizations in and around Tucson. Most of the records for these organizations are housed at the Arizona Heritage Center in Tucson and include microfiche copies of *El Tucsonense*. However, information is cursory, and oftentimes an organization is mentioned in the discussion of other subjects.

COALICIÓN DE BORICUAS, INC. (PUERTO RICAN COALITION) (CB)

Coalición de Boricuas is a nonprofit organization founded in San Jose, California, by Gustavo Nuñez and others concerned with meeting the unique needs of the growing Puerto Rican population in Santa Clara County. The corporation operates primarily as an information and referral service for Puerto Ricans. The organization also provides assistance to Puerto Ricans who have complaints about employment discrimination.

The organization is a hierarchically structured corporation headed by a board of directors, who set organizational policy and goals. The board is assisted by an executive director in carrying out decisions. The organization has assumed an important role in the Hispanic life of this community. However, they have experienced funding difficulties in recent years, forcing the CB to relinquish a centrally located office in San Jose. Nevertheless, they continue to sponsor highly successful fund-raising activities, such as their annual picnic, and they cosponsor many programs and activities with other organizations in the city.

There is little printed reference material on this organization in spite of its visibility in San Jose. The primary reference source on the organization is the *Directory of Spanish Speaking Community Organizations* (1970). Although several interviews were conducted with officers of the CB, they were hard-pressed to share reference materials that would provide expanded information on the organization. No other sources were identified.

COALITION OF FEDERAL HISPANIC EMPLOYEE ORGANIZATIONS

(COFHEO) Based in Washington, D.C., the Coalition is an association of Hispanic employee groups in the federal work force. The focus of this organization is to organize Hispanic civil servants and represent their interests before the executive branch, Congress, the media, and the public.

The COFHEO played a major role in the appointment of the first Hispanic to the Federal Communications Commission. It also sponsored a symposium, "Hispanics and the Media," designed to call attention to the lack of positive coverage of Hispanics by mainstream media, particularly in the Washington metropolitan area. The organization was also part of the organizing group for Hispanic Heritage Week, a Washington celebration of Hispanic historical roots.

A summary of this organization's activities is contained in *Nuestro Magazine* (March 1982). The historical origins of the COFHEO are not indicated.

COALITION OF PUERTO RICAN WOMEN, INC. (CPRW) The Coalition

is an association of Hispanic women in New York City which works with Hispanic persons in hospitals, prisons, and other institutions. It also raises money for scholarships for Hispanic youths.

A summary of this organization's activities is contained in the archives of the Robert Kennedy Memorial in Washington, D.C.

COALITION OF SPANISH SPEAKING MENTAL HEALTH ORGANI-ZATIONS See NATIONAL COALITION OF HISPANIC MENTAL HEALTH AND HUMAN SERVICES ORGANIZATIONS.

COLLEGE OF ARCHITECTS OF CUBA IN EXILE ASSOCIATION (CA-CEA) A professional national organization founded in 1961 and based in Miami, Florida, the College has a membership totaling over 400 consisting of members of the Colegio de Arquitectos de Cuba (Cuban College of Architects) who reorganized in the United States. Membership is open to architects exiled from Cuba or Cubans who have become architects in the United States. Their goals are to seek Cuban "liberty" and to initiate and maintain research programs in architecture, city planning, social welfare, etc. The association sponsors exhibits and awards. It also regularly publishes *Architecture in Exile*.

The most recent reference source for the CACEA is the *Directory of Spanish Speaking Community Organizations* (1970). Further references may be available from the organization, including bylaws, articles of incorporation, copies of *Architecture in Exile*, and membership forms.

COLONIA HOLGUINERA (HOSPITALITY GROUP) (CH) The members of this club in Highland Park, California, include many South and Central American nationalities. The Club is open to all Latin Americans who wish to meet others like themselves. Club activities include parties with live Latin bands, athletic games such as soccer and baseball, and other social events.

This organization is an example of the many social clubs founded to make South Americans feel at home in the United States. There usually is little printed references to the history, goals, and purposes of these groups. Most often they are unincorporated and therefore lack articles of incorporation and bylaws. Whether this is the case with the CH is uncertain. Summary information is contained in the archives of Dr. Andre Simic, Department of Anthropology, University of Southern California.

COMISIÓN FEMENIL MEXICANA NACIONAL (NATIONAL COM-MISSION OF MEXICAN WOMEN) (CFMN) In 1970 a national Hispanic Issues Conference was held in Sacramento, California. A group of women attending the meeting decided to respond to the lack of organizations dealing with the problems of Mexican American women by founding this association.

The purposes of Comisión Femenil are to improve the status of Mexican American women, to treat issues which pertain to the Mexican American woman and her family, and to provide leadership training for the same. The organization is a hierarchically structured one headed by a board of directors. Under board supervision is a set of officers charged with responsibility for executing decisions. Assisting the officers are the several standing committees on education, health and welfare, and legislative issues. While CFMN is predominantly a California organization in terms of chapter locations and membership, there are now ten regional groups and five state groups located throughout the United States. The California chapters are situated in Fresno, Watsonville, Modesto, Los Angeles, Pasadena, San Gabriel Valley, Rio Hondo, Sacramento, and San Diego. The majority of the members are Mexican American women.

CFMN philosophy centers on the belief that the most effective means of enhancing the status of Mexican American women throughout the United States is via involvement in the legislative process. CFMN conducts various programs and activities which reflect this belief and the goals of the organization.

CFMN has been a longtime champion for the rights of Mexican American women. The organization was instrumental in the founding of the Chicana Service Action Center* (CSAC) in Los Angeles, which operates an employment counseling and manpower training program. The organization also maintains two bilingual child development centers in Los Angeles called Centro de Niños (Children's Center). Individual chapters develop their own local programs, such as the Fresno chapter's job training program, Working Opportunities for Women.

The CFMN has joined a number of class action suits as a plaintiff. In 1978–79 CFMN filed suit to stop forced sterilizations of Mexican American women. Subsequently, the organization also participated in a suit seeking continued Medi-Cal funding for abortions.

This organization likes to maintain a high political profile, and this has been the chief criticism of an otherwise productive group. In November 1977 CFMN representatives organized to promote CFMN leadership of the Latina agenda at the National Women's Year Conference in Houston, Texas. This was done at the expense of unity and caused dissension within the Hispana ranks. Again CFMN leadership, angered with what they saw as competition from the Mexican American Women's National Association's* (MANA) role in planning of the National Hispanic Feminist Conference in 1980, participated in organizing a boycott of the conference hotel. MANA, as the most prominent Mexican American women's organization nationally, was cosponsor of the event. The CFMN-assisted boycott seriously disrupted activities and alienated participants. CFMN then proceeded to try to wrestle conference leadership away from the organizing committee. They proposed the formulation of an ad hoc committee at the conference for purposes of decision making, with the majority of members from the CFMN. This committee was to be charged with further conference activities during and beyond the meeting. However, since the NHFC was the result of a government-funded grant awarded to the grant initiator and San Jose State University, this last move was unsuccessful.

Although CFMN critics disapprove of the organization's tactics, the organization is praised for its successful programs and earnest efforts on behalf of Mexican American women. They have also helped run effective political campaigns on behalf of Mexican American candidates, such as U.S. Congressman Edward Roybal and California State Assemblywoman Gloria Molina.

CFMN representatives participated in the National ERA March held in Chicago, Illinois, in 1980. At the CFMN annual conference held in April 1978, La

Mujer, Acción y Cambio, eleven resolutions were passed setting priorities for 1978–79. Latinas from California, Texas, Colorado, and Washington, D.C., were in attendance. The CFMN health committee has been active on a number of fronts. The committee presents papers on the health conditions of the Mexican American community at workshops throughout the state of California and the nation. The organization has issued a "pro-choice" statement reiterating the stance of the CFMN on the abortion issue. A brochure on issues relating to health care for undocumented persons was developed by this committee. Other committee actions include joining the national boycott of Nestle products and the production of a regular health column in the CFMN newsletter published bimonthly.

The most reliable reference on the CFMN's history is a document assembled by the organization, *Comisión Femenil History* (1978), available from the organization. A helpful summary is included in *A Guide to Hispanic Organizations* (1979). For purposes of this work, interviews with various women's organizations and Mexican American women's leadership were utilized as well as direct study and recollected notes by this author.

COMITÉ ESTADO 51, PUERTO RICO (COMMITTEE FOR PUERTO RICAN STATEHOOD) (CEPR) An issue that has stimulated extensive debate in Puerto Rico and on the mainland is that of statehood with the United States. Governors of Puerto Rico have been elected according to their stance on the issue, and violent acts have been committed over the pros and cons of the debate. This organization was founded in July 1980 in New York City by a group of Puerto Ricans who favor statehood rather than an independent or commonwealth status. Among the founders were Mario Figueroa and Carlos Semanete.

The main goal of the Committee is to educate Puerto Ricans in the United States on the positive aspects of Puerto Rican statehood. Among these espoused advantages are the gain of full political rights of citizenship, including the right to vote for the president, and equal treatment with regard to federal programs.

The CEPR is a hierarchically structured organization with an executive director, president, vice-president, and executive secretary, who serve as the group's official spokespersons. All Americans are eligible for membership if they are at least sixteen years of age and are familiar with the workings of the U.S. and Puerto Rican governments. The organization encourages the utilization of non-violent means for the espousal of committee views and is not affiliated with any U.S. political party. Committee members participate with other prostatehood groups in Puerto Rican parades in northeastern United States cities such as Philadelphia and New York. The Committee also produces pro-statehood leaflets and, along with these, circulates articles written in the United States and Puerto Rico promoting statehood. The organization also distributes cloth emblems and membership cards depicting a U.S. flag with fifty-one stars. The slogan of Comité Estado 51, Puerto Rico is "Statehood Now."

Reference sources for this organization include the CEPR bylaws, various statehood articles circulated by the Committee, committee-produced leaflets, and the organization's membership card.

COMMUNITIES ORGANIZED FOR PUBLIC SERVICE (COPS) In the 1970s the Catholic Church became a catalyst for many of its religious servants to undertake a doctrine of political activism in the areas of civil and human rights. Organizations of nuns and priests committed to spiritual and economic renewal of the Mexican American community emerged. Las Hermanas* (LH) and Padres Asociados por Derechos Religiosos, Educativos, y Sociales* (PADRES) were the most notable. At the same time, more Hispanics were advanced to positions of prominence within the Catholic hierarchy, such as Juan A. Arzube to auxiliary bishop in Los Angeles, Robert F. Sanchez to archbishop of Santa Fe, Manuel Moreno to auxiliary bishop of Los Angeles, and in May 1978, Patrick Flores to bishop of El Paso.

Of all of the religious activists, the most aggressive and innovative may have been Patrick Flores, who helped found a Mexican American Cultural Center (MACC) in San Antonio and raised $500,000 annually for its support, and was instrumental in the creation of COPS for the purpose of involving grass-roots parishioners in social change. Also instrumental in the formation of this group was Ernesto Cortes, Jr.

The leaders received training from Saul Alinsky's Industrial Areas Foundation (IAF) in Chicago. Alinsky preached a doctrine of confrontation and sometimes disruption as a way of provoking social change. In theory this conflicted with the *Pedagogy of the Oppressed* (1970) methodology of Paulo Freire, which advocated dialogue and nonviolence as a process for understanding and cooperation. So although Freire's book became the intellectual handbook of the Mexican American movement, impatience and anger gave way to Alinsky's confrontational tactics.

COPS challenged the city of San Antonio, forcing the City Council to build curbs and drainage ditches in Mexican American neighborhoods. The organization protested the awarding of $1.3 million in federal funds to the Pecan Valley Country Club, lobbied for more money from state government for San Antonio schools, and worked for the election of progressive champions of the poor to the City Council. COPS represented a radical departure from the organizations of the 1960s. And while COPS took on the established powers, it was also accused of seeking power for itself. Whether this was the case with COPS is questionable. What is certain is that the organization has followed a path of well-disciplined political activism in the name of the Hispanic Catholic hierarchy. Its sister organization in Los Angeles, United Neighborhoods Organization* (UNO), has chosen a more conservative approach, focusing on neighborhood organization for community physical and economic well-being as opposed to electoral politics.

The sources for the COPS history include Rodolfo Acuña, *Occupied America* (1981), and Jose Amaro Hernandez, "The Political Development of Mutual Aid Societies in the Mexican American Community: Ideals and Principles" (Ph.D.

dissertation, University of California, Riverside, 1979). Neither of these references included information on organizational structure and membership.

COMMUNITY SERVICE ORGANIZATION (CSO) CSO was one of many organizations founded in California in the late 1940s and early 1950s by returning Mexican American servicemen anxious to participate actively in American society and improve the status of the Mexican American community. Recognizing a lack of opportunity for leadership in existing assistance programs, dedicated Mexican Americans decided to form their own community organizations. The CSO, founded in 1947 in Los Angeles, was one of the first of these organizations.

The organization began by attacking a series of problems confronting the East Los Angeles community, including poor educational opportunities and police mistreatment of Mexican American youth. From an original membership of 15, the CSO grass-roots participation quickly grew to over 250 people meeting in a local elementary school to discuss these local issues of concern to the Mexican American community.

CSO recognized as a priority the unresponsive municipal government. They supported the election of Edward Roybal to the Los Angeles City Council and were defeated. Undaunted, CSO sought the seasoned political savvy of Fred Ross and embarked on a massive voter registration drive to ensure Roybal's victory in the next election. Sixty-three CSO members were sworn in as deputy registrars, and 12,000 Mexican American citizens were registered by the end of the year. House meetings were organized where neighbors invited neighbors into their homes to listen to a representative of the CSO. The organization succeeded in registering 40,000 voters in East Los Angeles and increased its membership to 3,000. And in 1949, the first Mexican American in sixty-eight years was elected to the Los Angeles City Council. The recognition of this community's political potential gave impetus for future political mobilization of Spanish-speaking citizens.

The CSO soon moved from the political arena, where they had experienced much success, to a concern with providing the Mexican American community with mutual aid services. The CSO no longer overtly or formally supported a candidate for political office. Informally, they organized unofficial fund-raising activities for candidates sensitive to Mexican American community concerns. The CSO chose a direction reminiscent of the early organizing efforts of the Mexican American community. The mutual aid approach was seen as a way of solidifying its membership and pursuing long-term goals. Some of the mutual aid programs initiated by the CSO and its approximately thirty California chapters included death benefit insurance, a credit union, a buyer's club, and consumer complaint center.

Although contemporary published references for this organization are brief, the CSO has played a dramatic role in the grass-roots organizational efforts in the Mexican American community. Many leading associations and individuals can trace their roots to the early CSO, including Cesar Chavez. Contemporary

Mexican American historians and social scientists have paid considerable attention to the CSO, however scarce the documented record, and among them are F. Chris Garcia, *La Causa Politica: A Chicano Politics Reader* (1974); Leo Grebler, Joan W. Moore, and Ralph C. Guzman, *The Mexican American People* (1970); Julian Zamora, *La Raza, Forgotten Americans* (1966); Rodolfo Acuña, *Occupied America* (1981); and Michael David Tirado, "The Mexican American Minority's Participation in Voluntary Political Associations" (Ph.D. dissertation, Claremont Graduate School and University, 1970).

CONCILIO REGIONAL DE ORGANIZACIONES PUERTORIQUEÑOS DEL OESTE See WESTERN REGIONAL PUERTO RICAN COUNCIL.

CONFEDERACIÓN DE PROFESIONALES CUBANOS (CONFEDERATION OF CUBAN PROFESSIONALS) (CPC) In the early 1970s in the rapidly growing and increasingly influential Cuban community in Miami, there was a need for an organization to provide special services for professionals seeking to establish themselves in a professional capacity. In 1970 the CPC was formed in Miami to assist Cuban professionals in preparation for Florida licensing examinations, particularly for medical, legal, and accounting certification.

The CPC is made up of professional associations with delegates assessed a twenty-dollar fee to cover operational costs. The organization holds monthly board meetings and an annual meeting of officers.

A summary of this organization is included in *A Guide to Hispanic Organizations* (1979).

CONFEDERACIÓN DE UNIONES OBRERAS MEXICANAS (CONFEDERATION OF MEXICAN LABOR UNIONS) (CUOM) CUOM was founded March 23, 1928, in Los Angeles, California, as a response to substandard working conditions and wages. The original members of the CUOM were persons affiliated with the Committee of the Federation of Mexican Societies (CFMS) in Los Angeles, which was made up of mutual aid and benefit societies in southern California.

CUOM formulated a constitution that was formally adopted by the organization at their convention in 1928. The constitution was modeled after the Regional Confederation of Labor in Mexico's (CROM) constitution and included a declaration of principles which in part stated:

1. That the exploited class, the greater part of which is made up of manual labor, is right in establishing a class struggle in order to effect an economic and moral betterment of its condition, and at last, its complete freedom from capitalistic tyranny.

2. That in order to be able to oppose the organization each day the more complete and intelligent of the exploiters [*sic*], the exploited class must organize as such, the base of its organization being the union of resistence, in accord with the rights which the laws of this country concede to native and foreign workers.

3. That the corporations, possessors of the natural and social wealth, being integral parts of the international association of industry, commerce, and banking, the disinherited class must also integrate by means of its federations and confederation into a single union of all the labor of the world.

The constitution also called for a central committee made up of two delegates from each of the representative locals. The central committee administered all functions of the Confederation between conventions and was authorized to "make solidarity agreements with labor organizations, national and foreign, . . . but always without weakening in any manner the autonomy of this organization and the nationality of its components." The first central committee was composed of Elias S. Garcia, secretary general; Enrique Toral, secretary of the interior; Pascual S. Diaz, secretary of the exterior; Armando Flores, secretary of the treasury; Jesus M. Olguin, secretary of education; Manuel Olmos, secretary of record; Lucas A. Raya, secretary of English; Manuel F. Cabanillas, secretary of agriculture; Alberto R. Telles, secretary of labor; Rafael Gutierrez, secretary of the press. Manuel Olmos and Armando Flores were designated general organizers.

Twenty-one locals sent delegates to the Confederation's first convention, held May 5, 6, and 7, 1928. A delegate from the Regional Confederation of Labor in Mexico (CROM) was also in attendance. The constitution formulated at this convention not only emphasized the class struggle but also stated that "the industries must be in the hands of those who are capable of maintaining said industries in production."

Articles 5 and 6 of the general program of the new constitution directed the Confederation to study and determine, in accordance with the Mexican government, the best systems of repatriations for Mexican workers as well as to bring pressure to bear on the Mexican government to regulate and limit Mexican labor into the United States, especially given the large appetite for Mexican labor among American businesses.

Membership within the Confederation fluctuated with the demands of seasonal labor since it included both agricultural and industrial workers in rural and urban contexts. The total membership was between 2,000 and 3,000 persons in May 1928, with 200 actual dues-paying members in March 1929.

Interest seemed to have waned after 1930 due to a series of events such as the Great Depression, forced deportation and voluntary repatriation of thousands of Mexican and Mexican Americans, and the difficulties of maintaining an urban and rural federation of unions, mutualist associations, and social clubs under one banner. So on July 15, 1933, the Confederation reconvened as the Confederación de Uniones de Campesinos y Obreros Mexicanos del Estado de California (Confederation of Mexican Peasant and Workers Unions of the State of California) (CUCOM), composed of fifty member unions, mutualist associations, and social clubs. By 1934 this new spinoff organization had 10,000 members. Among the leaders of the new group were Guillermo Velarde, Jose Espinosa, and Bernard Lucero. Most left-wing organizers were attracted to CUCOM, which took the leadership in six of the eighteen strikes called during 1935. This activity was centered in Orange and San Diego counties.

In January 1936 the CUCOM led in forming the Federation of Agricultural Workers of America, which was joined by eleven locals of Filipino, Japanese, and other nationalities. In the spring of 1936 CUCOM led a walkout of 2,600 celery workers in Los Angeles County. Parades and picket lines were teargassed, union members beaten and arrested. And in 1937, when urban unions began to pay more attention to these rural unions, CUCOM entered into negotiations with other cultural labor unions to form an alliance. In 1937 they sent delegates to Denver and joined the United Cannery, Agricultural, Packing, and Allied Workers of America (UCAPAWA).

It is necessary to consult a variety of sources to assemble a progressive history of this union from CUOM to CUCOM. Rodolfo Acuña, *Occupied America* (1981) reports on the CUCOM but does not trace its origins to CUOM. Acuña does indicate that leaders of CUOM were involved in the formation of CUCOM. A primary reference source for Acuña's documentation of the CUCOM is Stuart Jamieson, *Labor Unionism in American Agriculture* (1976). The most important sources for the CUOM's history are *Mexicans in California: Report of Governor C. C. Young's Mexican Fact-Finding Committee* (1930), a report prepared by the State Department of Industrial Relations; and Ronald W. Lopez, "The El Monte Berry Strike," *Aztlan-Chicano Journal of the Social Sciences and the Arts* 1:1 (1974), a reprint.

CONGRESO DE LATINOS UNIDOS (UNITED LATINS CONGRESS) (CLU) In the 1970s the Delaware Valley experienced a rapid increase in its Hispanic population. There was a need for a coordinating organization to serve the community and to familiarize the government with the social and economic problems of the area's Hispanic peoples. Congreso de Latinos Unidos, also referred to popularly as El Congreso, was created in the Commonwealth of Pennsylvania on September 29, 1977, to fill this need.

The goals of the organization are multifold and include the deliverance of human and social services to the Hispanic community of the Delaware Valley, advisement to government institutions regarding the needs of the community, and service as an organized voice on behalf of the community before state and county governments.

Congreso de Latinos Unidos is a hierarchically structured organization governed by a fifteen-member board of directors. To serve on the board one must be eighteen years of age or older, a U.S. citizen, and reasonably fluent in both English and Spanish. Also, board members must have experience in human services delivery and be elected by the membership. The board meets monthly to determine organizational policy and to oversee the functioning of the corporation's various committees. Next in line is a set of officers, including a president, vice-president, secretary, treasurer, and general counsel, who are elected by the board from among its own members. The president sees to the execution of the board's decisions. There is an executive director who serves as a chief administrator and operations officer. There is also an executive committee, which advises the board of directors in managing the corporation. Other committees are formed by the board on an ad hoc basis.

One of the chief programs of CLU is Centro Nuevos Caminos, an alcoholism treatment program. The Center is located in the city of Philadelphia and is funded by the National Institute of Alcohol Abuse and Alcoholism. This Center provides assistance to its clients in the areas of therapy, psychiatric and medical examination, education and prevention, vocational and educational outreach, and other support services.

References for this organization include the CLU bylaws (1977) and CLU's substance abuse program brochure.

CONGRESO, EL, See NATIONAL CONGRESS OF HISPANIC AMERICAN CITIZENS.

CONGRESO NACIONAL DE ASUNTOS COLEGIALES (NATIONAL CONGRESS OF COLLEGIATE AFFAIRS) (CONAC) In the late 1960s a group of Mexican American educators began to meet informally to discuss new forms of postsecondary and nonformal education. This focus of discussion was generated by a unanimous concern for the expansion of educational opportunities for the Spanish-speaking population of the Southwest. CONAC was formed in Washington, D.C., in 1971 as a result of these meetings.

The organization's goals include the improvement of the educational, social, and economic well-being of Spanish-speaking persons in community and junior colleges. Further, CONAC aims to secure the provision of adequate and effective education for the Hispanic community. This is a hierarchically structured organization. The board of directors is composed of representatives from states with large Spanish-speaking populations such as California, Texas, Arizona, Colorado, New Mexico, and New York. CONAC employs an executive director, who is in charge of overseeing organizational projects. CONAC employs three permanent staff members in its Washington, D.C., headquarters and employs project staff on an ad hoc basis. Membership in CONAC is open to persons involved in educational institutions and education-related, community-based programs. CONAC, in 1979, had a total membership of some 1,500 community and junior college faculty, administrators, and students. In 1972 CONAC became affiliated with the Council of the American Association of Community and Junior Colleges (AACJC). In 1974 CONAC became affiliated with the American Council on Education (ACE) and the American Society for Engineering Education (ASEE).

Since its founding CONAC has undergone a change in focus and activities. Upon its establishment CONAC functioned as a national register for educators, social scientists, educational trainers, researchers, and management specialists from the United States and other countries. CONAC's early activities included the collection, research, analysis, and assessment and dissemination of data relevant to bilingual, bicultural education. CONAC also was involved in the identification and recommendation of model approaches to meet the needs of Spanish speakers and assistance to organizations seeking solutions to the educational problems of Spanish speakers in the United States.

In 1974 the organization broadened its educational scope to include other countries, and in cooperation with the office of internal programs of the AACJC, CONAC undertook a comparative bilingual research project in Latin America. It has since participated in a number of international projects, most of which have involved the development of community college programs and personnel adapted to the individual nation's needs and conditions. In aiding international education departments, the use of appropriate technology and analytical approaches are emphasized, according to the organization. In all, CONAC has consulted with sixty countries, including the Ivory Coast, where it helped develop a national system of community colleges.

Domestically, CONAC has conducted several projects focusing on the preparation of Mexican Americans at the doctoral level for administrative positions in community and junior colleges. Additionally, CONAC has sponsored numerous seminars, workshops, and colloquia related to the Spanish-speaking student. It plans in the future to assist in the preparation of more Spanish-speaking administrators, bilingual teachers, counselors, librarians, financial administrators, and science personnel for community colleges.

CONAC maintains a library with some 800 volumes on multicultural Hispanic education. Organization publications include *Fomento Literario*, a triennial journal; *Boletin*, an irregularly published newsletter; plus monographs and occasional papers. CONAC utilizes Aztec symbols such as Texcatlipoca, the Aztec god of knowledge, to represent its goals and purposes.

The journal and newsletters serve as excellent references for this organization. Also, CONAC has compiled an organizational history which is available from the organization in pamphlet form (n.d.).

Primary sources for this work consisted of the CONAC-completed HAVO questionnaire, CONAC membership advertisement and application form, and the history pamphlet.

CONGRESSIONAL HISPANIC CAUCUS (CHC) The formation of the Congressional Hispanic Caucus was formally announced in Washington, D.C., in December 1976. A group of Hispanic members of the House of Representatives got together to work toward Hispanic involvement in the newly elected Carter Administration. The development of a national policy that reflects the concerns and needs of the nation's Hispanic population is one of their major priorities.

The Hispanic Caucus works to reverse the exclusion of Hispanics under previous administrations by focusing on two goals: the development of legislative and budgetary priorities; and the encouragement of greater Hispanic participation at all policy-making levels of government. These objectives would encompass the monitoring of legislative action to assure appropriate inclusion of Hispanic concerns. The CHC works with a coalition of groups both inside and outside of Congress to accomplish these goals.

CHC founding members include the Caucus's first chairman and guiding spirit, Representative Edward R. Roybal from California, Representative E. Kika de la Garza from Texas, and Resident Commissioner-Elect Baltasar Corrada of Puerto Rico. Members vote their conscience on all congressional issues but are expected to consult each other and vote as one on Hispanic issues.

The Caucus held its first annual fund-raising dinner in 1978. Close to 900 people attended from throughout the United States. First Lady Rosalynn Carter was the keynote speaker, and Joan Mondale, wife of the vice-president, acted as dinner chairperson. The dinner raised $80,000 for the Caucus. This money was used for educational functions, research development, and the establishment of a statistical clearinghouse on data pertinent to Hispanics. With the success of this first dinner, the annual fund-raiser has become the most important "event" in the Hispanic community, continuing to draw larger numbers of guests each year. The "event" is also televised over the Spanish International Television Network (SIN) for home viewing and participation.

The CHC publishes *Avance*, a bimonthly newsletter. *Avance* reports on organizational activities, features articles by Caucus members, and provides data on the Hispanic population. In 1979 *Avance* announced the availability of a directory compiled by the Caucus of approximately 100 Hispanic state and national elected officials from Arizona, California, Colorado, Missouri, New Mexico, New York, and Texas.

Since its initiation, the CHC reports that it has dealt with issues relating to bilingual education, immigration, fair housing, census procedures, police brutality, and affirmative action. According to *Avance* the Caucus has been influential in expediting investigations into more than 200 cases of alleged police brutality against Hispanics. Moreover, the CHC has been instrumental in defeating amendments by the House of Representatives that would result in the elimination of federal bilingual education programs. One of the most startling successes of the Caucus was its extensive mobilization of the Hispanic community nationwide to defeat the Simpson-Mazzoli immigration reform legislation. However, the bill was reintroduced in 1984; the CHC was forced to mount another campaign; and, in spite of the overwhelming response from the Hispanic community, it passed in the House of Representatives. This legislation was determined by the CHC and major Latino groups to be decidedly anti-Hispanic.

There are a variety of primary sources on the CHC, including editions of the *Avance* newsletter. Also, there is a helpful summary by Raul Yzaguirre, "The Hispanic Congressional Caucus: A New Sign of Unity," *Avance* (1977). An early reference was the December 8, 1976, press release issued by Congressman Roybal announcing the formulation of the CHC.

CONGRESS OF ORGANIZATIONS OF PUERTO RICAN HOMETOWNS (COPRH) As a national organization founded in 1958 and based in New York

City, COPRH serves as a liaison agency for Puerto Rican organizations and state and muncipal authorities. Membership is restricted to Puerto Rican organizations, fifty-seven of which presently comprise its membership. The organization has a permanent staff of twelve. The Congress meets three times a year.

COPRH, as a coordinating organization for its member groups, seeks to improve the status of Puerto Ricans through a unified approach to community efforts. Its activities include job training classes, voter registration and civil rights programs, special education classes, and the sponsorship of a summer camp for Puerto Rican children.

References to the Congress's history are scant. An attempt to solicit further information from the organization was unsuccessful. The sources used for this work include the archives of the Robert Kennedy Memorial and the *Directory of Spanish Speaking Community Organizations* (1970).

COUNCIL OF MEXICAN AMERICAN AFFAIRS (CMAA) This organization was founded in Los Angeles in 1953 to represent a cross-section of the Mexican American community and to organize all Mexican American community organizations under one permanent coordinating body. The organization was founded as a nonpartisan, nonsectarian, and nonprofit citizens organization dedicated to the development of leadership among Americans of Mexican descent and to coordinate the efforts of all the various organizations and groups concerned with the betterment of the Mexican American in the Los Angeles area.

As originally established, CMAA's governing board consisted of thirteen members at large and twelve representatives of the house of delegates, which listed forty-four member organizations. Some of the organizations were social, some made up of veterans, and some community service programs. The membership consisted mainly of Mexican Americans described as individuals desirous of improving the social, economic, educational, and cultural conditions of this population. They included business, professional, and labor leaders.

CMAA emphasized cooperation, unity, and a better way of life for Mexican Americans. Conferences were held on youth problems and delinquency, narcotics, education, and job opportunities and training. The organization maintained an office and full-time executive director. Yet CMAA's efforts to unite the many organizations in the Mexican American community failed. A fund-raising campaign was unsuccessful, and member organizations refused to pay their dues. A twenty-five dollar membership fee had to be paid in order for an organization's delegate to vote on business matters and policy. CMAA could not raise a quorum of delegates in order to elect officers or transact business. The organization soon fell into debt. The CMAA office was closed and the staff dismissed.

There was renewed interest in CMAA in 1963, and it was reorganized under a new leadership and approach to serving the Mexican American community. This new leadership, composed of successful Mexican American professionals and businessmen, chose instead to function as a high-level pressure group rather than as a grass-roots organizing body. The organization sponsors political banquets and community forums to honor public officials and to support Mexican Americans in public office.

There are two secondary reference sources on this organization of wide circulation: Julian Samora, *La Raza, Forgotten Americans* (1966); and Michael Tirado, "The Mexican American Minority's Participation in Voluntary Political Associations" (Ph.D. dissertation, Claremont Graduate School and University, 1971).

CRUSADE FOR JUSTICE (CFJ) The Crusade for Justice was one of the more prominent radical organizations of the 1960s to come out of the Mexican American movement. The founder and president of the Crusade, Rodolfo "Corky" Gonzales, was an influential Mexican American leader among urban youth. He was a professional boxer who had won a Golden Gloves championship and was a contender for the featherweight championship from 1947 to 1955. He was born in 1928 in Denver, Colorado, the son of migrant sugar beet workers. In the late 1950s and early 1960s, he became a leader in the Democratic Party of Colorado, serving as the first Mexican American district captain in 1957. Corky Gonzales was also active in the Mexican American community. He operated a bail bond business and auto insurance agency. Eventually, in 1963 his involvement led him to organize demonstrations against police brutality. After being fired as the director of one of the Denver War on Poverty's youth programs in 1966, Corky Gonzales founded the Crusade. Originally housed in an old, red brick building in a condemned neighborhood in Denver, the CFJ later managed to buy an old church and establish a Mexican American center.

The basic goals and objectives of the CFJ were to develop a civil rights organization. However, it soon became evident that the primary problem affecting Mexican American youth was their early educational experience. Neighborhood *barrio* youth were frightened by the schools, where their ethnic identity was challenged. The psychological impact of the Mexican American historical experience was eloquently expressed in the popular epic poem *I Am Joaquin* by Corky Gonzales, which was developed into a powerful film for classroom use. Education, then, became the primary focus of the CFJ, although other civil rights issues continued to be addressed.

The CFJ encourages total family involvement in its activities, sometimes hosting weddings and other traditional family events. It has also established a school, Tlatelolco, designed to educate from preschool to college. The Crusade published a newspaper, *El Gallo, La Voz de la Justicia* (The Rooster, the Voice of Justice). Membership in the Crusade consists mainly of Mexican Americans in Denver, Colorado. There has been no recordkeeping on the actual size of membership throughout the organization's history. Likewise, there is no evidence of CFJ structure, decision making, or officers other than its president, Rodolfo "Corky" Gonzales.

The Crusade has housed a school, curio shop, bookstore, and social center.

It has offered educational courses, an art gallery for exhibition of neighborhood art, a nursery, a gymnasium, a legal aid service, a major ballroom for social and other activities, shops, and library. The Center has also administered a job skills bank, neighborhood police review board, health and housing social worker, bail bond service, and a theater.

On March 27–30, 1969, the Crusade sponsored the First National Chicano Youth Conference at Denver. The purpose of the Conference was to promote greater unity and cultural awareness among the youth. Approximately 1,500 youths representing numerous Mexican American student organizations attended. From this Conference came El Plan de Aztlan (The Plan of Aztlan), a document espousing ethnic nationalism and self-determination among Mexican Americans in the entire Southwest. In addition, the Plan brought together all Mexican American student organizations under the name of the Movimiento Estudiantil Chicano de Aztlan* (MECHA).

The CFJ also organized the Chicano United Conference in Denver on August 29–30, 1969. This Conference provided the impetus for massive school walkouts throughout the Southwest on September 16, Mexican Independence Day. And on March 25–29, 1970, the Second Annual National Chicano Youth Conference was held in Denver. The most important resolution adopted by the participants called for the formation of an independent Mexican American political party and a national moratorium against the war in Vietnam. On the last day of the Conference the formation of the Colorado state branch of the Partido La Raza Unida* (PLRU) was announced, and the Chicano Moratorium was held in Los Angeles on August 29, 1970.

The Crusade has been a victim of considerable harassment by police and other local authorities because of its activism. On March 17, 1973, an outburst of shooting and an explosion took place in an apartment building owned by the CFJ. Corky asked for an investigation of the incident by the U.S. Justice Department. Police contended that there were numerous weapons in the building, and the mayor of Denver refused to support a Justice Department investigation. Corky contended that several members of the crusade had been shot, arrested, and brutalized by police. This event marked a steady deterioration in relations between the CFJ and Denver city officials.

In the late 1960s and early 1970s, the Crusade was the most prominent of Chicano movement organizations. Its leader, Corky Gonzales, was sought after on college campuses throughout the country. Certainly the crusade was instrumental in calling national attention to the plight of Mexican Americans in the Southwest. And although it appears that the Crusade has declined in influence in recent years, its historical impact cannot be denied. Corky's poem *I Am Joaquin* remains a classic documentation of the passions and pain of that decade of struggle.

Contemporary references to the crusade include Elizabeth Sutherland Martinez and Enriqueta Longeau y Vasquez, *Viva la Raza* (1974); Rodolfo Acuña, *Occupied America* (1972); Christine Marin, *A Spokesman of the Mexican American*

Movement: Rodolfo "Corky" Gonzales (1977); Carlos Larralde, *Mexican American Movements and Leaders* (1976).

Also, it is almost certain that the CFJ maintains an extensive archive on its activities in the Center. Old copies of *El Gallo* and other references to its activities appearing in local and national magazines and newspapers must form a part of its library collection.

CUBAN ASSOCIATION, INC. (CA) This organization was founded in Gary, Indiana, for the purpose of uniting Cuban families in the area. The organization fosters social and cultural relations, assists newcomers in adjusting to the community, and helps individuals seek employment.

The Association is a membership organization and admits any individual who subscribes to its goals. It publishes *Estrella Cubana* on a monthly basis.

Estrella Cubana should provide information on the organization's activities. Also, local newspapers may contain references to this group. The CA failed to respond to requests for information. A summary of its activities can be found in the archives of the Robert Kennedy Memorial in Washington, D.C.

CUBAN DENTAL ASSOCIATION IN EXILE (CDAE) This Association is typical of many such professional organizations founded by Cubans in exile. These groups were made up of Cubans who came to Miami in the 1950s and 1960s and organized for professional reasons and to sustain their Cuban identity. CDAE seeks to ensure full use of the talents of its members and to help them with any orientation to practice in the United States.

A summary of this organization is contained in the archives of the Robert Kennedy Memorial in Washington, D.C.

CUBAN LICEUM OF DETROIT (CLD) This is a local social organization founded in 1971 and based in Michigan. It has a permanent staff to respond to a membership of approximately 120 families. Annual dues are twenty-four dollars. Solicitation for membership requires the signature of two members and approval by the board of directors. Officers of the CLD include a president, vice-president, and secretary.

The principal objective of the organization is the promotion of social and cultural Cuban activities in Detroit and surrounding areas. The Liceum provides English-language classes for Cuban Americans. The CLD holds annual general membership meetings. It publishes a monthly, *Cuban Liceum Echos*, with issues dating back to 1973.

Information on the CLD's organizational functions are summarized in the organization's publication. The most available summary of the CLD's activities can be found in the *Directory of Spanish Speaking Community Organizations* (1970).

CUBAN MEDICAL ASSOCIATION IN EXILE (CMAE) Similar to other Cuban professional organizations, the CMAE is made up of physicians who chose to leave Cuba after the revolution that led to the Marxist-oriented Castro government. Most of these physicians were prosperous members of the former Cuban professional elite. They joined the mass exodus of the early 1960s and reestablished themselves mainly in Miami, Florida.

The Association promotes the professional interests of its members and strives to sustain the Cuban cultural heritage in the United States. It also provides assistance to newcomers to the profession.

A summary of this organization's activities is contained in the archives of the Robert Kennedy Memorial in Washington, D.C.

CUBAN NATIONAL PLANNING COUNCIL (CNPC) In 1972 the Reverend Mario Vizcaino and a small group of Cuban Americans generated the concept of a nonprofit organization in Washington, D.C., to assist the Cuban community in its efforts to communicate professionally and effectively with government officials. Formally organized in the same year, the organization has as its primary focus to identify the social, economic, and cultural needs of Cubans in the United States and to assist in their adjustment to American society. CNPC has emerged as a multiservice agency structure and assumes a leadership role in providing employment, education, community, and economic development services to the Cuban American community.

The structural organization consists of a national board, with its executive committee composed of a president, vice-president, treasurer, and secretary. The CNPC also has six regional boards located in Florida, New York, New Jersey, Chicago, Washington, D.C., and California. Each board elects a representative, who together with the regional board president holds a seat on the national board. Thus, there are twelve directors, two from each regional board, representing their respective communities before the board's executive committee.

The CNPC has taken an active role in the development of an effective community. As a part of its activities it has developed programs which meet the needs of their target population. In instances where there has already been an existing organization, CNPC found it profitable to join them in their goal. As a result, some CNPC board members are also members of multiple boards and committees, such as the Dade Monroe Mental Health Board, Miami Mental Health Association Board, National Minority Advisory Council to LEAA, and the National Hispanic Coalition for Better Housing. CNPC has also cosponsored other such organizations, such as the National Coalition of Hispanic Mental Health and Human Services Organizations* (COSSMO), Asociación Nacional Pro Personas Mayores* (ANPPM), National Council of La Raza* (NCLR), and the National Puerto Rican Forum* (NPRF).

The CNPC has been primarily responsible for the early research on Cubans sponsored by the Department of Education and Welfare. In 1973 CNPC published the monograph, *The Cuban Minority in the United States: Preliminary Report on Need Identification and Program Evaluation*, by Raphael Prohias and Lourdes Casals. This work represented an important first step for information gathering on the Cuban population. In 1977, under a grant from the National Institute of Mental Health, the CNPC conducted a project aimed at researching the psychosocial stresses and resources of Cubans residing in the areas of Miami and Union City, New Jersey, the two largest concentrations of Cubans in the United States. CNPC also contracted with the U.S. Department of Health, Education, and Welfare to evaluate the impact that this department's services and programs have on Cubans in five target cities.

More recently, on the national level, CNPC played a major role in providing resettlement services to Cuban refugees. CNPC worked within and outside the Cuban community in providing assistance to the Marielitos (Mariel refugees) in adjusting to American life. CNPC utilized voluntary and contracted services to meet their needs. Halfway houses were established by the organization to provide food, shelter, social services, and employment counseling. In addition, CNPC worked with the federal retention centers continuing to provide needed assistance.

On the local level, CNPC participated in the reception accorded Mariel refugees in Dade County. Of primary concern was the assurance that the general stability of Dade County not be seriously affected by the massive influx of refugees. Drug counseling, English-language instruction, cultural orientation, and other social services were offered by the organization to the refugees settled in Dade County. CNPC provided English training and an employment program under the South Florida Employment and Training Consortium, a local Comprehensive Employment Training Act (CETA) agency. These same services were also provided to all Hispanics in the area.

CNPC has been the provider of a number of services for disadvantaged Hispanic youth. It selected as its target population youth who were not receiving assistance from other agencies. This target population was made up of school dropouts, those in trouble with the law, and the unemployed. The CNPC aimed, through its remedial programs, employment counseling, and seminars, to help the youth return to school, secure employment, or both.

Through the Padrinos program, youth counseling was also provided. Through Padrinos, the Spanish word for godparents, a person from the community adopts one or more youths for purposes of informally sharing their work and life. This is done through weekly sharing sessions for purposes of guidance and role modeling. In addition, the CNPC sponsors guest lectures for local groups on Hispanic culture and values. Musicians, artists, media professionals, and academicians have paved the way for greater communitywide understanding under the auspices of this organization.

In the legislative arena, CNPC's activities have centered around the establishment of single-member districts in Florida, especially for the election of state representatives and local representatives to school boards. Communication on these issues as well as all the activities of the organization is provided through its newsletter, *CNPC al Dia* (CNPC Update). Published in Spanish, the newsletter is distributed to the entire membership to keep them abreast of organizational activities.

The most useful references on the CNPC are the organization's newsletter and

Raphael Prohias and Lourdes Casals' report on "The Cuban Minority in the United States," published in 1973, and *Nuestro Magazine* (March 1982). For purposes of this work, CNPC newsletters nos. 2 and 3 (February 1980 and April 1980) were utilized, as well as a letter from the organization on its purposes and goals.

CUBAN WOMEN'S CLUB (CWC) This organization occupies an important role in the Miami Cuban community as a network organization and conscious-ness-raising group for mostly professional Cuban women. Although there is little readily available printed information on the CWC, it is well known among Miami's Cubans for its increasing influence in the social and political life of that city. From the ranks of its members have emerged some of the most prominent Cuban women—Silvia Unzueta, Maria Fernandez, and Yvonne Santa Maria, to name just a few. These women occupy positions in the fields of psychology, county government, and banking. They are representative of the women who founded the organization and have participated in its many activities for at least a decade.

CWC members actively participated in the International Women's Year Conferences and sent delegates to the National Hispanic Feminist Conference held in San Jose, California, in 1980. A slide presentation on the Cuban women's community of Miami, highlighting their achievements, was presented by members of this organization.

Although there is little reference material available on this group, information is contained in the archives of the Robert Kennedy Memorial in Washington, D.C. Also, the written narrative of the slide presentation is included in Sylvia Gonzales, *Hispanic Women 1980: A Feminist Anthology*, an unpublished document of the National Hispanic Feminist Conference, 1980.

E

EAST LOS ANGELES COMMUNITY UNION (TELACU) Formed in 1968 under the technical direction of the United Auto Workers (UAW), TELACU was incorporated as a public, nonprofit, equal opportunity agency striving to organize East Los Angeles community residents to negotiate for better resources from governmental and private institutions. In 1969, with an annual budget of $250,000, TELACU operated programs in the areas of housing, economic development, manpower, social services, and education. All programs and services focused on the unincorporated East Los Angeles community, where 90 percent of the population are of Mexican descent, over 30 percent speak Spanish, and 25 percent live below the poverty level (per capita income is approximately $4,000).

In 1972 TELACU became a Community Development Corporation to bring about economic and social change to the disadvantaged. First, federal funding was granted by the Community Services Administration and the Office of Economic Opportunity during the Nixon Administration. The three main organizers of TELACU were Glen O'loane, who lived in East Los Angeles and served as TELACU's first staff member through the auspices of the United Auto Workers (UAW), Estela Torres, a UAW official; and George Solis, another UAW-sponsored individual who served as the first chairperson of TELACU's board of directors.

In 1969 Esteban Torres, a high-ranking representative of the UAW, became TELACU's executive director and in 1972, the organization's first president. Mr. Torres provided leadership for five years, then left to become a President Carter appointee stationed in Paris in 1977 and in 1979 special assistant to the president for Hispanic affairs. He now serves as a U.S. congressman from California. David Lizarraga assumed the presidency of TELACU in 1977.

Other important figures in TELACU have included Leonard Rutkin, prominent in financial circles; Celestino Beltran, president of TELACU's Community Planning and Development Corporation; Roy Escarcega, a division vice-president; Ed Keefer, president of TELACU's savings company, Community Thrift and Loan; Carlos J. Garcia, general counsel; Peter Theobald, director of the international development department; Dr. David James Bellis, former director of TELACU's subsidiary, Community Rsearch Group; Luis Lopez, a more recent director of the Community Research Group; and Vice-Presidents Richard Polanco and Saad Hafiz.

The major thrust of TELACU's efforts has been to bring employment opportunities to East Los Angeles as well as a sense of cohesion and necessary commerce. TELACU seeks financial stability so that it can remain in operation even if all government funding were to be withdrawn. TELACU has been involved in the food stamp service, housing programs, job training, transportation and care of senior citizens, small business loans totaling $7 million, the production of Domingos Alegres (Happy Sundays), a free bimonthly cultural program, and a community revitalization project.

The Barrio Housing Project was a special program sponsored and organized by TELACU and the Community Development Administration (CDA), which singled out a specific area in East Los Angeles, called Maravilla, for housing development and improvement. The Maravilla program included the replacement of an already existing housing project, the building of a community facility to serve the Maravilla area, and the revitalization of several blocks surrounding Maravilla. The program established community confidence in TELACU and brought together Mexican American activists and residents to accomplish the project successfully.

Perhaps the organization's greatest endeavor has been the development of a $25 million industrial park where the Ford Foundation, Crocker National Bank, Wells Fargo Bank, the United Auto Workers, the Department of Housing and Urban Development, and other federal agencies have come together to improve employment and financial benefits to the East Los Angeles community. The park was projected to employ approximately 2,000 minorities from East Los Angeles, attract independent small businesses, and offer needed community services. The park was capital intensive with the long-term objective of expanding employment opportunities and becoming self-sustaining.

The East Los Angeles Community Union has an organizational structure of seventy-five departments headed by a fifteen-member board of directors and a president, executive vice-president, executive advisory board, legal counsel, personnel coordinator, and communications director. This group oversees TELACU Industries, Inc., the Finance Division, and the Community Development Division, all of which are further subdivided.

TELACU's program involvements are extensive and range from community thrift and loans, credit and mortgage corporations and home loan companies to several Comprehensive Employment Training Act (CETA) funded programs, immigration counseling, food cooperatives, and senior citizen ventures. TE-LACU is a closed corporate organization in that membership is granted to a select group of individuals either appointed or employed in particular positions within the organization. The success of TELACU can be attributed to its strong political relationships with federal administrations. TELACU has branched out to the San Fernando Valley, Orange County, and internationally through social and economic programs in Latin America.

The East Los Angeles Community Union has grown significantly since its inception as a public social welfare agency. It has become a multimillion-dollar corporation which has developed political power and influence through its relationships with governmental agencies and private industry. TELACU has developed manpower training programs with the U.S. Departments of Labor and Commerce, has worked on housing projects with the Department of Housing and Urban Development, and has been active with the Office of Economic Opportunity as well as with the former Department of Health, Education, and Welfare. In 1981 TELACU reached total assets of $50 million. Its profit-making companies continued to provide resources for support of three social service programs. In February of that same year, the TELACU Family Health Center, serving 4,000 low-income people a year with comprehensive primary health and preventive care, was opened. Stationers Corporation became a major tenant of TELACU Industrial Park, bringing its total employment level to 1,300. Construction also began on a three-story office structure, the park's last phase of development. The completed park, which was to offer an employment level of 2,000, was yet to be completed. Subsequent *Los Angeles Times* articles in March of 1982 disputed the wisdom and potential success of the industrial park.

Additionally in 1981, TELACU opened a new office in Fresno, California, to serve the needs of rural communities in the state's central valley. The TELACU First Urban Development Corporation was created to provide loan guarantees and technical assistance to small business people. Working with the Bank of America, it established a $1 million revolving loan fund for commercial revitalization of greater East Los Angeles. TELACU also expanded its network of thrift and loan companies with the inauguration of two new southern California branches.

TELACU is a highly centralized technical organization, and personnel working for it are required to possess the highest professional qualifications and expertise. Yet, there has been much criticism of the organization's professional judgment. TELACU's activities are extensive, but it may have overextended itself. Intensive reviews of its expenditures came under scrutiny of the *Los Angeles Times* in March of 1982, and intensive federal audits became public which involved alleged political contributions and financial improprieties.

The most useful resource for this organization is the *Los Angeles Times*, especially for the years 1977–82, and the *Los Angeles Herald Examiner* for 1978. Additional references include in-house publications such as *TELACU To-*

day and *TELACU: Community Development for the Future*. *Nuestro Magazine* (March 1982) gives a summary of its activities. Further information is available from the organization's communications department.

F

FEDERATION OF HISPANIC ORGANIZATIONS OF THE BALTIMORE METROPOLITAN AREA, INC. (FHOBA) This nonprofit organization was founded in March 1977 in Baltimore, Maryland. Since an estimated 10,000 households in Baltimore are Hispanic, a group of local Hispanics saw the need for an organization to coordinate and inform the area's existing Hispanic organizations of common concerns. These founders included Aurelio F. Goicochea, Victor E. Davila, and Carol L. Gonzales. One of the main goals of the organization is to facilitate communication among the city's Hispanic population. Further, the Federation seeks to research and articulate the needs of the Hispanic community.

The Federation of Hispanic Organizations of the Baltimore Metropolitan Area is a hierarchically structured organization headed by a board of directors, which sets policy. The membership is composed of local Hispanic cultural, social, and political associations, including those typical of various South American constituencies such as the Club Peru of Baltimore (CPB). The member organizations constitute the Federation assembly, and each association has one delegate vote at meetings. Officers are elected to two-year terms at the annual assembly meetings in March. The organization maintains its offices at the Community College of Baltimore, Harbor Campus. There, two CETA-funded workers and a volunteer staff conduct the organization's business.

The Federation engages in a number of programs and activities which reflect the organization's goals. In 1977 Federation representatives began negotiations with the city of Baltimore for funds to establish an information and coordination project in the Hispanic community. In January 1979 the FHOBA signed a one-year contract with the Baltimore City Board of Estimates for $10,000 to establish this project. The project's activities included translation services, the collection of data about the Hispanic community and its needs, and assistance to service agencies for expanding their services to the Hispanic community. In the field of advocacy, Antonio Diaz, FHOBA founder and first speaker of the assembly, testified before the Subcommittee on the Census and Population regarding the needs of the Hispanic community in being accurately counted. For this, Spanish-language census forms were required. The Federation offers classes for children in Spanish language and Hispanic culture. In addition, FHOBA conducts high school diploma equivalency classes for young dropouts and adults. Each year the organization sponsors a Hispanic festival in Baltimore at which member organizations contribute food, games, and entertainment. The money raised by individual organizations is retained for their own use.

The Federation publishes a bilingual monthly newsletter, *El Hispano*. In 1976 it ran a one-hour, once-a-week radio program, but this was soon abandoned due to lack of funds. The organization's operating funds are derived from city government, Comprehensive Employment Training Act (CETA) grants, and other fund-raising activities.

The most important reference to this organization's activities is its newsletter, *El Hispano*. For purposes of this work, *El Hispano* issues for February, March, and June 1979 were utilized, and the testimony of Antonio Diaz, speaker before the Subcommittee on the Census and Population, House of Representatives, as presented in written form for distribution.

FORUM OF NATIONAL HISPANIC ORGANIZATIONS (FNHO) Based in Washington, D.C., the Forum is an advocacy coalition that was established in 1975. The organization is made up of thirty-two member associations seeking to increase participation at all levels of government. FNHO promotes a unified approach to Hispanic issues. To do this, it has sought funding for and initiated a program of support for individual organizations in their efforts to provide equal treatment and access for Hispanics.

The Forum has established eight task forces for the study and preparation of positions on legislative matters to come before Congress. They cover the areas of banking, housing and economic development, education and labor, including health, employment and training, and migrant issues, general government, civil rights, entitlements and social services, international affairs and foreign trade, and immigration and refugees. The task forces are made up of three members from the various member organizations and include representation from Congress and the executive branch of government. In January 1982 a press conference was held on Capitol Hill where Forum members presented the task force structure and the organization's legislative agenda to the media.

A primary source for this organization is *Nuestro Magazine* (March 1982). A major reference source on the Forum is the office and materials collection of the National Council of La Raza* (NCLR), which has figured prominently in its establishment.

FRENTE POPULAR MEXICANO (POPULAR MEXICAN FRONT) (FPM) The FPM was founded in Chicago in 1935 as a chapter of the Mexican-based organization of the same name. The Frente sponsored meetings, discussions, and lectures attended by more than 200 people. The organization operated out of the University of Chicago Settlement House in the Back of the Yards.

The primary objective of this organization was to protect Mexican workers. However, their activities extended beyond labor issues to anti-Franco protests during the Spanish Civil War and to anticlerical attitudes. Their anticlerical stance so alienated the Catholic organizations that the church published *El Ideal Católico Mexicano* (The Ideal Mexican Catholic) in 1935 as a specific challenge to the Frente. But the Frente never had a wide following and eventually disappeared.

The sources for the FPM's history include Rodolfo Acuña, *Occupied America* (1981); and Louise Año Nuevo Kerr, ''The Chicano Experience in Chicago: 1920–1970'' (Ph.D. dissertation, University of Illinois at Chicago Circle, 1976).

G

GRAND COUNCIL OF HISPANIC SOCIETIES IN PUBLIC SERVICE

(GCHSPS) This organization serves as an umbrella for fourteen New York State societies comprised of Hispanics in public service positions. Founded in 1960 and with its principal office in New York City, the Council provides free training seminars in preparation for civil service examinations and qualifying tests for other types of public and government employment.

The Council is funded by annual dues of $100 per organization, as well as by grants and contributions. The organization holds annual meetings. Officers include a president, vice-president, and executive assistant.

The primary source of information on this organization is *A Guide to Hispanic Organizations* (1979).

GRAN LIGA MEXICANISTA DE BENEFICIENCIA Y PROTECCIÓN (GREATER MEXICAN CHARITY AND PROTECTIONIST LEAGUE)

(GLMBP) This organization was an outgrowth of El Primer Congreso Mexicanista* (PCM) held in Texas in 1911 and was made up of the membership of the various societies represented at the Congress.

The GLMBP was organized to provide long-range solutions to the multiplicity of Texas-Mexican problems. The Congreso had decided to create an ongoing, statewide organization with local chapters and named it La Gran Liga Mexicanista de Beneficiencia y Protección.

According to its constitution, La Gran Liga would have these objectives: (1) carry out culture and moral instruction among its members; (2) protect its members when treated unjustly by the authorities; (3) protect them against unlawful acts by other persons; (4) create a fund for the organization; and (5) prevent the exclusion of Mexican children from Anglo American schools. Its motto was "Por la Raza y para la Raza" (By the Race and for the Race).

Structurally the GLMBP was composed of a central governing board of directors, with each local chapter having their own board. The central and local boards would have the same official structure: director, vice-director, secretary, treasurer, and master of ceremonies. At the first election the director and vice-director became president and vice-president. The central board was elected annually by delegates from the local chapters to the annual convention on September 16. The central board had only the power to carry out those policies already written into the constitution or adopted at the conventions, including the power to hire agents to start local chapters in places of its own choosing, although each delegate was supposed to carry out the task in his local community. The rest of the constitution spelled out the requirements for membership and the rights and obligations of the members. The organization was not limited to U.S. citizens or to males. The first board of directors was composed of Nicasio Idar, president (Laredo), Basilio Soto, vice-president (San Antonio), Geronimo Jimenez, treasurer (Laredo), Lisandro Peña, secretary (Laredo). A master of ceremonies was not elected, and all of the delegates were designated voting members.

La Gran Liga was given responsibility for monitoring the treatment of Mexicans in Texas and for representing them against unjust treatment. Although the ideals of the organization were laudatory, their organizational efforts failed. The coalition concept struggled against the need at that time for local organizations to develop their own strength and autonomy.

Historical references for the GLMBP include contemporary works such as Jose Amaro Hernandez, "The Political Development of Mutual Aid Societies in the Mexican American Community: Ideals and Principles" (Ph.D. dissertation, University of California at Riverside, 1979); and Jose Limon, "El Primer Congreso Mexicanista de 1911: A Precursor to Contemporary Chicanismo," *Aztlan* 5: 1 and 2 (1974).

GREATER WASHINGTON IBERO-AMERICAN CHAMBER OF COMMERCE (GWIACC) This organization was founded to promote the establishment and expansion of Hispanic businesses in the Washington, Maryland, and Virginia area. A nonprofit association, it strives for greater business and community development opportunities for its members and other Hispanics. The Chamber was established in 1977 and is based in Washington, D.C.

One of the more important goals of the GWIACC is the establishment of a community development corporation to revitalize Hispanic sections of metropolitan Washington. As part of this focus, the Chamber visualizes a minority enterprise small business investment company to help capitalize Hispanic entrepreneurs. Organizational funding comes from a fifteen-dollar annual membership dues and the U.S. Department of Commerce's Office of Minority Business Enterprise.

In spite of its relative youth, the Chamber has a solid record of accomplishments. The organization has provided management and technical assistance to more than seventy-five individual Hispanic businesses and was instrumental in aiding various firms to obtain $10.5 million in procurements in the first five years of its existence. It was instrumental in the expansion of the United States Hispanic Chamber of Commerce* (USHCC), helping to make it a viable national organization. And within the Washington area, it served as liaison between local Hispanic businesses and public officials, particularly the mayor's office.

Most significantly, the Chamber has directed its vision toward the larger world community. Chamber representatives sit on an international committee of eighteen member countries created to establish wider and more constructive ties between the Hispanic business community and the international business community. Available references indicate a business membership of forty, with six working committees. However, the GWIACC is continually growing in membership and programs.

References to the GWIACC activities can be found in *A Guide to Hispanic Organizations* (1979); and *Nuestro Magazine* (March 1982). Although helpful, these references contain only summaries of the organization.

GRUPO DE ARTISTAS LATINO AMERICANOS (LATIN AMERICAN ARTISTS' GROUP) (GALA) Founded in 1976 in response to the artistic and cultural needs of Washington's growing Hispanic community, the group's objectives are twofold: (1) to preserve, promote, and expand the use of Spanish and the cultural awareness of Hispanics living in the United States; and (2) to contribute toward a cross-cultural understanding between this country's Spanish-speaking and English-speaking communities. The founders of the organization were Hugo Medrano and Rebecca Read.

GALA has sixty-one member subscribers, a staff of nine, and sixty volunteers. The economic status of its membership ranges from the low- to the middle-income bracket. Its members are of Spanish and Latin American backgrounds. Its board of directors has ten members and is responsible for all general policies. The executive board is made up of a president, vice-president, secretary, and treasurer.

The organization has established a professional bilingual repertory company in Washington, D.C., through which it trains Hispanics in the theater arts. Through it, also, GALA exposes North American audiences to the performing arts of Hispanic groups from throughout the United States and other countries. The organization has, in addition, established an information center making literature and material on the performing arts available to the Spanish-speaking community. Community outreach includes conferences, art expositions and lectures, acting workshops, poetry readings, dance and music recitals, concerts, and street theater. In March 1979 GALA initiated the Community Outreach Program for the Elderly Spanish Speaking (COPES) for those over fifty years of age. Participants receive training in acting, diction, lighting, and stage setting and some instruction in the history of the theater.

In 1981 GALA received the District of Columbia's Mayor's Art Award. It was the first of these awards to be presented. With help from the Mexican

Embassy, GALA brought a Mexican director to Washington to direct a play. A commitment was also made to bring a Puerto Rican director to Washington.

GALA's major impact has been its ability to unite the local Latino community with the city's international community. This is due to the role theater plays in bringing people together. The organization receives operational funds from the U.S. Department of Labor, National Endowment for the Arts, Commission on the Arts and Humanities, Mobil Oil Foundation, and private donors.

A summary of this organization's activities is contained in *Nuestro Magazine* (March 1982). Primary reference sources provided by GALA for this work included their completed HAVO questionnaire; a short summary issued by GALA entitled, "What Is GALA?"; GALA's bylaws; and *Blanco y Negro* 1:4 (May 1979).

GUANTE NEGRO MUTUALISTA (BLACK GLOVE MUTUAL AID SOCIETY) (GNM) There is no recorded founding date for this organization in any of the references identified. However, it was probably founded in the late 1800s or early 1900s. It was organized in Eagle Pass, Texas, as a secret order dedicated to tactics of terror and violence to collect monies from rich families. These monies were then distributed to the poor and distressed.

In all probability there was more fear generated in the minds of the organization's victims than actual violence committed by this Robin Hood-like group. Their *modus operandi* consisted of male members dropping a black glove at the doorstep of a rich man's house in the middle of the night. That was a sign that money was to be donated for a specified cause. Many responded to these tactics out of fear for lives and property.

This kind of vigilante Robin Hoodism was most certainly in response to the dire circumstances affecting Mexicans of that period in south Texas. In addition, another kind of violent vigilantism was rampant at the time and chiefly directed toward Mexicans and the poor by the more wealthy majority population.

This organization is briefly described in Jose Amaro Hernandez, "The Political Development of Mutual Aid Societies in the Mexican American Community: Ideals and Principles" (Ph.D. dissertation, University of California at Riverside, 1979).

H

HACHEROS See LEÑADORES DEL MUNDO.

HERMANAS (NUNS) (LH) This organization was founded in 1970 by a group of Hispanic lay and religious women in Houston, Texas, who saw a need for greater justice for the Hispanic community and believed in its achievement through ministry. The prime mover behind the LH, however, was Sister Gregoria Ortega, a community leader who actively supported walkouts of Mexican American students in Abilene, Texas, in the fall of 1969. Sister Gregoria was a champion of various human rights causes in the notoriously anti-Mexican American climate of west Texas. In all probability these activities were the reason for her expulsion from two dioceses.

Whether this was part of a larger movement in the worldwide church or simply that of Latin American religious who were influenced by the U.S. civil rights movement is debatable. Perhaps it was Latin America's cry for human justice that demanded response from this country's religious minorities. Whichever the motivation, an increasing number of nuns and priests were influenced by the liberation theology of Latin American writers and intellectuals Paulo Freire and Gustavo Gutierrez. In this atmosphere of intellectual questioning and conflict between the religious doctrine of submission and continued human injustice, many priests and nuns identified more closely with movement issues such as the rights of farmworkers and undocumented workers as well as prison reform.

Today the major goals of Las Hermanas include engaging Hispanic women in active ministry among their own communities and assisting non-Hispanics in becoming more effective in the Hispanic apostolate. Other purposes concern gathering supporting evidence of social injustice and supporting and encouraging each other in dealing with conflicts of cultural identity.

Las Hermanas is a hierarchically structured, four-tier organization. These units include the national, regional, state, and local groups. The national organization is headed by a three-member coordinating team composed of Sylvia Sedillo of Denver (the national headquarters), Margarita Castañeda of New York City, and Sara Gonzalez Segovia of San Jose, California. The twelve regional units are designated as Washington–Montana, Oregon–Idaho, Utah–Nevada, New Mexico, California, New York, Arizona, Texas, Minnesota–Wisconsin–Iowa, Illinois–Indiana–Michigan–Ohio, New Jersey, and Colorado. There are fifty state chapters and several hundred local groups. Las Hermanas supports and works with other organizations such as Padres Asociados por Derechos Religiosos, Educativos, y Sociales* (PADRES) and the United Farmworkers of America* (UFW). Las Hermanas annually holds a national assembly at which goal evaluation, constitutional revision, and election of national coordinators are conducted. The theme of the 1980 conference, for example, was "Vision del Futuro de Las Hermanas (1980–1990)" (Vision for Las Hermanas' Future).

Las Hermanas programs and activities, in reflecting the organization's goals, are mainly of a social and religious nature. Group discussions for members are scheduled on such topics as community organization and networking, higher education for the Hispanic woman, immigration, women as single heads of households, and job training and employment. LH also offers spiritual retreat programs, workshops, and in-service evangelization. In addition, the organization provides workshops for working in the Spanish-speaking apostolate and leadership training. Las Hermanas activities also include group prayers and liturgy. The organization supports itself, in part, through forty-dollar fees for attending its assembly and by its ten-dollar annual membership dues.

A contemporary reference on the LH is Rodolfo Acuña, *Occupied America* (1981). Primary sources for this work included Las Hermanas conference brochures, the organization's application form, the LH 1980 national assembly announcement, a completed HAVO questionnaire, and the *Encyclopedia of Associations* (1979).

HISPANIC HEALTH COUNCIL (HHC) The Council is based in Hartford, Connecticut, but it is a national organization, founded for the purpose of providing advice and assistance to Hispanics on health issues. A relatively young organization, the HHC distinguished itself in the early 1980s with the release of a study on sterilization and its effect on Puerto Rican families and the community. It organized the first crisis intervention program for Hispanics who are victims of stress, especially working with local police and emergency rooms to service this need.

The organization has conducted a major study on the health and mental issues affecting Puerto Ricans. This study was funded by the National Institute for Mental Health and was instrumental in advancing more scientifically based information and an understanding of the Puerto Rican community. Recently, the Council has expanded its activities to include a Hispanic Health and Professional

Organization as well as a library and resource center to inform Puerto Ricans better about health issues.

The brief reference to the Council's activities that appears in *Nuestro Magazine* (March 1982) gives no history of the organization's founding. Other references may be available in the form of source materials produced by the Council from the organization.

HISPANIC HIGHER EDUCATION COALITION (HHEC) The Coalition is a nonprofit organization established in 1978 to provide greater outreach to federal higher education programs for the Hispanic community. HHEC's objectives include the promotion of educational equity and excellence for Hispanics in postsecondary education, structuring incentives for community service programs throughout the country to address Hispanic educational needs better, and substituting present state grant authority with a total federal discretionary authority.

The HHEC leadership consists of a board of directors with a chairperson, vice-chairperson, and secretary-treasurer. Also, there is an executive director, staff associate, and support staff. Coalition members include the following: Aspira of America* (AA), El Congreso Nacional de Asuntos Colegiales* (CONAC), Incorporated Mexican American Government Employees* (IMAGE), The Latino Institute* (LI), League of United Latin American Citizens* (LU-LAC), Mexican American Legal Defense and Education Fund* (MALDEF), Mexican American Women's National Association* (MANA), National Association for Equal Education Opportunities (NAEEO), National Council of La Raza* (NCLR), Puerto Rican Legal Defense and Education Fund, Inc.* (PRLDEF), Secretariat for Hispanic Affairs* (SHA), Society of Hispanic Professional Engineers* (SHPE), and the Spanish American League Against Discrimination (SALAD).

HHEC has submitted several proposals to congressional committees on higher education and has proposed the creation of a National Center for the Study of Relations between Mexico and the United States. It is often called upon to testify before congressional committees and representatives. In general, it works with higher education interest groups and Congress.

Primary references for this organization include the organization's newsletter, *Hispanic Higher Education Coalition*, and the *HHEC News*. For this work, the April 25, 1979, August 30, 1979, and December 14, 1979, issues of the newsletter were utilized as well as the November and December 1981 issues of *HHEC News*.

HISPANIC INSTITUTE IN THE UNITED STATES (HIUS) The Hispanic Institute was founded in 1920 and is headquartered in New York City. It has approximately 300 members and operates with a staff of two. Its membership consists of educators, students, and others interested in Hispanic culture.

The Hispanic Institute was founded to serve as a center for the study of Hispanic culture, to promote interest in the Spanish and Portuguese civilizations, and to foster cultural relations between the United States and all Hispanic nations. HIUS sponsors lectures, readings, and discussions on literary, historical, and cultural topics. The Institute also maintains a library of over 6,000 volumes and a clipping collection on Hispanic literature and linguistics.

There are various sections of the Institute which include the Brazilian, Portuguese, and Sephardic as well as Hispanic components. The organization publishes a quarterly, the *Revista Hispánica Moderna*. Originally this organization was known as the Instituto de las Españas.

References to the activities of the HIUS can be found in the archives of the Robert Kennedy Memorial in Washington, D.C., and in *A Directory of Voluntary Organizations* (1980). The HIUS's quarterly and other organizational publications describe the association's activities.

HISPANIC ORGANIZATIONS OF PROFESSIONALS AND EXECUTIVES (HOPE)
HOPE was established in Washington, D.C., to serve as a national forum for Hispanic professionals and executives. HOPE's principal objectives are to enhance opportunities for economic and political participation and involvement by its members in the American capitalist system. HOPE seeks to establish linkages among the various national and international professional and executive and economic sectors with a view toward improving the Hispanic community. In addition, HOPE fosters the development of growth of individuals, professionals, and executives as well as serving as a catalyst in the formation of private enterprise endeavors and significant community programs.

HOPE is the sponsoring organization of the Hispanic First Federal Credit Union. Membership in the Hispanic First Federal Credit Union is limited to those persons affiliated with HOPE, but these are two distinct organizations. HOPE is a hierarchically structured organization governed by a chairperson, secretary, treasurer, executive director, general counsel, and eight-member board of directors.

Primary references for this organization consist of various HOPE brochures and pamphlets available from the organization.

HISPANIC POSTAL EMPLOYEES AND FRIENDS (HPEF)
In May 1979 a group of concerned postal employees met in Los Angeles, California, to discuss employment issues. In addition to their own personnel problems, the group discussed obstacles encountered by Hispanics in seeking employment within the Postal Service. They decided to form an organization to address those issues.

An immediate goal of the organization was to create a realistic awareness of Hispanic employment problems within the Postal Service. It was their experience that upward mobility programs did not markedly affect career advancement and enhancement for Hispanics. In addition, Hispanics were conspicuously underrepresented in the Postal Service in relation to their numbers in the general population.

Problems explored by this organization are related to areas of hiring, recruitment, testing, interviewing, selection, procedures, training, and promotion. A secondary but vital priority is to attempt to fill a vacuum in the social-recreational life of Hispanic postal employees through this association. To accomplish this, the organization sponsors dances, banquets, picnics, trips, sports activities, and cultural events.

Services provided by HPEF to its members and the community at large cover areas such as dissemination of postal employment information, instructions on how to take the postal entrance exam, provision of interview counseling, assistance during employee probationary periods, encouraging advancement strategies in the form of courses and other instruction, and maintaining standards of conduct relating to attendance, sick leave, and discipline.

The structural organization consists of nine directors who collectively are known as the board of directors. The members of the board are the president, vice-president, secretary, treasurer, director of public relations, and four directors who are elected at large by the general membership. Membership within the organization is open to both rank-and-file and managerial employees of all races and creeds.

The sources utilized for this work were provided by the organization and consisted of interim HPEF bylaws and the *Hispanic Postal Forum Newsletter* (November 30, 1979 and September 1980). The most useful references on this organization are its newsletters.

HISPANIC PROFESSIONAL ACTION COMMITTEE (HPAC) This organization started as an ad hoc committee of professional Hispanics in Tucson, Arizona, sometime around January 1983. The purpose of HPAC appears to be the discussion and advancing of issues, and more so of individuals, so as to have an impact upon the social, economic, and educational well-being of the large Mexican American community of that city. Among the founders of the group are Maria Urquides, an educator; Arnold Elias, the Tucson postmaster; John Huerta, a local businessperson; Diego Navarette, vice-president of Pima Community College; and Joel Valdez, Tucson's city manager.

HPAC continues to operate in an ad hoc fashion or as an "un-organization." However, the framework for the group follows those of a voluntary association. HPAC is a membership organization comprised of an assembly of community people who share common interests and represent diverse elements of the Mexican American business and professional sectors. Thus HPAC's literature indicates that membership is restricted to only those individuals the organization deems reflective of a certain community leadership. In other words, this organization appears to be a closed, "unstructured gathering of peers"; a network designed to advance the objectives of the group and its members. So although the group purports to advance issues or concepts of greater benefit to the Mexican American community, once again its literature states, "admission requirements will be strict enough to ensure that prospective members share similar philosophical positions and commitment." While these requirements are appropriate enough for a voluntary association, the literature further stresses "anonymity" and confidentiality. Spokesperson John Huerta writes in a January 7, 1983, memorandum of a concern that an open association may result in "the day when an open discussion cannot take place." This air of secrecy and anonymity combined with other aspects of the organization gives the appearance, albeit on a smaller scale, of an association not unlike the Tammany Hall political circle in New York. But as stated in the Introduction to this work, this kind of activity by many Mexican American and other Hispanic organizations of the 1970s was not uncommon. In Tucson, this may open the group to criticism from other sectors of the population, most notably the poor and disenfranchised Mexican American. Also, it may exclude prominent Mexican Americans who exercise leadership beyond that perceived or defined by this group. A prospective member must have a sponsor who continues to be responsible for the applicant *throughout* the admission process. Although not specifically stated, it can be assumed from the above that admission standards are rigorous.

But some events in Tucson give an even more insightful look at the workings of this group. When Governor Bruce Babbitt refused to appoint John Huerta to a seat on the Arizona Corporation Commission, HPAC member and publisher of the local *Tucson Daily Citizen* Gerald Garcia mounted a press campaign critical of the governor. Garcia, chairperson of Acción '80's* (A's) even went so far as to publish an open letter of criticism with his and the city manager's signature in the *Citizen*. Another HPAC member, Frank Felix, sought a position as a vice-president at the University of Arizona. Felix, a fairly recent graduate Ph.D. from that university and with little previous experience at the higher levels of academia, managed to secure an assistant vice-presidency after an active campaign of marches and protests. And in 1984 another HPAC member, Edith Sayre Auslander, was appointed to the Arizona Board of Regents. In subsequent newspaper interviews, she credits this network for her appointment. Thus, the political influence of this group is evident. And they have had a great deal of assistance in establishing credibility from the powerful Arizona congressman Morris K. Udall.

Officers for the organization include a chair, vice-chair, secretary, and treasurer. There are also four-at-large members who, together with the officers, comprise a governing committee. This committee, in turn, provides guidance and direction to the group. However, it is indicated that agenda items, the approval of prospective members, and interim decision making are concentrated in this governing body, providing it with an inordinate amount of organizational authority. The chair and vice-chair serve as convenors of the group, while the membership is allowed final vote approval of decisions.

The group definitely responds to a need in the contemporary political reality of this community. Early Tucson remained fairly free of the divisive polarization and blatant racism experienced by other Mexican American communities in Arizona. But the city's Hispanic community did not readily realize the professional opportunities afforded by the expanded growth of the 1950s and 1960s. The city does have a tradition of Hispanic business and civic leadership, as illustrated in the history of one of its earliest organizations, the Alianza Hispano Americana* (AHA). And Tucson can boast of one of the few cities of its size to appoint an Hispanic city manager. Still, this city is made up of an education-conscious Hispanic community, and as more Mexican Americans attain higher education, competition for professional advancement increases. Within this climate, it seems appropriate for Hispanic professional, voluntary associations to form for the purposes of advancing their members. It is assumed that within this context a sensitive programmatic response to areas of concern to this community on the part of individuals who have attained professional and decision-making positions would result. In principle, the intent is exemplary and does not differ from the approaches advanced by similar special interest groups throughout social and civic history. In practice, however, there is always the danger that professional advancement may come at the expense of group needs and in favor of personal or selective group advancement. And because the issues that HPAC has chosen to publicly challenge have succeeded in polarizing a community where previously this was nonexistent, the universal goals and objectives of this organization tend to provoke further scrutiny.

Officially HPAC is politically nonpartisan and excludes officials and announced candidates for office from its ranks. According to the organizational literature, this enables HPAC to refrain from political endorsements or participation in political campaigns. Again, in practice individual members including HPAC officers have taken public, partisan political stands which reflect on the organization as a whole. In fact, Spokesperson Huerta and another highly visible member, Lillian Lopez Grant, have advocated in local newspapers throughout 1983 and 1984 that Hispanics should move into the camps of the Republican Party for purposes of power brokering.

HPAC makes a point of emphasizing the need for gender balancing in the membership as well as equal participation on the basis of age, professions, and capabilities. Yet, of its list of members, only nine of forty-nine members are women. This may reflect a lack of professional Hispanic women in Tucson or neglect on the part of the organizational leadership to identify these women. Whatever the reasons for low Hispana representation, it is an important first step that this goal is included in HPAC's organizational framework.

Currently the organization is in the process of changing its name. It is felt that the "PAC" in HPAC reflects a political purpose for the group. Again, the organization shows a concern for potential loss of direction and control should membership be too open. And finally, there is too a fear of imbalance in professional representation should issues become too focused.

Primary references for this organization consist mainly of in-house memoranda, especially those of April 31, 1983, and January 7, 1983, which outline the organizational concept and structure of HPAC. Further references to its activities can be found in the local *Arizona Daily Star* and *Tucson Citizen* for the years 1983 and 1984 which relate to the historical origins of the group.

HISPANIC YOUNG ADULT ASSOCIATION See PUERTO RICAN AS-SOCIATION FOR COMMUNITY AFFAIRS.

HISPANOS ORGANIZED TO PROMOTE ENTREPRENEURS, INC. (HOPE) This organization was founded in Detroit, Michigan, as a local business development organization to aid minority firms and was funded by the Office of Minority Business Enterprise. The association provides management and technical assistance to new or existing minority firms and assists them with capital acquisition, accounting, and other business services.

There were no printed identifiable references to this organization in the contemporary literature. There are miscellaneous notes on the group contained in the archives of the Robert Kennedy Memorial in Washington, D.C.

HOUSTON CUBAN ASSOCIATION (HCA) This is a local social organization founded in 1966 and based in Houston, Texas. The preservation of the Cuban heritage in the United States is a major goal of the organization and is encouraged through the sponsorship of social and cultural activities. It publishes *El Cuba Libre* (Free Cuba), a bimonthly newsletter. Membership is open to individuals of Cuban origin.

The most useful references to the activities of this organization are its newsletters. A published source is the *Directory of Spanish Speaking Community Organizations* (1970), which only summarizes the HCA.

I

INCORPORATED MEXICAN AMERICAN GOVERNMENT EMPLOYEES (IMAGE) In the early 1970s a group of Mexican American federal government employees met in Denver, Colorado, to discuss ways in which they could assist the same to increase their representation in civil service. IMAGE was formed as a national, nonprofit organization in February 1971 as a result of these meetings. IMAGE's main goal is to help effect an increase in job opportunities for Mexican Americans in government service. The organization seeks to promote the advancement of Hispanics already within the civil service as well as to expand the total number of Mexican Americans in government employment. In facilitating these aims, IMAGE has an additional objective of increasing communication among Mexican American civil servants.

IMAGE is a hierarchically structured national voluntary association. While it was originally organized by federal employees, it soon expanded to include others in state, county, and city governments. There is a thirteen-member national board of directors overseeing the organization. This board decides policy and recommends constitutional changes to the general membership for approval or rejection. In addition, the state chapters have boards of directors which meet annually to discuss matters of state concern. Individual local chapters require thirty members in order to affiliate with national IMAGE, and these members must represent at least three levels of government. IMAGE, which began as a local Denver organization, now includes 3 additional Colorado chapters and more than 120 chapters in forty states. The headquarters for IMAGE are in Arlington, Virginia. Membership is open to any Hispanic government employee who supports the goals and objectives of the organization. Associate membership may be granted to Hispanic nongovernment persons who are committed to IMAGE's agenda; and intermediate membership is open to youths employed in part-time government jobs.

IMAGE has established tremendous credibility inside and outside of government and serves as one of the chief organizational representatives of the Hispanic community. Because it is so widely respected, IMAGE has been invited to serve on advisory committees to the regional directors of the U.S. Departments of Health, Education, and Welfare, Housing and Urban Development, and Labor, and to the Office of Economic Opportunity and ACTION. Representatives of IMAGE in Colorado serve in an advisory capacity to the Denver Regional Council of Governments, the Metro Denver Urban Coalition, various departments within the city and county governments, and state agencies. And under a Department of Health, Education, and Welfare grant IMAGE has established a talent bank through which job applications filed by Hispanics are matched with job announcements.

This organization assists in providing Congress, the president, and other interested or involved organizations with information on how the federal budget and other legislative actions will affect the Hispanic community. In addition, IMAGE of Maryland piloted a litigation fund project called HELP (Hispanic Legal Project) to serve as a model for other IMAGE chapters. National IMAGE established the National IMAGE Training Institute to provide competency-based training courses in affirmative action, employment, and management-related areas. Training classes began in December 1981.

These are only examples of the content and variety of IMAGE programs. This organization represents a sophistication and altruism symbolic of the changing mood of Hispanic organizational life. Whereas in the 1960s and early 1970s this organization might have been described as moderate, its productive activism has served as a model for the future.

IMAGE has not only expanded its mission beyond the Mexican American community to serve all Hispanics but it has also increased its private sector capability. IMAGE's Wall Street chapter hosted a conference with top Hispanic businesspersons, "Hispanics in the Corporate World," in December 1981.

The organization fought successfully in the early 1980s against the elimination of the federal Hispanic Employment Program created as part of the Federal Equal Employment Opportunity Program. And finally, IMAGE presented to President Reagan a documented petition asking for an investigation into the underrepresentation of Hispanics in federal agencies. The action culminated three years of research by California IMAGE's Economic Development Project. The 1980s portends an increase in IMAGE's visibility, and the organization has entered the decade with heightened activism on behalf of Hispanics.

Detailed references for IMAGE include the organization's bylaws, IMAGE's national constitution, IMAGE convention brochures, and IMAGE's services and objectives brochure. Also reference to its activities can be found in *Nuestro Magazine* (March 1982).

INQUILINOS BORICUAS EN ACCIÓN (PUERTO RICAN TENANTS IN ACTION) (IBA) In the early 1960s the Boston Redevelopment Agency issued an urban renewal plan which would have led to the displacement of many

residents of Parcel 19 in South Boston, a low-income neighborhood with numerous Hispanic and elderly residents. Inquilinos Boricuas en Acción was founded
by a group of local residents and church members who opposed the city government's plans for their community. The organization was formally chartered
under Massachusetts law in 1968.

The IBA's objectives have changed since its founding. Originally the organization aimed at improving the housing conditions in the neighborhood, pre-
venting the displacement of low-income families, and providing low-cost housing
for the elderly. Later the IBA expanded its goals to include designing and
providing attractive and usable neighborhood open spaces, redirecting rush hour
traffic, expanding economic and commercial activities in the area, and raising
public and private capital to provide new health and school facilities.

IBA is a hierarchically structured organization headed by a twenty-member
board of directors, which make decisions regarding policy and action. Board
members are elected by the organization's general membership: community residents over the age of eighteen who have paid their one-dollar membership fee.
IBA has over 400 members. The board employs an executive director, who
informs its members on the agency's progress.

IBA has developed a number of programs and activities reflective of its goals.
The organization sought and secured funding to construct and rehabilitate numerous family dwellings. At this writing, the IBA was managing 489 units and
had plans to develop 187 more. The organization has formed two subsidiary
corporations for the overall management of its housing interests.

Aside from community advocacy and housing management, IBA operates
Escuelita Agueybana, a bilingual day care program for preschoolers. Also, the
organization administers the Areyto Cultural Project, which provides the community with cultural presentations and conducts visual arts, communications,
and music workshops. In addition, IBA functions as a brokering service coordinating special services of other agencies such as medical care and hot lunches.

IBA is headquartered in the Inquilinos Boricuas en Acción Human Services
Administration Building, a six-story office building rehabilitated at a cost of
$250,000. The organization's current operating budget is in excess of $3 million.

The primary references for this organization were provided by IBA and consisted of the completed HAVO questionnaire and an ''Inquilinos Boricuas en
Acción'' overview sheet.

INSTITUTE OF PUERTO RICAN UNITY (IPRU) As a regional service
organization founded in 1971 and based in Los Angeles, IPRU attempts to raise
the socio-economic status of Puerto Ricans in California by providing services
in job placement, housing, education, mental health, etc. The organization's
membership is open and consists of 200 members. Dues are twenty-four dollars
annually. IPRU has a staff of two. It is affiliated with the Western Regional
Puerto Rican Council* (WRPRC). Officers include a president, executive vice-
president, and executive secretary. The organization has published a newsletter

since 1973. Among its other activities are a scholarship program and the maintenance of historical archives.

Sources on the IPRU's history should be contained in the organization's archives. Also, the newsletters are helpful references to the organization's activities. The reference used for this work was the *Directory of Spanish Speaking Community Organizations* (1970). The IPRU failed to respond to a request for more detailed information.

INSTITUTO INTERNACIONAL DE COOPERACIÓN Y SOLIDARIDAD CUBANA, INC. (INTERNATIONAL INSTITUTE FOR CUBAN COOPERATION AND SOLIDARITY) (ICOSOC) This Institute was founded in 1979 to provide benefits to exiled Cubans which are not provided by any other group or persons and especially to those outside densely populated Cuban enclaves.

It is evident from materials describing the organization that although its primary purpose seems to be the provision of services and networking to the exiled Cuban community, there is a strong political direction underlying the association. This is specifically indicated in that ICOSOC membership is open to all Cubans who are committed to the goals of the organization which include outright rejection of Marxist-Leninist political doctrine. Therefore, while maintaining a strictly nonpartisan position, the ICOSOC succeeds in interjecting politics into their organizational philosophy.

The goals of the organization as stated in membership materials and exactly quoted here are:

(a) ICOSOC will not undertake any activity which is currently being addressed by another organization in order not to duplicate efforts;

(b) ICOSOC does not propose to develop into a massive agency competing with the function of immigration and exile agencies;

(c) ICOSOC rejects outright Marxist-Leninist political doctrine while maintaining a nonpartisan position, taking into account that ICOSOC's work is aimed toward practical projects promoting greater solidarity amongst the Cuban exiled community;

(d) ICOSOC will dedicate itself primarily to those projects which dedicate themselves to the entire, or major part, of the exiled and immigrant population, avoiding individual cases except in exceptional instances of need.

ICOSOC's bylaws expand on the above goals by pledging to provide legal, psychological, and general counseling to Cubans who migrate to other countries, to assist in the reunification of Cuban families, to seek the release of Cuban political prisoners, and to assist Cubans to leave Cuba and immigrate to the country of their choice.

The organization offers three kinds of membership: regular, patron, and honorary member. Regular membership is open to all Cubans dedicated to the organization's goals who pay the twenty-four dollar annual membership dues and are approved by two-thirds of the members of ICOSOC's board of directors. Patrons of the organization may be of any nationality but committed to the goals of the association. An annual membership fee of forty-eight dollars is assessed each patron. An individual wishing to be a patron of the organization must submit a written request and be approved by two-thirds of the members of the board of directors. Patrons may attend ICOSOC international assemblies but may not vote. Finally, honorary members are selected by unanimous vote of the board of directors. Honorary members may be of any nationality and recognized contributors to the arts, religion, civic, or political affairs who identify with ICOSOC's goals. Honorary members are also invited to international assemblies of the organization but may not vote.

The international assembly of ICOSOC draws from the regular membership and constitutes the supreme body of the organization. The international assembly is made up of the board of directors and three regular delegates from each country or region. The international assembly meets every two years to discuss activities of the organization, approve the proposed plan of action, approve current dues schedule, modify or expand the bylaws, elect the board of directors, and conduct other business.

The board of directors is charged with implementing the decisions taken by the international assembly and is composed of a president, two vice-presidents, secretary, vice-secretary, treasurer, vice-treasurer, and auditor. The board of directors meets a minimum of twice a year.

Sources of information on this organization include ICOSOC's detailed by-laws, informational pamphlets, and correspondence with the organization. No historical background is given except that the founders were Cubans situated in a variety of countries. Names listed on the informational pamphlets include Reinol Gonzales, Carmen M. Marth, Baston Cantens, Arnoldo Muller, Francisco Echevarria, Eduardo Garcia, and Enrique Osle, S. J., and may reflect the founders or current leadership.

INTERSTATE RESEARCH ASSOCIATES (IRA) IRA was born out of the civil rights struggle of the 1950s and 1960s. It developed rapidly into the foremost nonprofit Hispanic research foundation and consulting firm. The board and staff of IRA realized that government agencies at all levels were not equipped to understand and design programs affecting Hispanic communities, particularly Mexican Americans of the Southwest. They recognized that much of the monies assigned as governmental response to problems voiced by agitated minorities were contracted to research and consultant firms, the majority based in Washington, D.C. The resultant studies and pilot programs greatly influenced national public policy and governmental decision making.

IRA was officially incorporated in February 1968 in Washington, D.C., a year after serious conversations had taken place on the idea of establishing a nonprofit Mexican American foundation. The discussion group included individuals who would later command national prominence but at the time were not in a position to finance the operation. However, these planners decided to organize as a board and incorporate their vision.

The original board included Alex Mercure, then director of a migrant assistance program in New Mexico. Mercure was well known in Office of Economic Opportunity (OEO) circles and later became an assistant secretary of agriculture in the Carter Administration. There was Esteban Torres from Los Angeles, California, who was working as an United Auto Workers (UAW) international representative out of Washington and with little previous experience in domestic antipoverty programs. Torres went on to become the powerful head of the East Los Angeles Community Union* (TELACU) in Los Angeles, U.S. ambassador to UNESCO, special assistant to President Carter, and finally, U.S. congressman from California. Henry Santiestevan was an editor for a labor magazine of the Industrial Union Department of the AFL-CIO who later became the executive director of the Southwest Council of La Raza, forerunner of the National Council of La Raza* (NCLR). The board also included Jack Alford of New York, director of the Suffolk County Long Island Council of Churches, and Tomás Atencio, a social worker from Colorado who later founded the Academia de la Nueva Raza, an institution dedicated to academic discourse and the preservation of Hispanic literary and philosophical tradition. The best known of the group were Texas State Senator Joe Bernal, who had distinguished himself in the field of bilingual education, and Judge Alfred F. Hernandez of Houston, Texas, national president of the League of United Latin American Citizens* (LULAC).

There were others who supported the group's vision. Outstanding among them were Raul Yzaguirre and Richard Bela, both employees of the federal OEO office in Washington. These two individuals chose initially to remain in the background because of their federal employment, but Bela did offer legal assistance to the group.

Because the national consciousness of the time was essentially black-oriented, the IRA nucleus found it difficult to secure either public or private monies to subsidize the organization. The new foundation lacked start-up capital and a track record, so banks werre unwilling to provide loans. Finally, through the intervention of Esteban Torres, the UAW lent IRA temporary office space. Tom Karter, a former government manager and free-lance consultant, volunteered time to IRA, as did Eric Reuther, a nephew of labor leader Walter Reuther. By the end of 1968, the organizing group realized that if IRA was to succeed it would need a full-time administrator. Raul Yzaguirre was persuaded to take on the task of executive director.

Raul Yzaguirre, a native of San Juan, Texas, and active in the American G.I. Forum* (AGIF) and other Mexican American activities, was hired in 1966 by the Migrant Division of the Office of Economic Opportunity, where he worked as a program analyst reviewing project proposals. It was while at OEO that Yzaguirre recognized a need for a national organization. At OEO he worked alongside Rick Bela, who also shared his vision.

The second person to join the IRA staff was Sylvia Gonzales. The Tucson,

Arizona, native had worked for Congressman Morris K. Udall in his Washington office, served as a chief investigator for the U.S. Commission on Civil Rights 1968 hearings in San Antonio, Texas, and helped design the Mexican American Education Study of the Commission. Immediately prior to joining IRA, she had worked in Valencia, Venezuela. It was Gonzales, then, who brought an expanded Pan-American vision to IRA and designed the foundation's logo to reflect this. She became IRA's chief administrative officer.

The third person to join the organizing staff, in May 1969, on a full-time basis was Richard Bela, a native of New Mexico raised in the mining communities of that state and in El Paso, Texas, who had earned a law degree from the University of Texas. Rick Bela joined the OEO Migrant Division as a community action program specialist, and it was here that he became friends with Raul Yzaguirre. Bela had contemplated a national Hispanic institute fashioned after the many Washington-based public policy and public affairs institutes for some time. Meeting Raul Yzaguirre and sharing his concept brought it closer to reality. Richard Bela became IRA's corporate counsel.

The final person to join the core staff of IRA was Bettie Baca in December 1969. Prior to joining the IRA Washington offices, she had been project staff on IRA's first major program, a U.S. Department of Commerce and Economic Development Administration grant for a jobs skills study in south Texas. Bettie Baca was a native of Colorado who earned her university degree there. Most important, she had consulting firm experience as a former staffer of Leo Kramer, Inc., one of the most prominent of Washington, D.C., consulting establishments at that time. She was hired as program developer for IRA.

Like so many of the Hispanic organizations conceptualized in the 1960s, IRA believed that the community had the ability to solve its own problems and in fact was a major resource for solving many of the country's problems. This was especially so in the area of inter-American affairs. But what the community did lack were the credentials and expert training that expanded educational opportunities would later provide. Thus, IRA sought out the best-trained and credentialed Mexican Americans and Latinos, provided training experiences for others, and developed educational motivation and opportunities programs for the Hispanic community.

IRA began its drive toward public recognition by working as subcontractors to other more established firms. By 1970 the firm had secured its first big contract for $300,000. By 1971, IRA had tripled its business and had also spun off a profit-making arm, InterAmerica Associates. IRA maintained a policy of working with local community organizations and not competing with these for contracts. The organization developed as a national, technical assistance research foundation for local communities and, even more important, as a lobbyist at the national level for the Mexican American cause.

Although IRA's life span was short, during its brief success in the nation's capital it especially helped bring the plight of Mexican Americans into the national consciousness. IRA figured prominently in antiwar efforts of the period as well as in other civil rights marches, movements which had heretofore ignored the needs of Mexican Americans. It assisted in the founding of the first Mexican American university, Jacinto Treviño, and was the impetus behind the founding of the Hispanic community's first formal lobby, National Congress of Hispanic American Citizens* (NCHAC), El Congreso. The original board of El Congreso was composed of IRA veterans, including Richard Bela, Sylvia Gonzales, and Raul Yzaguirre. IRA served as a meeting place and home away from home for the many Mexican Americans coming to Washington "from the field" seeking federal assistance. Reputations were made and strategies hatched within its confines. Jose Angel Gutierrez of Partido La Raza Unida (PLRU), Mario Compean of the United Farmworkers of America* (UFW), and Juan Patlan of the Mexican American Unity Council* (MAUC), all Texas-based organizations, were regulars, as were David Hackett and David Ramage of the Center for Community Change in Washington, D.C. IRA epitomized the times and, most important, the self-initiative of minority communities by solving their own problems through understanding the funding system.

But the successes of IRA would not have been possible had not the original core staff made exceptional sacrifices. Although salaries were assigned, for over a year these individuals collected only a minimal percentage of the designated amount. After this first year, personal circumstances forced Sylvia Gonzales and Richard Bela to seek paid employment. Rick Bela moved to the Civil Rights Commission's Texas office, and Sylvia Gonzales took a position in the director's office of the U.S. Civil Service Commission in Washington. Raul Yzaguirre stayed on, living and supporting his family with the assistance of food stamps and other government assistance. Bettie Baca also continued with IRA until her marriage to Manuel Fierro in 1970. Later, when IRA prospered, Richard Bela was invited back as part of the new management team.

Sylvia Gonzales and Bettie Baca were not invited to participate in the new IRA, yet their contributions were especially unmeasurable in terms of the long-range success of the foundation. Incurred wage debts with each for over $10,000 resulting from the original policy of collecting only partial payment on salaries were forgiven.

IRA's success transformed the organization's philosophy and structure. Most notable was the lack of female representation in its leadership hierarchy. The new management team included Juan Gutierrez, IRA senior associate in charge of the San Antonio field office; Tony Gutierrez, the general manager of the organization; Gil Florence, head of IRA's manpower division operating out of Dallas, Texas; and Yzaguirre and Bela. Although women were excluded from IRA's management team, by vote of the board of directors Sylvia Gonzales was brought on to the IRA board.

Several reasons have been given for the decline of IRA. Some felt it was due to the growing isolation of its executive director. Others attributed it to its rapid climb and ensuing power bureaucracy, which pushed it further away from its earlier constituencies. Many felt that the spirit of extended family that had predominated during the early years had given way to competing philosophies and their concomitant power struggles. One thing is certain, its seemingly close association with the political policies of the Johnson New Society threatened the ideologically wary Nixon people who had come to power in the early 1970s. The country was changing under Richard Nixon, and IRA seemed to be out of the mainstream of this change. Government contracts always went to other consulting firms more in keeping with the new Republican philosophy. Then, too, the feminist movement was beginning to emerge in the early 1970s as a powerful force, and IRA was decidedly out of sync with this new movement. Mexican American women listened to these female voices and questioned the lack of women in IRA's decision-making process. More and more they felt that IRA's problem solving excluded the problems of women.

After IRA's decline, Juan Gutierrez assumed sole responsibility for its profit-making arm, InterAmerica Associates, and transformed it into a successful business. The new InterAmerica is fulfilling its Pan-American vision through contracts with Latin America. It remains strictly nonpartisan and addresses its problem solving to monies available for critical areas as defined by the federal bureaucracy rather than initiating funding ideas for social change.

Interstate Research Associates concerned itself with the multiplicity of issues affecting the Mexican American community. The diversity of projects undertaken was reflective of its goals. Mostly, IRA launched several projects geared toward the needs of the steady stream of Mexican American migrant workers. But IRA also worked on innovative approaches to problems of elderly Hispanics, most notably through their Community Center Program for the Chicano Aged. IRA initiated technical assistance and training projects as well as consumer education programs. The organization also took in student interns through its Stanford-in-Washington program, which served Stanford University Hispanic students. Overall, IRA was recognized as a leading resource in the areas of manpower training, migrant education, Headstart, and bilingual education. At its peak, IRA operated out of Washington, D.C., with field offices in south Texas, Dallas, Denver, Phoenix, San Francisco, and Kansas City.

The most detailed reference for IRA is the March 1973 issue of *La Luz Magazine*. However, the history presented in this source focuses on the reorganized IRA and leadership and gives little information on the early organizational years. More accurate insights into this early history of the organization is presented in a variety of in-house reports and board meeting minutes and numerous other unpublished documents and publications, including public relations pamphlets. Personal association and recollections of this author were utilized for this work as well as in-house memoranda and other documents.

K

KANSAS STATE UNIVERSITY MEXICAN AMERICAN ALUMNI ASSOCIATION (KSUMAAA) This association is typical of many such alumni groups now forming in institutions of higher education around the country where Hispanic recruitment has suffered. The KSUMAAA was founded in 1978 in Manhattan, Kansas. Its primary purpose is to provide scholarships and information concerning educational opportunities for Hispanic students at Kansas State University.

In early 1981 the Association dispensed three scholarships and expanded its membership to over 100. Since that year of realized activity, the organization has continued to grow and award more scholarships. Its expanded program of activities includes annual banquets, a newsletter, recruitment, and support for Hispanic students and relevant curricula at that university.

There are few readily available reference sources on this organization. A brief description of the KSUMAAA activities is contained in *Nuestro Magazine* (March 1982). This organization is typical of many such groups now forming at universities situated within cities with a significant Hispanic population.

L

LATIN AMERICAN ASSOCIATION (LAA) The Association was established in 1972 as a response to the lack of available services to meet the needs of the growing Hispanic population in Atlanta, Georgia. The services provided by this organization consist of employment referral, an elderly volunteer program, and other social services. The organization also publishes a monthly newspaper, *Gaceta Latina* (Latin News Gazette). The LAA is made up of Puerto Ricans (25 percent), Cubans (25 percent), other Hispanics, including Guatemalans, Panamanians, Peruvians, Mexicans, and Brazilians (40 percent); the remaining ten percent are from the Virgin Islands.

The organization structurally consists of a board of directors, executive director, assistant director, and coordinators. The board is a policy-making body and works through board committees. There is no information provided on the founders and leaders of the organization other than the listing of a director, Lino H. Dominguez.

The primary reference for this organization consisted of a completed HAVO questionnaire.

LATIN AMERICAN CHAMBER OF COMMERCE OF NEVADA, INC. (LACCN) From late 1975 to early 1976 a group of Hispanic business owners met to discuss the need for a statewide chamber of commerce to advance the commercial and business interests of the Hispanic community in Nevada. Among the group's leaders and founders were Arturo Cambeiro, the LACCN's first president and recipient of the Small Business Administration's Man of the Year Award for Nevada, 1979, Otto Merida, Enrique Salzano, Gil Flores, Agustin Menedez, and Jorge Valladares. This organization was incorporated as a statewide association in Las Vegas, Nevada, on May 17, 1976. The primary goal of the Chamber is to develop projects to stimulate the expansion of national and international trade in Nevada, ultimately increasing economic opportunities in the Hispanic community.

The Latin American Chamber of Commerce of Nevada is a hierarchically structured organization headed by a nineteen-member board of directors, which sets corporation policy. Assisting the board with Chamber operations are an executive director and several vice-presidents representing northern and southern Nevada. The organization maintains offices in Reno and Las Vegas, both of which were opened in March 1978. The organization holds annual meetings in July for the election of board members and officers. In 1976 the Chamber had a total of 50 members, and by 1980 this number had risen to 200. The majority of the members are business owners of Cuban or Mexican descent.

The Latin American Chamber of Commerce of Nevada sponsors a number of programs and services which reflect the organization's goals. The LACCN's initial activities were focused on developing Latin American tourism and commerce in Nevada. In this process the Chamber has collaborated with the state's major casinos and hotels by offering expert assistance in the areas of advertising, marketing, promotions, employee relations, and Latin American customer policy handling. In the field of marketing the Chamber advises business concerns on Latin American and Hispanic consumer trends in the United States and abroad. Its communications and public relations services produce press releases, kits, and brochures in Spanish and serve as liaison between Nevada business establishments and the Latin American community. Another major effort of the Chamber is the establishment of a foreign trade zone in north Las Vegas to stimulate an increase in national and international trade brought to Nevada. In this project the chamber is being assisted by the Clark County and Nevada State governments and by Opportunities Industrialization Centers of America, Inc.

Operating funds for the Chamber's services and projects come from its monthly membership dues, ranging from fifteen dollars for corporate members to five dollars for affiliated members. The organization is further assisted in its operations by funds from local, county, and state governments. The Latin American Chamber of Commerce of Nevada publishes a monthly newsletter, *Mundo Mercantil*.

The best sources of information for LACCN are the newsletters. Other reliable sources include the *Nevada World Trade and International Association Newsletter* 1:1 (May 1980); and *Vida Nueva: The Bilingual Magazine* (April–May 1980, and June–July 1980). Detailed information on the organization was extracted from the LACCN bylaws, an informational leaflet, and the completed HAVO questionnaire.

LATIN AMERICAN MANUFACTURERS ASSOCIATION (LAMA) This Association is a national trade organization formed in February 1973 to help Hispanic-owned businesses obtain federal contracts. The organization has over 200 member firms and is housed in Washington, D.C. LAMA lobbies government agencies and the private sector on behalf of its members. Operating monies come from monthly dues of twenty-five dollars from members and grants from the U.S. Department of Commerce's Office of Minority Business Enterprise and the Department of Transportation. Principal officials of the organization include a chairperson, president, and executive director. The Association publishes a quarterly, *LAMA*, and holds national conventions.

A brief synopsis of this organization can be found in the archives of the Robert Kennedy Memorial in Washington, D.C. Also, the organization is summarized in *A Guide to Hispanic Organizations* (1979).

LATIN AMERICAN RESEARCH AND SERVICE AGENCY (LARASA)

The Latin American Research and Service agency was established as a nonprofit organization in Denver, Colorado, in March 1964. LARASA organized for the major purpose of assisting individuals and families to make a more effective use of community services. LARASA provides services to members which include employment referral, workmen's compensation, social security, educational opportunities, housing, medical care, court procedures, welfare services, and job training information.

LARASA has developed Headstart centers, which provide low-income children with preschool training in preparation for regular school attendance. LARASA also sponsors Latin American Student Clubs in cooperation with the Denver Public Schools. Students are encouraged toward academic achievement as well as extracurricular activities that are school-related. The Clubs emphasize pride in the students' cultural heritage and stress the need for higher education. The organization also sponsors conferences, forums, and workshops dealing with a number of topics of interest to the community. The conferences and meetings provide the opportunity for the exchange of ideas and information.

Membership in this organization is open to any person who subscribes to LARASA's goals. Members who have paid their dues in a timely fashion and thereby are in good standing are eligible to vote on LARASA business. All members are informed of the corporate activities, notified of annual meetings, and supplied with annual reports. Membership is comprised of three types: regular membership with dues of five to ten dollars annually; supporting membership, ten to twenty-five dollars annually; and sustaining membership, twenty-five dollars or more.

LARASA is a hierarchically structured organization headed by a president, executive director, assistant director, education coordinator, secretary, and board of trustees. The board is made up of twenty members. Some of the past officers of LARASA include Bert Gallegos, president; Charles Tafoya, executive director; Tony Lovato, assistant director; A. A. Archuleta, education coordinator; and Marian D. Garcia, secretary.

In May 1965 LARASA was admitted as a United Way affiliate under the Mile High United Fund for the purpose of securing funding for the study of problems within Denver's Latin American population. Other funding for LARASA comes from membership dues and individual, business, and organizational contributions.

Research on this organization was facilitated by Senator Polly Baca Barragan of Denver. Senator Baca Barragan allowed access to her extensive files on organizing activities within Denver's Hispanic community. Some of the reference sources included organizational brochures and leaflets as well as meeting notes.

LATIN CHAMBER OF COMMERCE (LCC) This national organization was founded in 1965 and is currently based in Miami, Florida. The LCC is affiliated with the U.S. Department of Commerce and serves area businesses, promotes international relations, educates against crime and drug abuse, and arranges bilingual programs.

The LCC has a permanent staff of twenty-five and a membership of nearly 2,000. Its annual dues are sixty dollars. Its leadership hierarchy includes a president, vice-president, and secretary. Membership is open to individuals with an established business and must be approved by the executive board. LCC has published since 1968 two monthlies, *Industria y Comercio* (Industry and Commerce) and *Supplemento* (Supplement).

The source for this organization was the *Directory of Spanish Speaking Community Organizations* (1970).

LATINO INSTITUTE (LI) In November 1974 the Chicago Latino community faced continuing social and institutional discrimination and experienced high unemployment and underemployment, substandard housing, and high student underachievement and dropout rates. That same year Carolyn Bergan, David Duster, Burton Hales, Fidel Lopez, and Frank Seevers founded the Institute to address the socio-economic needs of the Latino community. These leaders possessed the skills and experience in business, fund-raising, and program organizational development to make the Institute a viable reality.

The Institute seeks to facilitate improved communication between the Spanish-speaking and non-Spanish-speaking communities, as well as to serve as an advocate for the Latino community. To accomplish this, the Institute focuses on leadership training, advocacy, information and referral, organizational development training, radio broadcasting, networking, coordination of major cultural events, and coordination of workshops and seminars. The Institute also provides consultation to non-Latino agencies and conducts action-oriented research of social and educational issues significantly affecting Latinos, other minorities, and low-income people.

The Latino Institute is a hierarchically structured organization presided over by a board of directors charged with setting policy. There are five directors under the board's supervision: executive, program, communications, advocacy, and research. Although the founders of the organization were primarily non-Latino, the majority of the members and leaders are Hispanics.

In July 1979, the Latino Institute Research Division was established for the purpose of providing documented bases of support for the Institute's advocacy efforts. Too often, community groups have been accused of lacking the ammunition to support their charges of discrimination and institutional neglect. The Institute's Research Division was established to counter those charges.

The Latino Institute has conducted a number of programs and activities reflective of its goals. Their organizational leadership program identifies and trains leaders among parents of school-age children. This program aims to increase involvement of Latino parents in their children's education. The Institute has developed parent advisory councils in a number of Chicago school districts. It also operates a technical assistance program which provides information and skills development to Latino community-based organizations. In addition, the Latino Institute maintains a data bank on Latinos as well as an information and referral service.

In the early 1980s the Latino Institute established an office in Washington, D.C. It also produced an in-depth study on Latinos and philanthropy which significantly influenced how the philanthropic community views Latinos. The Institute assisted in organizing in southeast Chicago a social action coalition of black, white, and Latino people. This coalition succeeded in starting a million-dollar health clinic and a school, which opened in September 1981. The LI has also worked with the Mexican American Legal Defense Fund* (MALDEF) in researching and preparing briefs for cases that focused on winning appropriations to provide legislative representation heretofore denied Latinos.

The Institute has completed major studies on developmentally disabled Hispanics in Illinois and on the dissemination of Title I federal monies to the public schools. The first study was presented to the Governor's Planning Council for recommendations. The second study helped change the criteria for allocation of money so that more funds could be sent to the public schools. This effort was done in conjunction with several community-based organizations.

The Latino Institute has been particularly interested in researching further and advancing the educational model of Brazilian educator Paulo Freire. The Freire model is a community dialogue methodology for learning. In October 1981 the Institute convened the first national conference on Educación Liberadora (Liberating Education). This created a network of adult education programs for Latinos throughout the country using the Freire concept.

Funding for the Institute comes from private contributions and foundation grants. The organization publishes *Latino Institute Bulletin*, a quarterly newsletter.

The LI has printed an organizational history and philosophy sheet which is available from the organization. The Aspira of America* (AA) of Illinois newsletter *Informa* (September 1979) provides an excellent reference for LI activities in that state. *Nuestro Magazine* gives a brief summary of activities in its March 1982 issue. Primary reference for this work was the completed HAVO questionnaire.

LÁZARO CÁRDENAS SOCIETY (LCS) This organization was founded by members of the Los Angeles Mexican community soon after World War I. LCS was named after a revered socialist president of Mexico. The organization had a strong political orientation, revealed through its commitment to social welfare and organized community action. The organization provided low-rate insurance benefits for the community and effort and action on behalf of community issues such as the lack of school buses and other facilities. The municipal facilities available to Mexicans were inferior to those found elsewhere in the city. The founders of LCS recognized that community organization for social action was the only way to remedy their grievances.

Identified references gave no information on the founders, membership, or organizational structure of the LCS. The organization is described summarily in Michael Tirado, "The Mexican American Minority's Participation in Voluntary Political Associations" (Ph.D. dissertation, Claremont Graduate School and University, 1970); and Richard Thurston, "Urbanization and Socio-Economic Change in a Mexican American Enclave" (Ph.D. dissertation, University of California at Los Angeles, 1957).

LEAGUE OF UNITED LATIN AMERICAN CITIZENS (LULAC) Formed in Corpus Christi, Texas, on February 17, 1929, the organization was created by the merger of three local mutual benefit associations: Council Number 4 of the Orden Hijos de America* (OHA), the Knights of San Antonio, and the League of Latin American Citizens of Rio Grande Valley. Prompting the founding of LULAC was the general discrimination against Mexican Americans in the Southwest. This condition was evident in social, residential, and institutional segregation. Too, there was much hostility toward Mexican Americans, which took the form of violent acts committed against this population in Texas.

The founding members of LULAC were Ben Garza, Alonso C. Perales, Manuel C. Gonzalez, J. T. Canales, Mauro Machado (the first five LULAC presidents), E. H. Marin, A. de Luna, and J. Luz Saenz. A number of these men were sons of immigrant, working-class families. Nonetheless, most of them attained a higher education or established themselves as businessmen. Among the men who have served as LULAC national president are nineteen lawyers, a doctor, a university educator, a certified public accountant, an architect, and an engineer. A number of others were wealthy businessmen.

LULAC was formed to help secure and defend rights for Mexican Americans guaranteed in the U.S. Constitution. Emphasis was placed on the rights and privileges, duties and obligations, of citizenship as a means of improving the socio-economic and political status of Mexican Americans. Methods of action were to be taken within constitutionally prescribed means. English-language proficiency was viewed as a necessity for the effective exercise of citizenship, and English was adopted as the official language of the organization. Membership was open to male U.S. citizens who had reached the age of eighteen. Auxiliaries were established for women. The first male-female council appeared in El Paso, Texas, in 1963.

During the initial years there were a few Anglo members, although Mexican Americans constituted the vast majority. In the 1970s there was an increased effort to include other Hispanic Americans. Membership today cross-cuts ethnic, class, political, and national boundaries. The membership includes professionals, business men and women, and tradesmen and laborers. Corporations and other enterprises are also encouraged to become participating members by contributing fifty dollars or more annually.

By 1942 there were 37 councils in Texas plus a few in California and New Mexico. In the 1960s a number of councils were organized in Indiana, Illinois, and Michigan. In the early 1970s councils were established among Cuban Americans in Florida and Puerto Ricans in New York. Today there are more than 380 councils in twenty-six states, the District of Columbia, and Puerto Rico. There are approximately 100,000 members.

The organization is comprised of local, district, state, regional, and national units. Each of the groups holds annual assemblies, elects its own officers and executive boards, and makes decisions pertaining to its area of concern. Members are grouped according to age and sex. In addition to womens' auxiliaries, there are also junior LULAC councils organized in each chapter, which serve to train youths for eventual participation in adult councils. LULAC members are charged a four-dollar initiation fee and pay monthly dues to their local, district, state, regional, and national units.

The national organization has a published constitution and bylaws including articles on legal provisions, philosophy, aims and purposes, financial considerations, and offices. The organization has a number of official symbols including the acronym LULAC, a motto, emblem, seal, flag, banner, membership pin, colors, prayer, and hymn. The flag used is the U.S. flag, the prayer Washington's prayer, and the hymn "America."

Throughout its fifty-two-year history LULAC's major activities have centered on education, employment, and civil rights. LULAC has also initiated social and legal action on behalf of the Hispanic population. It functions as both a protector and provider of services to this community. LULAC's interest in educational processes and institutions is reflected in its involvement in suits to end segregation of Hispanics in southwestern schools. In 1948 LULAC entered the Delgado case, which resulted in the closing of segregated Mexican schools in Texas. LULAC promotes education as a solution to many of the problems of Hispanics. In 1957 "Little Schools of the 400" were established by LULAC for preschool English-language training. By 1959, 800 children were enrolled in twelve schools. During Lyndon B. Johnson's administration the program was taken over and funded by the federal government as Project Headstart.

LULAC has always advocated the awarding of educational scholarships. In the 1940s local councils raised money and distributed awards. In 1975 the LULAC National Scholarship Fund was established, combining council and corporate contributions, and by 1978, $170,438 had been awarded to 449 students. The organization also operates the LULAC National Educational Service Centers, providing counseling and college and occupational planning to post-secondary students. LULAC has operated eleven of these centers with an annual budget of over $2.1 million. Federal funding for this program has required service to low-income students of all ethnic groups.

Employment has been another area of focus for LULAC. During World War II, LULAC fought to open jobs in the defense industry to Mexican Americans. Also, it has interceded on behalf of migrant workers. In the 1960s LULAC filed several class action suits alleging discrimination in public hiring, such as the case against the Santa Ana, California, police and fire departments. In 1964 LULAC began Operation SER (service, education, and redevelopment) in conjunction with the American G.I. Forum* (AGIF). The project seeks to train Mexican Americans in job skills necessary to find and retain employment. At this writing, there were 134 projects in 104 cities.

Civil rights has been the third major area of concern of LULAC. From its founding the organization has been concerned with Mexican Americans' voting rights. LULAC filed a suit against the governor of Texas to eliminate property ownership as a qualification for voting. In the 1950s LULAC took the Pedro Hernandez case to the U.S. Supreme Court, appealing his life sentence on the basis that never had a Mexican American sat on a jury in Jackson County, Texas. The plaintiffs won both cases. In the 1960s LULAC members formed the State of Texas Mexican American Legal Defense Fund. This group was awarded a $2 million Ford Foundation grant. The organization today is known as the Mexican American Legal Defense and Education Fund* (MALDEF). LULAC attorneys continue to serve as "watchdogs" over events with important implications for Hispanics.

LULAC publishes a monthly news magazine called *LULAC*. This is published at LULAC's publications office in Washington, D.C., where its national data processing office is located. LULAC assemblies and conventions incorporate a number of social, cultural, and recreational activities such as banquets, dances, parties, golf and tennis tournaments, and city tours.

LULAC relies on a variety of sources for funding of its programs and activities. LULAC has received monies from business and corporations such as Kraft Foods and Coors Beer, as well as from a variety of federal agencies such as the Community Services Administration, and from private foundations including Ford. Additional revenues are derived from membership dues and council fundraising drives.

LULAC has been an effective spokesperson on behalf of Hispanics. To continue to effect change for Hispanic citizens, LULAC has targeted the 1980s as the "Decade of the Hispanic." The 1980 census was utilized to determine the impact of increased numbers for the Hispanic population on politicians and government agencies. As the largest ethnic minority, Hispanics should require greater attention from city, state, and national officials determining public policy, reasoned the LULAC leadership. The organization sees an even greater role for itself through the establishment of closer ties with the Mexican government and people. LULAC sees its function as assisting in the resolution of common U.S.– Mexican concerns and, in turn, the Mexican government encouraging the U.S.

government to resolve and assist in the improvement of social, economic, and political conditions within the Hispanic community.

LULAC has been perceived by some Mexican Americans as a conservative organization due to its espoused American patriotism, its commitment to working within the system, and its seemingly assimilationist goals. However, in its knowledge and manipulation of American juro-political rules and symbols, LULAC has achieved a great deal. As a matter of fact, due to its actual, if not perceived flexibility and adaptability, LULAC has been able to remain a viable organization under changing social and political conditions. In the early 1980s LULAC's leadership seemed to be moving the organization toward greater activism. Whether the association can maintain its effectiveness in light of this philosophical variation merits continued study.

Most contemporary works on the Mexican American people contain some references to LULAC. Also, many Texas, California, and other southwestern states' newspapers have published articles of one kind or another about LULAC. The primary references used for this work include the LULAC Constitution and Bylaws for 1977, the *LULAC 50th Anniversary History* (1979), and various editions of *LULAC*.

LEÑADORES DEL MUNDO (WOODMEN OF THE WORLD) (LM) The LM, also referred to as Hacheros (Axemen), attracted mostly middle-income Mexican Americans in the state of Texas. Many of them were civil servants and included employees of the U.S. Post Office and the water works, clerks of the municipal offices, janitors of the U.S. Immigration Service, plumbers and electricians, as well as veterans of World War I.

References give little historical information on this organization. From the material available, it can be assumed that the LM was founded sometime around 1910. The organization was an affiliated Masonic body, which contributed to their middle-class status and ability to secure "good" jobs. Local lodges of the Hacheros were spread out in the towns along the Rio Bravo River, including Eagle Pass, Laredo, and Del Rio. Historian Jose Amaro Hernandez says that according to former members of the order, there was widespread acceptability by the Catholic Church to membership in these Masonic provident associations in Eagle Pass.

A summary reference on the LM is contained in Jose Amaro Hernandez, "The Political Development of Mutual Aid Societies in the Mexican American Community: Ideals and Principles" (Ph.D. dissertation, University of California, Riverside, 1979).

LICEO CUBANO (CUBAN LYCEUM) (LC) This is a regional organization founded in 1968 and based in San Jose, California. Its goals include the preservation of Cuban customs and culture in the United States. It sponsors social, cultural, and recreational activities. The organization meets monthly. The LC is primarily a social organization intended to provide a meeting place and social network for Cubans in San Jose.

A summary of the LC is included in the *Directory of Spanish Speaking Organizations* (1970).

LIGA FEMENIL MEXICANISTA (MEXICAN WOMEN'S LEAGUE)

(LFM) The Liga was founded in Texas at El Primer Congreso Mexicanista* (PCM) held on September 11, 1911, in Laredo. The Liga also met on October 15, 1911, to debate the selection of a more specific name for the organization. However, no name change was made. Biographies of several Mexican heroines were read at this meeting, including those of Josefa Ortiz de Dominguez, Leona Vicario, and Dona Manuela Aguado de Abasolo.

The officers of the new organization were: president, Jovita Idar; vice-president, Professor M. D. J. de Leon; secretary, Professor Soledad F. de Peña; treasurer, Professor Maria Renteria; general counsel, Maria Villarreal; voting members, Professors Luisa Cabrera, Rita Tarvin, and Aurelia Peña and Mrs. de Silva.

The female representation at the Congreso was comprised mainly of schoolteachers. Therefore, members of La Liga promoted the discussion of educational issues at the Congreso meeting. The organization immediately undertook a project to provide free instruction to poor Mexican children who could not afford to attend school. Although La Liga did not continue beyond its founding year as an active national organization, it is significant to the history of organizational efforts among Hispanic women.

References for this entry include Rodolfo Acuña, *Occupied America* (1981); and Jose E. Limon, "El Primer Congreso Mexicanista de 1911: A Precursor to Contemporary Chicanismo," *Aztlan* 5:1 and 2 (1974).

LIGA PROTECTORA LATINA (LATIN PROTECTIVE LEAGUE) (LPL)

The Liga was founded in 1914 in Phoenix, Arizona, by a group of Mexicans opposing the discriminatory Claypool-Kinney Bill. This bill was introduced into law in November 1914, with the provision that no firm could hire more than 20 percent aliens and prohibiting anyone who was deaf or dumb or did not speak English to be employed in a hazardous occupation. The bill was the result of a long struggle between Arizona mine owners and organized labor, which opposed Mexican labor in the mines. The Liga was organized and led by Ignacio Espinosa, Pedro G. de la Loma, and Jesus Melendez. By May 1915, the Tempe lodge had eighty members and had established a bureau to provide employment referral and financial assistance.

When miners organized a strike in Ray, Arizona, the Liga supported them. They involved themselves extensively with the education and protection of Mexicans. By 1917 the Liga had thirty lodges focusing on political and legal action to protect Mexican rights, increased financial mutual aid for members, and greater emphasis on education. La Liga supported striking miners at Jerome, Globe,

Miami, and Clifton-Morenci. The organization initiated a series of meetings with then Arizona Governor Thomas Campbell calling for night classes, especially in mining areas. When Campbell's opponent in the race for governor tried to revive the 80 percent bill, La Liga supported Campbell's candidacy.

At its third annual convention members established a commission headed by Amado Cota Robles to lobby the state legislature for bilingual education at the primary level. Night classes in Spanish, arithmetic, geometry, geography, and Mexican history were begun under Cota Robles's leadership. Emphasis was on learning English and on reading. By 1919 lodges had been established in Arizona, California, New Mexico, and Philadelphia. Circa 1920 dues were raised to a three-dollar initiation fee and monthly dues of one dollar and twenty-five cents, causing poor members to protest.

A summary reference to the activities of the LPL is contained in Rodolfo Acuña, *Occupied America* (1981).

LIGA PROTECTORA MEXICANA (MEXICAN PROTECTIVE LEAGUE)
(LPM) This organization was founded in 1921 by a group of Mexican immigrants in Kansas City facing expatriation after World War I. The Mexican community organized the Liga to protect the right of residency respective to their legal immigrant status.

The Liga Protectora was a grass-roots organization in structure which served a number of functions during its two years of existence. These included finding jobs for the unemployed and providing food and clothes for the needy. When the postwar depression ended and the threat of expatriation was eliminated, the organization lost its major reason for existence and dissolved in 1923.

Sources for information on the LPM include Paul Ming Chang-lin, "Voluntary Kinship–Voluntary Association in a Mexican American Community (Master's thesis, University of Kansas, n.d.), as presented as a primary reference in Miguel David Tirado, "Mexican American Community Political Organizations," *La Causa Politica: A Chicano Politics Reader*, ed. F. Chris Garcia (1974).

LITTLE HAVANA ACTIVITIES CENTER (LHAC) This local service organization was founded in 1973 and based in Miami, Florida. The LHAC is a United Fund affiliate with four local branches in Dade County. References to the organization indicate a permanent work staff of eight and membership of over 1,700 persons of Cuban descent. The membership is open to individuals sixty years or over. There are no dues. The LHAC provides services to senior citizens which include a variety of referrals, counseling, free meals, transportation, arts and crafts, and educational, civic, and recreational activities. Officers include a president, vice-president, secretary, and treasurer.

The primary reference for this organization is the *Directory of Spanish Speaking Community Organizations* (1970). However, since this is a United Way of Dade County agency, it is certain that further information can be obtained in the form of United Way reports and program descriptions as well as in-house documents available by provision of the LHAC. The organization failed to respond to the HAVO questionnaire.

M

METROPOLITAN SPANISH MERCHANTS CO-OP (MSMCOP) This organization was founded in 1967 as the Metro Spanish Merchants Association. The impetus behind the creation of the association was the recognition that the average Puerto Rican grocer in New York City worked 108 hours a week. The Co-op was designed to lower grocer's costs by use of cooperative techniques. The Co-op has over 100 members and receives support from the Puerto Rican Forum* (PRF) for its efforts. The Co-op is housed in the Bronx Terminal Market in the Bronx.

Information on the MSMCOP can be found in the archives of the Robert Kennedy Memorial in Washington, D.C.

METRO SPANISH MERCHANTS ASSOCIATION See METROPOLITAN SPANISH SPEAKING MERCHANTS CO-OP.

MEXICAN AMERICAN BUSINESS AND PROFESSIONAL WOMEN'S CLUB (MABPW) This organization was founded in 1974 in Dallas, Texas, to upgrade the image of the Mexican American working woman through personal development, civic involvement, and bilingual-bicultural awareness. The goals of this civic group as stated in their literature are to promote interest in business and professions generally, through educational, scientific, and vocational activities. As a way of achieving its goals, the organization provides its members with workshops on self-development, rape prevention, job application, conflict management, and housing and health careers. The organization also makes available organizational scholarships. Money for these scholarships is raised locally through the sponsorship of a Cinco de Mayo celebration dance for Mexico's May 5 Independence Day. Other activities of the MABPW include a children's

Christmas party for needy families and La Feria del Rio (The River Fair), a celebration of Mexico's September 16 Independence Day.

Initially the organization was founded with forty members, but membership has increased steadily. The scope of this organization is local, district, state, and national. The structure of the MABPW is set up in hierarchical order to include a president, first vice-president, second vice-president, recording secretary, corresponding secretary, and treasurer. Some of its more prominent leaders have been Veronica Salazar, Mary J. Roque, Maria S. Castillo, Gloria Rodriquez, and Mary Helen Alvarado. However, references do not indicate these to have been the founders.

Membership in the MABPW is restricted to women who are either full- or part-time students in four-year educational institutions and to women who are full- or part-time employees in a business or professional capacity. Members must subscribe to the ideals and goals of the organization as well as support the Equal Rights Amendment. The organization's dues are thirty-four dollars annually and include fees for local, state, and national participation, a name tag, a gold-filled pin, and a subscription to the state and national magazine.

The primary reference for this organization was a completed HAVO questionnaire.

MEXICAN AMERICAN COMMUNITY SERVICES AGENCY (MACSA)

Historic conditions of institutional discrimination against Mexican Americans in northern California still existed in the 1960s. Discriminated against in education and employment, many Mexican Americans lived in poverty, lacking adequate nutrition, health care, and housing. These conditions pertained to both rural and urban Mexican American populations in Santa Clara County and its major city, San Jose. This part of California is known for its agriculture, and many Mexican Americans comprised the backbone of the crop pickers. So although Mexican Americans were numerous, there were no agencies addressing their specific needs. MACSA was established in 1964 in response to these conditions. It received a start-up grant from the Rosenberg Foundation in the amount of $20,000 and was the first Mexican American agency to be formed in Santa Clara County.

MACSA's major purpose is to identify and define educational, employment, and other social needs of Mexican Americans and to devise programs and services to meet these needs. More specifically, MACSA's goals are to locate resources for programmatic implementation in social services, develop leadership in planning for services, analyze significant social policies, and create community awareness regarding the implications of these policies. Other goals of MACSA are to coordinate voluntary and public services, provide assistance to agencies trying to improve services to the Mexican American community, and organize demonstration projects, programs, and services for Mexican American families.

In 1966 the Rosenberg Foundation ceased to fund MACSA, concluding that the agency's mission had been accomplished. That same year MACSA was accepted as a member agency of the United Way of Santa Clara County and was awarded a $29,482 grant. In 1976 MACSA's budget was $431,014, and by 1978 its annual funding totaled $935,377. By this time, MACSA was receiving funds from the Comprehensive Employment Training Act (CETA), the U.S. Department of Education, United Way, and the Santa Clara County and California state governments. More than $900,000 of MACSA's 1978–79 budget was targeted for salaries, payroll taxes, employee benefits, office and equipment rentals, office supplies, and travel.

Membership in MACSA is divided into two types, voting and nonvoting. The board of directors comprise the voting group. They vote on all questions of policy and programs pertaining to the agency and are responsible for MACSA finances. Board members serve staggered three-year terms and nominate and vote on their replacements. Nonvoting members assist in membership recruitment for the board, participate on standing and ad hoc committees, and carry out duties as directed by the board.

The MACSA bylaws specify a fifteen-member board of directors to govern the agency. In the early 1980s, however, the organization began to experience internal difficulties, and this resulted in continued inability to fill board seats. For the majority of the agency's existence, MACSA was run by its charismatic executive director, Jose Villa. Villa, essentially a product of his times, developed his leadership capabilities during the turbulent 1960s. So while not lacking in creative leadership, he was notably weak in administrative and management skills. The board, during Villa's tenure, was viewed by those outside the agency as a rubber stamp for Villa's personal goals and objectives. And frequently these were called into question by the Mexican American community which the agency served. But Villa did provide innovative community leadership under which MACSA experienced considerable expansion.

In early 1980 the board expressed a desire to assume greater responsibility for the operational and policy-setting activities of the agency. This provoked a crisis in Villa's leadership that eventually forced a change. Villa resigned and a national search was conducted for his replacement. Rosa Maria Hernandez, an administrative assistant to Villa, emerged as a leading candidate. Although Hernandez lacked formal management training, she had served the agency well since its beginning. Her candidacy was championed by several board members with the rationale of demonstrating support for upward mobility for MACSA employees. The appointment of Hernandez would demonstrate to other staff that an individual, because of exemplary performance, could climb through the ranks and be rewarded with not only recognition but increased responsibility and compensation. Rosa Maria Hernandez was selected as the new executive director, and the agency entered into a transformational period. In considerable contrast to Villa's charismatic style and his unconventional staff, in particular Jack Brito, Hernandez brought in several low-key administrators to run the agency.

At the same time Esther Medina Gonzalez was elected board president. The new board officers included Manuel Sandoval, Emily Ortega, and Sylvia Gonzales. The agency began to chart a course of long-term problem solving. Consultants were brought in to assist the board in defining goals and priorities, and the agency seemed to be heading on a new and even more expansive course.

Early into her board presidency, however, Medina Gonzalez challenged the administrative capabilities of the new director. Individual board members began to assume greater authority over the day-to-day operation of the agency, allowing little latitude to its director. Board members Gonzales and Ortega suggested that an outside evaluation of the director's performance be conducted and either training be provided to correct any weaknesses or she be dismissed. This was, of course, in the event that she be found remiss in her duties. Although an evaluation was never conducted, because of these two members' opposition to outright dismissal, the direct intervention into the duties of the director was held in check until the departure of Sylvia Gonzales from the board in 1981. New board members supportive of the president were appointed.

In 1981, although she no longer held the position of board president, Medina Gonzalez continued to exercise a good deal of influence over the agency and especially those members she had assisted in appointing to the board. Some board members, while not calling into question Medina Gonzalez's judgment, felt that an outside evaluation of the director was both legally and ethically correct. MACSA entered into a period of extreme turmoil culminating with a formal complaint to the primary funding agency, United Way, the resignation of the executive director, a purging of the agency staff, and resignation of half of the board, including the then board president, Maria Elena Chavez. Medina Gonzalez was appointed the executive director by the new officers of the board, and the board continued to lack full representation according to the agency's bylaws.

Since the appointment of Medina Gonzalez, the agency's one-time staff of over sixty including officers, resource staff, and project staff has sharply declined. MACSA had employed over the years a highly diversified staff of Mexican Americans, Filipino Americans, and Anglo Americans. Presently, MACSA projects are of a more limited scope, and staff makeup is no longer as diversified.

MACSA, as an agency, has played a significant role in the organizational efforts of Mexican Americans in Santa Clara County. For years, the agency ran the Luchessa Day Care Center, which provided bilingual bicultural preschool training and health and day care services to 132 migrant children and other health care education for parents. The Center held the first direct state contract with the California Department of Education to provide ongoing services to migrant children through a continuing funding source.

An ongoing MACSA educational program is Project Independence, which treats the unemployment problems of youths in the largely Mexican American neighborhoods of East San Jose. It has assisted in the training and job placement of over 125 youths between the ages of sixteen and eighteen.

MACSA has always devoted much of its program impetus to the elderly. In order to do this it sometimes funds existing projects. One of these was Todos Amigos, a program which provided transportation and other personal services to Mexican and Filipino senior citizens in the community of Gilroy and within the Franklin McKinley district in San Jose. So while the agency was founded to provide needed services to Mexican Americans, as this program demonstrates, it has assisted the needy of various ethnic groups. And the agency continues to serve the elderly through its Minority Senior Outreach Program.

MACSA utilizes Aztec symbols to represent its programs and activities. The agency has published its bylaws and a personnel manual for its employees. Aside from its services to the community, MACSA participates in other social and cultural activities. The agency holds banquets, picnics, and holiday parties for its staff members. Also, MACSA enters floats in the annual September 16 Mexican Independence Day Parade.

This agency has undergone considerable transformation since its inception. Overall, it has contributed much to the development of the Mexican American community in San Jose. Whether MACSA's difficulties were reflective of internal differences among its leadership, the result of insecurities and anxieties provoked by changes in national priorities, or simply due to the lack of formal professional training and experience of its managers are considerations that require further examination.

Sources for this organization include MACSA interoffice memoranda; MACSA board meeting minutes; interagency communiqués; bylaws of MACSA, the MACSA personnel manual; MACSA executive director's progress reports (1964–69); interviews with former Executive Director Rosa Maria Hernandez and former Board President Maria Elena Chavez; and personal recollections of this author as a MACSA board member (1979–81).

MEXICAN AMERICAN ENGINEERING SOCIETY (MAES) This organization was established as a nonprofit voluntary association in Placentia, California, in 1974 by a group of local Mexican American engineers. MAES focuses on the relatively low representation of Hispanics in engineering and the sciences. These engineers founded MAES to help increase the numbers of Hispanic professional engineers and scientists working to solve the nation's social and technological problems. The organization's founders include Manuel Castro, a professional engineer, and Ralph de la Parra, an expert on ecological and water resources.

MAES's main goal is to foster cooperation among government, industry, academic, and professional communities toward improving educational and employment opportunities for Mexican American scientists and engineers. Other MAES goals include promoting the placement and advancement of Mexican American engineers and scientists and providing assistance to Mexican American scientists and engineers starting or expanding technological businesses. MAES also seeks to bring national attention to the achievements and contributions of Mexican Americans in science and engineering.

MAES is a hierarchically structured national organization headed by a board of directors, which determines policy and controls finances. The organization is also served by a set of officers, including a president, vice-president, treasurer, and secretary. MAES has a total of twelve chapters nationwide, six professional chapters and six student branches. The professional chapters are located in Los Angeles in Orange County (the national office); San Diego; Ventura County, California; Houston, Texas; Idaho Falls, Idaho; and Seattle, Washington. The student branches are located on the campuses of the University of California at Irvine; California State University at Fullerton, Long Beach, and San Jose; the University of New Mexico at Albuquerque; the University of Texas at El Paso; the University of Houston; Arizona State University at Tempe; and the University of Colorado at Boulder. Professional membership is open to all persons holding degrees in science or engineering, practicing science or engineering professionally, or working in management in science or engineering fields. MAES has a membership of over 250. Approximately 95 percent of the members are Mexican American, and the majority are at middle to high income levels. College and university students pursuing degrees in engineering or sciences are eligible for student membership.

As a national organization MAES engages in a number of activities directed toward the realization of its goals. Professional members make presentations at educational institutions, from primary to postsecondary levels, at PTA meetings, and in Mexican American community neighborhoods regarding the work they are involved in and the opportunities for minorities in engineering and the sciences. MAES representatives also speak before the National Academy of Sciences on the need for increasing the participatory role of Hispanics in science and technology. The organization also sponsors tutorial programs providing minority science and engineering students guidance, instruction, and counseling by professionals in their chosen fields. MAES holds an annual National Symposium on Engineering, where representatives from industry, government, business, and education are invited to participate in seminars and the presentation of papers. A number of social activities such as banquets and receptions are also part of the symposia.

Student members engage in a number of activities in addition to assisting in the coordination of the National Symposium on Engineering. Campus organization members at the University of California at Irvine, with the statewide MESA Project (Math, Engineering and Science Achievement) sponsored by business corporations, tutor and counsel local high school students interested in science and engineering careers. Through the Minority Introduction to Engineering Programs (MITE), MAES student members escort students on tour of industrial plants. In addition, a MAES student newsletter is printed at the University of California at Irvine announcing opportunities available to minority engineering and science graduates, available scholarships and grants, and new developments in the technological fields.

MAES receives funding from industry. Some of the corporations providing financial assistance to the organization are Hunt-Wesson and Bechtel Corporations. The achievements of a number of MAES leaders including Joe Flores,

Ralph de la Parra, and Manuel Castro are mentioned in *Viva: A Salute to Hispanic Americans in Science and Engineering*, published by Domingo Nick Reyes and Associates.

An excellent reference for this organization is "Viva," an announcement brochure for the Fourth National Symposium on Engineering. Also, subsequent brochures provide a useful reference. The membership application contains information on the organization as well as the various student newsletters. For this work, each was utilized as well as the organization's completed HAVO questionnaire.

MEXICAN AMERICAN LEGAL DEFENSE AND EDUCATION FUND (MALDEF) MALDEF was founded in 1967 by Peter Tijerina, an attorney who served as state civil rights chairman for the San Antonio, Texas, League of United Latin American Citizens* (LULAC) Council No. 2. During his time in LULAC he participated in its "traveling squad," which visited cities and sites of alleged civil rights violations. During 1967 Tijerina became aware that the Ford Foundation would be willing to consider a proposal for a five-site Mexican American Legal Defense Fund based in Texas. With help from the NAACP Legal Defense Fund (LDF), a seed grant to fund writing the proposal was obtained from the Marshall Field Foundation. Utilizing LULAC contacts, Tijerina met with community organizations throughout the Southwest, which resulted in the formation of New Mexico, Arizona, California, and Colorado committees. The final committee was established in Texas. Carlos Codena was named president of the board, and Peter Tijerina was appointed executive director. It was in May 1968 that MALDEF received its first funding from the Ford Foundation of $2.2 million over a five-year period. As the organization developed, its supporters grew to include over 120 private corporations and foundations including Atlantic Richfield, IBM, and Western Airlines.

The organization's goals are to aid in the protection of Mexican Americans and other minorities' civil rights through legal means. Under the general heading of civil rights, MALDEF has been involved in cases concerning equal employment, bilingual education, police brutality, Chicana rights, immigration, and many others. Through its many activities, MALDEF has come to be recognized as the leading advocacy organization for Mexican Americans.

In 1973 attorney Vilma S. Martinez became MALDEF's president and general counsel. She had worked with the LDF in New York, was selected as a member of the Census Bureau's Advisory Committee on the Spanish Origin Population during 1975, and had received the Rockefeller Youth Award in 1977. She was also appointed to the California Board of Regents after joining MALDEF. Martinez oversaw the national expansion and financial solvency of the organization.

MALDEF's organizational structure consists of officers, a board of directors, and other members, all of which come under the heading of board members. Board membership includes women and men of various ethnic groups from diverse occupational backgrounds such as professors, business executives, politicians, and attorneys. Membership to the board of directors is limited to two-year terms to ensure that new people and new ideas are constantly injected into the agency's governing body.

The election of board members occurs during the annual spring meeting. Staff personnel such as secretaries, counselors, and attorneys are hired continuously. The policies of MALDEF are set by the board of directors and are implemented by the president and general counsel and staff. When Martinez became president she decentralized the running of the organization by delegating responsibility for day-to-day cases to staff attorneys. MALDEF utilizes indigenous symbols from Mexico and South America to represent its tasks.

MALDEF has five offices in operation: the founding branch in San Antonio, Texas; the Los Angeles office established in 1969; the present home office in San Francisco, first directed by Mario Obledo in 1970; the Denver, Colorado, branch opened by Ken Padilla in 1971; and the Washington, D.C., branch established in 1973 with Juan Rocha as director. There was also an Albuquerque, New Mexico, office (1972–76) directed by Ray Vargas.

MALDEF has aided in the protection of Mexican American civil rights by litigation and by developing special programs. One of its prime interests is educational equity. For example, in 1974 MALDEF won the *Serna* v. *Portales* case concerning the development of bilingual education classes in New Mexico, and in 1976 winning suits were brought against various school boards in Texas alleging segregation of Anglo students from Mexican American and black students. In the mid-1970s job discrimination in colleges and universities was MALDEF's focus: *Crofts* v. *Board of Governors* (1974) demanded high-level jobs and better student services for Mexican Americans in all California community colleges, and in 1975, *Guerra* v. *Board of Trustees* challenged teacher hiring and promotion practices in the California State University system. MALDEF was also involved in the much publicized *Bakke* v. *Regents of the University of California* (1975) case of alleged "reverse discrimination."

MALDEF's interests also include employment rights. Two separate suits—*Mandujano* v. *Basic Vegetable Co.* (1974) and *Alaniz* v. *Tillie Lewis Foods* (1976)—resulted in new jobs, training opportunities, and fair hiring and promotion policies for the large working Mexican American population in California. Other suits were brought against the Denver Fire Department, San Antonio's Kelly Air Force Base, and other institutions for their discriminatory employment practices. In the area of immigration, the *Loya* v. *Immigration and Naturalization Service* case helped limit mass immigration raids in Texas and California.

MALDEF sponsors a number of special projects such as the Chicana Rights Project (CRP), which consists of litigation, research and publication, and community education units; the Mexican American Equal Rights Project established to document disenfranchisement of Mexican Americans in Arizona, Texas, and New Mexico; the Legal Intern-Extern Project, which trains Mexican American law graduates in civil rights skills and helps them set up practices in local communities; the Community Education and Activation Program (CEAP), which informs the Mexican American community of the legal rights and the services that are available to them; the Headstart Preschool Project; and a Comprehensive Employment Training Act (CETA) job program.

In the 1980s MALDEF's CEAP launched an extensive campaign to make sure that all Hispanics in the United States were counted during the 1980 census. This would allow for a data base for determining the amount and location of funding for various programs as well as legislative representation. Other activities include educational grants for law students, individual and group counseling, legal seminars for Mexican American lawyers, fund-raising dinners, art exhibits, social and cultural gatherings, annual conventions, and a quarterly publication called *MALDEF*.

In 1981 MALDEF achieved a major victory with the passage of the Voting Rights Act in the House of Representatives. MALDEF pressed Hispanic issues in the hearing as well as lobbying for its passage, all necessary processes involved in the review of the act. MALDEF also pushed for its passage in the Senate. MALDEF joined with Representative Augustus F. Hawkins (D–California) in providing resources and organizing affirmative action hearings throughout the country. MALDEF has submitted formal comments to suggest proposed changes and to influence the legislative process in a way that would be most beneficial to Hispanics and affirmative action. Also in 1981 MALDEF joined in the *Doe* v. *Plyler* case before the Supreme Court dealing with the educational rights of undocumented children.

The early 1980s brought an end to Vilma Martinez's tenure as president and general counsel of MALDEF. She was replaced by Joaquin Avila. The activities of MALDEF through its first ten years have affected both the Mexican American communities and the community at large. This organization has not only brought attention to Mexican American problems but has also improved employment and educational conditions for blacks, women, and Mexican Americans alike. The organization represents a gathering of resources and individual talents working toward ending discriminatory practices within the employment, educational, housing, economic, and other American institutions.

MALDEF has received prominent mention in a number of contemporary references including the *Los Angeles Times*, *New York Times*, and *Washington Post*. It has been mentioned in *Time* and *Newsweek* as well as *Nuestro Magazine* (March 1982). The *Encyclopedia of Associations* (1979) gives a summary of MALDEF's activities. And the *MALDEF* newsletters provide detailed reviews of the organization's activities. For purposes of this work the MALDEF newsletters (1978–80) and the completed HAVO questionnaire were used as primary references.

MEXICAN AMERICAN POLITICAL ASSOCIATION (MAPA) This organization initially began in 1958 as a loose association of former more activist members of the Community Service Organization* (CSO). In 1960 it was formally established in Fresno, California, as a nonprofit, nonpartisan political organization. MAPA finally organized on a statewide corporate basis on May 2, 1963.

MAPA arose out of the disillusionment experienced by Mexican Americans with the Democratic Party in the 1954 and 1958 California state elections. Edward Roybal had run for lieutenant governor in 1954 and was defeated. Subsequently, Henry Lopez, a young attorney, ran for secretary of state and was also defeated in an election that had produced a Democratic landslide. As a result of these defeats, the organization was founded by Edward Roybal, Bert Corona, Eduardo Quevedo, and Frank Casado.

The Fresno meeting produced MAPA's objectives as the following, as quoted directly from the literature:

1. To see the social, economic, cultural, and civic betterment of Mexican Americans and other persons sympathetic to their aims.

2. To take stands on political issues and present and endorse candidates for public office.

3. To launch voter registration drives throughout California.

4. To encourage increased activity within the political parties.

So while its parent organization, the CSO, continued to work within the Democratic Party, MAPA concerned itself primarily with electing Mexican Americans to public office and supporting candidates from both parties. MAPA seeks to serve the Mexican American community through the articulation, advancement, and advocacy of the political interests of this population.

MAPA has played a major role in increasing Mexican American political representation in California. The election of two state assemblymen, one congressman, three superior court judges and three municipal court judges of Mexican descent can be directly attributed to MAPA.

MAPA pushed for East Los Angeles incorporation, which gave greater home rule powers to the largely Mexican American population of East Los Angeles. But MAPA's most notable success may have been the election of Edward Roybal to Congress. Congressman Roybal has served not only his district well but the entire Hispanic population nationally. And the organization has pressed for legislation beneficial to the Mexican American community and has launched several voter registration drives and programs of political education. MAPA has been involved in all sorts of issues ranging from police brutality to school discrimination.

In the beginning the membership consisted mainly of middle-class, albeit activist, Mexican Americans. This had affected the organization's efforts to promote political organizations and social action. Recognizing this, the organization has made strenuous attempts to increase its lower-class participation. These efforts include collaboration with more grass-roots organizations and locating meeting sites in lower-class neighborhoods.

Another aspect of Mexican American organizational attempts that this organization sought to avoid was that of the "patron" style of leadership. This refers to the cult of personality leadership with its cadre of loyal followers resulting in dictatorial and oppressive leadership, the kind one witnesses frequently in Latin America, where an autocratic and militaristic few rule the masses. Because of Mexican Americans' susceptibility to personalistic leadership, in which loyalty resides first with the chosen leader and then with the organization, MAPA's bylaws sought to decentralize the organization's structure, with each chapter assured autonomy within its assembly district.

However, in 1983 the organization experienced serious factionalism with the election of its new state president, Fernando Chavez, son of farmworker leader Cesar Chavez. Chavez challenged incumbent Julio Calderon. Charges were made that the United Farmworkers of America* (UFW) had paid MAPA's membership fees for UFW members immediately before the election so that the new members could vote for Chavez. The dissenting parties took their case before a San Jose court, and a scuffle even occurred between the Calderon and Chavez forces on the courthouse steps. The strife continued at the convention, and it appeared that, regardless of the sincerity of Chavez's motives, he was accorded the position of personalistic leadership, a probable transference from his father.

Whether the outcome of the 1983 election will have a serious impact on what attorney Manuel Ruiz has described as the "practical realities of local political autonomy" is yet to be determined. One thing is certain, Chavez, the father, has not hesitated in using his powerful organization in political campaigns of benefit to the UFW and Chavez's goals and objectives as he personally sees them.

The founders of MAPA believed in the conscientious respect for the autonomy of the local chapters. The 1983 election, however, has ushered in a new era of organizational politics for Mexican Americans in MAPA. Whether this thrust is truly representative of the needs, hopes, and aspirations of this community is still unclear.

MAPA is a hierarchically structured, three-tiered organization. MAPA units include the state and regional apparatus and the local units. Chapters exist in a number of cities in California and elsewhere. MAPA has strategically established an organizational chapter in every assembly district with a sizable Mexican population and has a membership of over 5,000 persons, who are primarily Mexican American-identified and of low to middle income. MAPA has both a membership application fee and annual membership dues. The organization has seriously reached out to women to join their ranks and, as an incentive, offers dual membership for wives of members at no extra cost. MAPA officers include a national president, first vice-president, and second vice-president.

The 1983 state convention was held in San Jose, California, and received extensive coverage in the *San Jose Mercury News*, which serves as an excellent source on the intricate machinations and political maneuvers that took place during that campaign. Other sources for this work included a completed HAVO questionnaire; Richard Santillan, "Third Party Politics: Old Story, New Faces," *The Black Politician* (1971); *A Guide to Hispanic Organizations* (1979); a July 1980 newsletter of the MAPA Santa Clara County chapter; Michael David Tirado,

"The Mexican American Minority's Participation in Voluntary Political Associations" (Ph.D. dissertation, Claremont Graduate School and University, 1970); and Maurilio Vigil, *Chicano Politics* (1978).

MEXICAN AMERICAN STUDENTS ORGANIZATION See MOVIMIENTO ESTUDIANTIL CHICANO DE AZTLAN.

MEXICAN AMERICAN UNITY COUNCIL (MAUC) The Unity Council was founded in 1967 in Prospect Hill, San Antonio, Texas, as a community development corporation with a mini-grant from the Ford Foundation. MAUC was incorporated as a nonprofit organization in the state of Texas in 1970 by a group of young Mexican American residents of the Prospect Hill barrio, a neighborhood with an 88 percent Mexican American population. The founders shared a common concern for improving the unhealthy conditions existing in the area: high unemployment, a high incidence of substance abuse, overcrowding, and inadequate municipal services. With the failure of politicians to settle these issues as promised, MAUC was initiated as a community-based effort to address these problems.

The goal of MAUC is to establish an independent Mexican American institution for the purposes of educating the community in the use of the American political process, identifying the felt needs of the community, especially socioeconomic and health needs, and advocating for the service of those needs.

MAUC is a hierarchically structured organization governed by a fourteen-member board of directors composed of experts central to MAUC pursuits and representatives from the community and its local organizations. The board chairperson is Ignacio Perez. The board's decisions are executed by a number of project committees overseen by Executive Director Juan J. Patlan. The committees include housing, child care, health care, employment and training, and economic development.

MAUC conducts a number of programs and activities reflective of its goals. In the area of housing, MAUC has obtained federal funds for the construction of twenty-eight new homes at affordable prices. In addition, with government funds MAUC has remodeled a number of homes utilizing local Mexican American contractors, who in turn hire MAUC-trained workers. MAUC has also established a comprehensive child care center, Escuelita del Sol (Little Sunshine School). The nursery offers programs for children in motor, social, and verbal skills development; culture, heritage, and language reinforcements; and individual and group therapy. The center also provides guidance sessions for parents and seeks to inform the community of the needs of neglected and abused children.

In the field of health care MAUC operates two programs under contract with the Bexar County Hospital District. The mental health program deals with the psychological effects of poverty on individuals and treats alcoholism and drug addiction. MAUC has a maternity program aimed at the reduction of the high rate of infant mortality in the barrio. And the organization has articulated the need for a central health clinic to service primary medical needs free of charge.

The Unity Council also operates a training and employment program providing counseling on job-related problems and family budgeting. The program includes training and placement in construction jobs such as carpentry, plumbing, and masonry.

In the late 1970s MAUC recognized the need for financial resources to build community economic development. An economic development department was established with goals of high-profit venture investment and creation of financial intermediaries for serving the community's economic needs. This resulted in the San Antonio Venture Group an SBIC (small business investment corporation) formed with funds from San Antonio financial institutions, the Small Business Administration, and the Community Services Administration. The San Antonio Venture Group has an initial investment potential of $5 million. While a number of MAUC's early investments failed, the corporation today is part owner of a successful McDonald's fast-food franchise. In addition, MAUC owns and operates two Mexican American restaurants and sixteen houses in a rental project subsidized by the federal government. Since 1969 the organization has raised more than $11 million for its community work. Aside from its profit-making ventures, MAUC receives funds from other government agencies such as the Office of Economic Development of the Commerce Department.

Since 1975 MAUC has operated out of an old building purchased from the city for $150,000 and renovated at a cost of $1 million. The Mexican American Unity Council's motto is ''A New Home in the Barrio.'' The organization utilizes Aztec symbols to represent its tasks.

MAUC is an excellent example of Mexican American self-initiative that has worked. It marks a trend toward economic development by many community organizations for the purposes of supporting social and other programs designed to alleviate Mexican American social, economic, and health ills. The leadership of MAUC has maintained a balanced perspective on socio-political events that has allowed for changes in approach and function as the times and national mood change.

Reference sources for this organization that are most helpful consist of in-house documents available from MAUC. For purposes of this work, MAUC's child care brochure, the MAUC statement of purpose, and a historical background pamphlet on MAUC were utilized.

MEXICAN AMERICAN WOMEN'S NATIONAL ASSOCIATION (MANA)

In October 1974, Mexican American women from a variety of political, educational, professional, and geographical backgrounds assembled in Washington, D.C., for the purpose of organizing a national forum for articulating their concerns. The resultant organization, the Mexican American Women's National Association, headquartered in Washington, is dedicated to the advancement of Mexican American women by fostering and promoting leadership among them.

The Association also strives to improve nationwide communication among Mexican American women and to achieve parity between Mexican American men and women. Above all, MANA wishes to create a national awareness of their presence and interests.

The first woman elected to chair MANA was Blandina Cardenas, then a Rockefeller fellow assigned to the office of Senator Walter Mondale and later a commissioner for children, youth and families in the Department of Health, Education, and Welfare during the Carter Administration. The early meetings were ad hoc discussion sessions. In September 1975 committees were identified and organizing committee officers were named. Bettie Baca Fierro, a civil rights activist from the mid- and late 1960s, was designated chairperson. Her tenure was followed by that of Evangelina Elizondo, a federal employee of the General Service Administration, and Gloria Hernandez of the U.S. Commission on Civil Rights. MANA's activities during its first three years of existence were run from living rooms, basements, and other makeshift headquarters. But the organization did not achieve a real sense of autonomy and self-sufficiency until the chairpersonship of Elisa Sanchez (1977–79), a vice-president of the Washington-based National Council of La Raza* (NCLR).

In 1975 MANA presented testimony before the National Commission on the Observance of International Women's Year, a hearing held in preparation for the 1975 meeting in Mexico City. Chairperson Baca Fierro testified to conditions among the "approximately 14 million" Hispanics in the United States which made the founding of MANA an obligation rather than a choice.

MANA addresses itself to the general issues of high unemployment among Hispanic workers (in 1975, the highest in the country), immigration problems serving to depress the job market, the youthfulness of the Hispanic population (median age 22.1), large Hispanic families, high dependency ratio of Hispanic women, low educational attainment and poor acquisition of English-language skills of Mexican American women, and the barriers to Mexican American women entering the work force.

Since 1977 MANA has held annual training conferences in Washington, D.C., at which Mexican American women from all sections of the country come to express solidarity in championing their rights and to learn to improve their political education skills. The training sessions also serve as an impetus for other Hispanic feminist organizations to organize and politicize in their communities.

Any person committed to the purpose and goals of MANA is eligible for membership. Initially, MANA attracted mainly professional women. However, as the organization's assertive leadership in promoting feminist rights evolved into unprecedented prominence in the Mexican American community, poor, grass-roots women joined MANA's ranks. Although the membership is predominantly Mexican American, other Hispanic and some Anglo women are active members. Current membership lists have indicated over 300 members nationwide.

With the passing of Sanchez's chairpersonship, Wilma Espinoza followed with a more aggressive style. Espinoza was a determined spokesperson representing a seemingly angry Hispana community. So while much attention was focused on MANA's claims and demands, the organization began to move into a period of diminished credibility.

MANA as an organization has grown into a sophisticated advocate for Hispana rights. After Espinoza's tenure, the organization settled into a decidedly less political role. It hosted its first conference outside of Washington and finally began to take on the appearances of a truly national association. The present leadership reflects this maturity and is expanding its leadership functions beyond the nation's capital by building up its national membership.

The primary reference sources relating to MANA's history include unpublished bylaws and meeting minutes, MANA newsletters, which are not widely available, and since 1978, the MANA "Profile," a public relations document outlining the organization's purpose, activities, and future goals, which is available from the association. The *Washington Post* ran an article on MANA's Training Conference for the year 1979, and Wilma Espinoza's remarks are included in a *New York Times* article on women's groups and the presidential campaign of 1980 by *Times* reporter Leslie Bennetts.

MEXICAN AMERICAN WOMEN'S POLITICAL CAUCUS (MAWPC)

The MAWPC is a statewide, affirmative action organization located in the state of Texas. It is not exactly known when this organization was established, but in 1976 the name was changed from the Chicana Women's Political Caucus to its present name. It was only briefly known by its former name. Its membership consists of 250 members spread throughout Laredo, Corpus Christi, and the Rio Grande Valley.

The organization has set up several goals for its members, and one of these is to provide avenues for more local and national political involvement of Mexican American women. In their efforts to do this they have been successful in influencing the appointment of three women to important political positions. Angie Flores was appointed to the assistant lieutenant governor's post, Helen Knaggs to the position of Republican lobbyist, and Carolina Rodriguez to the State Board of Education. Another set of goals for this organization is to recruit more members to work closely with Anglo organizations such as the National Women's Political Caucus in order to attain greater civic influence.

The structure of this organization is in hierarchical order, consisting of a state chair and vice-chairs located in separate cities. Vice-chairs have come from as widely scattered areas as Brownsville, Laredo, El Paso, Corpus Christi, Austin, and San Antonio, all during the same tenure in office. There is also a position of research director for MAWPC.

The organization has stated in its literature that it has had difficulty raising outside funding. But it is incorporated as an educational fund where monies would be channeled toward the offering of seminars and workshops. In May 1980 the organization sponsored a National Steering Conference in Houston, and in September of that same year they hosted a Career Option Seminar in San Antonio. The latter are indicative of the civic activities the MAWPC provides.

Primary reference sources for this work consisted of the organization's completed HAVO questionnaire and an unpublished project outline.

MEXICAN AMERICAN YOUTH ASSOCIATION OF STUDENTS See MOVIMIENTO ESTUDIANTIL CHICANO DE AZTLAN.

MEXICAN CHAMBER OF COMMERCE OF THE UNITED STATES (MCUS) The Chamber was legally incorporated as a nonprofit organization in the state of New York in December 1921. For a number of years prior to this time a group of Mexican and American businessmen had met in New York City on an annual basis to discuss mutual trade problems. The Mexican economy had experienced a decline since the Revolution of 1910, and both American and Mexican participants viewed the organization of a binational chamber of commerce as a means of promoting American investments in Mexico and of stimulating the Mexican economy. The American Chamber of Commerce of Mexico, Inc., served as a model for forming the Mexican Chamber of Commerce of the United States.

The founders of MCUS include Jose Miguel Bejarano, Sealtiel L. Alatriste, Charles Edmunds Kimball, Jr., Leo M. Blancks, Frederic G. Bastian, and Rene A. Womser. The organization had an initial membership of twenty-seven commercial enterprises. Of these charter institutions, eight were banks, including the Bank of America and the Banco Nacional de México. The remainder were predominantly transportation, motor works, law, metals, and communications firms.

The organization's primary goals are to help secure laws favorable to the development of increased trade and to seek the elimination of legal restrictions which inhibit commercial intercourse between legitimate American and Mexican business parties.

The Mexican Chamber of Commerce of the United States is administered by a board of directors with a board president and including such notables as the Honorable Jaime Peña-Vera, honorary Mexican president, and Miguel Aleman, honorary director and president of the Mexican National Tourist Council. Honorary general consul of Mexico, Alfred J. Lippman serves on the board as chairman and honorary American president. Annual membership meetings are held in the spring, when manufacturers, producers, importers, and businessmen come together to discuss mutual concerns. Previous guests of honor at annual meetings include Miguel Aleman, former president of Mexico; Jacob Javits, former Republican senator from New York; Robert H. McBride, former U.S. ambassador to Mexico; and Juan Jose de Olloqui, former Mexican Ambassador to the United States.

Most current records show the organizational membership consisting of 681 business corporations which pay annual tax deductible dues of $100. Business concerns represented range from producers of adhesives to those of traffic control equipment. In the membership directory the listing with the largest number of participants is for banking services with seventy-nine members. This is followed by the electrical equipment industry with forty-four representatives, the electronic equipment industry with twenty-eight members, and the food processing and packing machinery industry with twenty-seven members.

The Mexican Chamber of Commerce of the United States provides a number of services to its members. It carries out arbitration of disputes between members and helps establish connections between buyers and sellers in the United States and Mexico. The Chamber serves as a clearinghouse of information via the publication of a monthly digest explaining the financial, industrial, market, tariff, and trade laws of both countries. Also, the MCUS maintains a library with numerous trade and financial publications of the two nations. In addition, the organization represents its members before national and international business councils. The leaders of the organization are regularly invited to the presidential inaugurations in both Washington and Mexico City.

Aside from these activities, the MCUS participates in the annual Mexican Week held in New York City to commemorate the Revolution of 1910. During this time the Chamber sponsors social activities and business meetings. The organization also joins in trade fairs and expositions such as the International Commercial Exposition in Mexico City in 1922, the Eighteenth Annual Foreign Trade Convention in New York City in 1931, and the New York World's Fair of 1964. The organization uses both national Mexican and Aztec symbols to represent its activities.

The most useful reference source on the MCUS is an in-house publication, *The Mexican Chamber of Commerce of the United States* (1977).

MEXICAN CONGRESS (MC) The Mexican Congress was founded in 1938 in California as a federation of Mexican American organizations. The stated goals of the Congress were to work for the economic, social, and cultural betterment of the Mexican people; to have an understanding between Anglo Americans and Mexicans; to promote organizations of working people by aiding trade unions; and to actively fight discrimination.

In southern California, the organization concentrated primarily on reducing discrimination but also took an active interest in politics. Before the war, the MC waged an unsuccessful attempt to elect one of its members, Ed Quevedo, to the Los Angeles City Council.

During its peak years, the Mexican Congress claimed a membership of at least 6,000. Its popularity waned and finally, during World War II, it disappeared. Many reasons have been given for its demise, including generational conflicts relating to the organization's activities. Most historians attribute the decline to the Mexico-oriented perspective retained by most southwestern Mexican Americans up until World War II. From the historical record, however, this assumption is debatable. The Alianza Hispano Americana* (AHA) suffered a decline only after the membership's voting potential was bartered in the political arena and its leaders embezzled organization funds. But most interested historians have maintained that since the membership was mostly made up of recent immigrants, and since many of them expected to return to Mexico, they had little interest in establishing permanent affiliations in this country. So in all likelihood, this culturally nationalistic organization could offer only minimal appeal to a population challenged by the forced assimilationist climate of California.

This organization is discussed in two reference works, Michael David Tirado, "The Mexican American Minority's Participation in Voluntary Political Associations" (Ph.D. dissertation, Claremont Graduate School and University, 1970); and John Burma, *Spanish Speaking Groups in the United States* (1954).

MIDWEST CUBAN FEDERATION (MCF) A regional organization founded in 1967 and based in Kentucky, the organization coordinates the activities of midwestern Cuban associations. Presently, these include nine. The MCF also aids new refugees with relocation and employment.

The Federation sponsors and promotes activities designed to preserve the Cuban language and culture in the United States. It publishes political material on Cuba and maintains a small library. It also publishes a quarterly *Boletín*.

Two useful reference sources for this organization include the archives of the Robert Kennedy Memorial and the *Directory of Spanish Speaking Community Organizations* (1970). However, each gives only a brief summary of the MCF's activities. The organization's *Boletín* would be a better resource and are contained in the organization's library available from MCF. The organization failed to respond to a request for the same.

MIDWEST LATINO COUNCIL ON HIGHER EDUCATION (MLCHE) MLCHE was formed February 23, 1980, in Illinois to serve as a communication network among Hispanics in institutions of higher learning in the Midwest. This region includes, but is not limited to, Illinois, Indiana, Iowa, Michigan, Minnesota, Ohio, Wisconsin, Nebraska, Kansas, and Missouri. The Washington, D.C., area as well as New York and Florida have expressed an interest in participating in MLCHE. It may, then, have the potential for a national organization.

The concept for MLCHE was presented at the First Annual Conference on Latinos and Higher Education, which took place at Northern Illinois University in February 1979, by Mr. Ambrosio Medrano. The idea was well received, and subsequently Medrano worked with others to form the Council. Those who shared the concept for the organization included Dr. Gilbert Montez, who wrote an article in *La Red*, a newsletter published by the National Chicano Council on Higher Education* (NCCHE), in December 1979, where he recommended the establishment of the Council. Also, Dr. Vernon E. Lattin, director of the Center for Latino and Latin American Affairs at Northern Illinois University and coordinator of the Second Annual Conference on Latinos and Higher Education, presented the concept to the entire conference assembly, where it was favorably voted into existence.

At this same conference, a Council planning committee of seven persons including Lattin and Medrano was formed. The Council planning committee was to establish a set of priorities for the following year. It determined that a formal announcement of the founding and purpose of the Council should be sent to all college and university presidents and provosts and that a proposed constitution with projected short- and long-term goals for the 1980s should be drawn up.

References regarding this organization are few because of its recent formation at the time of this writing. Additional information may be available from Dr. Lattin at Northern Illinois University's Center for Latino and Latin American Affairs. Sources used for this work include a report/concept paper prepared by members of the Council planning committee. Also *La Red* (December 1979) is an important source.

MOVIMIENTO ESTUDIANTIL CHICANO DE AZTLAN (MECHA) Mexican American student organizational efforts matured through a number of developmental stages initiated in 1966 in specific regions of California and Texas, but eventually encompassed the Southwest, Midwest, Northwest, and eastern seaboard. In Texas, student mobilization efforts had roots in Austin, San Antonio, south Texas, and Houston. In California, student leadership was prominent in Los Angeles, the San Francisco Bay area, Santa Barbara, San Diego, Riverside, and the Central Valley areas.

Conditions prompting the mobilization of Mexican American student activism resulting in the formation of MECHAs throughout the country are varied, complex, and historically rooted in the socio-political and economic discrimination that exists in this country. The Mexican American student movement was part of a greater political movement within the Mexican community and involved farmworker labor issues in California, land grant disputes in New Mexico, and radical cultural institutions in Colorado. It was also part of a national movement for civil and democratic rights and the international movements of Third World liberation struggles.

More specifically, the Mexican American student movement sought political recognition and socio-economic rights for Mexican Americans who ranked below Anglos and blacks in income levels and educational attainment. The liberal presidential administrations and civil rights movement of the 1960s were conducive to increased demands by Mexican Americans for democratic and equal citizenship rights. These influences and the success of international liberation struggles in Mexico, Cuba, Vietnam, and Africa resulted in heightened national identity for Mexican Americans. Regardless of one's political affinity for the above-mentioned struggles, they did provide for an enhanced sense of empowerment for the underdog, and Mexican Americans oftentimes saw themselves as the oppressed underdog in the United States. "Power to the people" was a battlecry not lost to these astute student leaders.

Mexican American opposition to the disadvantaged status of Mexicans in American society translated into more specific goals by 1968. Material and spiritual support for Cesar Chavez and the California United Farmworkers became a priority, as did community involvement, bilingual-bicultural education, revitalization of cultural norms, legal defense, recruitment into institutions of higher education, equal employment opportunities, concern over alleged police brutality in the community, and the formation of a third political party, La Raza Unida. By 1975 concerns included the human and democratic rights of undocumented Mexican workers, mobilization against the *Bakke* reverse discrimination decision, and the formation of Marxist study groups on campuses.

MECHA had its strongest base in California. Among its founding members and student leadership were Moctezuma Esparza of Roosevelt High School, Alberto Juarez of East Los Angeles Junior College, Juan Gomez-Guiñones of the University of California at Los Angeles (UCLA), Luis Ortiz of UCLA, Susan Racho of UCLA, Armando Valdez in northern California, and Alberto Urista in southern California.

The selection of the term "MECHA" by most student organizations occurred in 1969 as a consequence of a conference held in Santa Barbara and signified a rejection of the term "Mexican American." Before this most organizations used the acronym UMAS (United Mexican American Students), others were known as MASA (Mexican American Student Association), and MAYO (Mexican American Youth Organization), and MAYAS (Mexican American Youth Association of Students).

MECHA has traditionally been hierarchically structured and consists of a chairperson, vice-chairperson, secretary, and treasurer. More recently, however, a collective "mesa directiva," or board of directors, has replaced hierarchical leadership as in the case of the University of California at Santa Barbara and Los Angeles and San Diego State University. In California, intercampus regional coordination is maintained through MECHA Central, a senate-type body of regional MECHA representatives.

MECHA chapters have been established on high school, college, and university campuses throughout the country and vary in the heterogeneity of the membership, organization objectives, ideological views, degree of maturity, age levels, class backgrounds, and aspirations. At the very least, they provide a collective cultural and social identity.

The early organizational efforts of MECHA student leadership focused attention on the needs of the Mexican American community and counted on the support of old and new left organizations as well as that of other Mexican American organizations such as the Mexican American Political Association* (MAPA), American G.I. Forum* (AGIF), and the League of United Latin American Citizens* (LULAC). Most significantly, MECHA's early organizational endeavors resulted in greater recruitment of Mexican Americans into institutions of higher education and the establishment of Mexican American curriculums, Mexican American studies departments, Mexican American centers and research units, Mexican American commencement ceremonies, and Mexican American campus newspapers. Ideologically, it resulted in the "Plan Espiritual de Aztlan," a "Chicano philosophical manifesto"; the concept of "chicanismo"; and heightened national and cultural identity. Organizationally, it was instrumental in staging high school walkouts, demonstrations, boycotts, strikes, and sit-ins for the purposes of attaining student demands. Politically, MECHA contributed to the emergence of class, student, and ethnic politics and established ties with workers in both Mexico and the United States.

There are several contemporary reference sources for MECHA. Most prominent among them is Juan Gomez Quiñones, *Mexican Students por la Raza* (1978). Also, Maurilio Vigil, *Chicano Politics* (1978) discusses MECHA. There are numerous newspapers, flyers, pamphlets, etc. distributed by the MECHA campus chapters that contain information on the activities of the individual chapters.

MECHA is an organization that experiences many peaks and valleys in its activities. Because student leadership is constantly changing, the organization on a particular campus may be very strong for a number of years and then go into decline. Then a strong student leader may emerge, revive the group, and the organization will move into prominence again until its next period of decline. This is true for most campus organizations that seem to require a strong issue to rally behind for maximum activism.

— N —

NATIONAL ASSOCIATION FOR BILINGUAL EDUCATION (NABE) It was at the Fourth Annual National Conference on bilingual education held in Chicago, Illinois, in 1975, that the conceptual framework for this organization was advanced. NABE was developed for the purpose of providing an advocacy force on behalf of the educational interests of U.S. language minorities. Its goals include, but are not limited to, the promotion and maintenance of bilingual bicultural education by integrating it into school curricula. NABE seeks to accomplish its objectives by lobbying school districts and legislative bodies, promoting professional standards in bilingual education, networking with others, and promoting research.

The organization has a membership of at least 3,500 persons of Hispanic, Asian, native American, and European descent and of diverse economic backgrounds. There are four types of membership: regular, made up of professionals in the field; associate, comprised of paraprofessionals, students, and community members involved in bilingual-bicultural education; institutional, including universities and colleges and related organizations; and honorary, conferred by the executive board to individuals of distinction in the field. The first two categories have voting status. Membership is given to any individual or institution interested in and supportive of bilingual-bicultural education and NABE's goals.

NABE is a hierarchically structured, nonprofit organization. It is headed by a national executive board consisting of six elected officers, a president, president-elect, vice-president, secretary, treasurer, and past president. The business of the organization is administered by the executive board and works closely with its affiliates to discuss, disseminate, and receive advice and information on relevant issues. The board provides technical assistance and support to affiliates, assists them with local legislation, and attends affiliate annual meetings. The executive board is also responsible for providing its affiliates and special interest groups with membership lists and, on occasion, use of its bulk mailing privilege.

Affiliates are states or geographical and political areas which have, with the approval of NABE, established a local organization consonant with NABE's national goals. There is an affiliate membership fee of $100 and an annual fee of $25. Affiliates are headed by a president responsible for advising and sharing information with the executive board. There are twenty-seven affiliates located in the states of Arizona, California, Colorado, Connecticut, Florida, Idaho, Illinois, Kansas, Louisiana, Massachusetts, Michigan, Minnesota, South Dakota, New Jersey, New Mexico, New York, Ohio, Oklahoma, Pennsylvania, Rhode Island, Texas, Virginia, Washington, Wisconsin, Wyoming, Puerto Rico, and the District of Columbia. There are ten special interest groups (SIGs) within NABE, which include Adult Bilingual Education, Early Childhood Education, Elementary Education, Higher Education, Legislation, Parent and Community Involvement, Research and Evaluation, Secondary Education, Special Education, and Vocational Education.

Each special interest group reflects areas of concern within bilingual education and involves the participation of teachers, parents, administrators, students, researchers, evaluators, legislators, and community members. SIGs report to the executive board and bring to its attention their respective areas of interest. Their leadership is comprised of a chairperson and vice-chairperson.

Standing committees are also a permanent component of NABE's structure. They coordinate the organization's primary functions and activities. There are eight standing committees, the Nominating and Election Committee, Conference Committee, Membership Committee, Socio-Political Concerns Committee, Fundraising Committee, Resolutions Committee, Publications Committee, and Public Relations Committee. Ad hoc committees act as standing committees on a short-term basis. They serve at the discretion of the board.

NABE publishes a journal three times a year and a bimonthly newsletter. The former has an editorial board, and the latter makes use of news reporters.

NABE has been influential in the integration of bilingual-bicultural education services at all levels of the nation's educational school curricula. In July 1979 it helped restore Title VII appropriations for bilingual education by lobbying congressional committees.

The major reference sources on NABE utilized for this work include NABE's "Manual of Operational Procedures 1979–1980" and their completed HAVO questionnaire. NABE holds annual meetings, and state affiliates hold state conventions with attendance in the thousands. These meetings are excellent sources of information on the organization's activities and are widely publicized.

NATIONAL ASSOCIATION FOR CHICANO STUDIES (NACS) Formed in 1972 in Pueblo, Colorado, the organization's primary aims are to promote cultural, educational, and political awareness in the Mexican American community. The NACS attempts to effect these goals by encouraging educational institutions to implement Mexican American studies programs or incorporate units on Mexican American history and culture into existing curricula. Another major activity of NACS is the training of Mexican American community leaders in the legislative process.

The Association is a hierarchically structured organization headed by a board of directors. Among the organization's founders and leaders are Irene Blea, Ricardo Romo, Alberto Camarillo, Alberto Mata, Carlos Navarro, Victor Nelson, Arturo Rosales, and Daniel Valdez. The Association has six regional chapters in northern and southern California, Colorado, New Mexico, west Texas, and the Midwest. NACS holds conferences annually, which present and serve as a primary impetus for the development of Mexican American scholarship. The majority of the organization's members are teachers and researchers.

NACS's funds are obtained from annual membership dues of thirty dollars for faculty and ten dollars for students. News regarding the Association's activities is printed in the monthly newsletter, *La Red*, published by the National Chicano Council on Higher Education* (NCCHE).

The most readily available reference source on NACS is *A Guide to Hispanic Organizations* (1979), which contains a brief summary of the organization's activities. Copies of the organization's conference programs at both the state and national levels are an important resource. A review of *La Red* should provide an overview of the activities of NACS through the years.

NATIONAL ASSOCIATION FOR PUERTO RICAN CIVIL RIGHTS (NAPRCR) This Association was organized in New York City to fill a void among Puerto Ricans and other Hispanics in the field of human and civil rights. The organization advocates full rights for Hispanics in employment, housing, and legal services. The NAPRCR also operates job training and job referral programs and executes agreements with employers and companies for the hiring of minorities.

A summary of this organization's activities is contained in the archives of the Robert Kennedy Memorial. An attempt to solicit further information from the organization was unsuccessful.

NATIONAL ASSOCIATION OF CUBAN AMERICAN WOMEN (NA-CAW) The NACAW was founded in 1972 in Washington, D.C., as a nonprofit, nonpartisan organization for the purpose of advocating the rights of Cuban American women in the United States. In November 1977 it was announced by NACAW President Dr. Ana Maria Perera that headquarters would be transferred from Washington to Miami, Florida, where it could service a larger number of Cuban Americans, but the move was not executed.

The main goals of NACAW are to work toward the solution of current problems facing Hispanic women. A major concern is to attain the representation and participation of women as leaders on national committees, task forces, boards, and conferences. A second concern is to gain support for bilingual-bicultural education at the local, state, and national levels from kindergarten to the university. As a way of achieving its goals, the organization acts as a clearinghouse for the dissemination of information on Cuban American women. In addition, NACAW works with other feminist organizations in ensuring a strong national platform to respond to the needs and concerns of women.

Membership within NACAW is not restricted but is open to anyone who subscribes to the goals and ideals of NACAW. The membership is mainly Cuban American, however. Each member pays annual dues of ten dollars. The money is used for organizational operating costs. The Association is hierarchically structured. There is a president, six chairpersons, a national director of public affairs, a treasurer, and an advisory board made up of forty-seven members located in forty-one different states.

Dr. Ana Maria Perera is founder and president of the organization. She had been active in the implementation of federal antidiscrimination laws such as the Women's Educational Equity Act (WEEA) of 1974. Until the Cuban Revolution, she was a delegate from Cuba to the Inter-American Commission on Women, an organization founded in Havana in 1928, and she was appointed to the New York-based Institute of Hispanic Research's Hall of Fame.

In spite of her many accomplishments, Dr. Perera has also been the target of the organization's harshest critics. Perera presided over NACAW in an autocratic fashion, allowing little amplitude for democratic participation and membership initiative. So although the organization boasts of an elaborate, democratically designed hierarchy, in actuality, it did not function as such. Dr. Perera demonstrated sincerity and commitment to the goals of the organization, but according to her critics, she was unwilling to entrust NACAW's mission to anyone else. Finally in 1980, the organization underwent some significant changes, and NACAW began to move toward a change in leadership and toward becoming a more democratic and task-oriented organization.

NACAW has found it profitable to unite with other women's groups in finding solutions to their most pressing problems. NACAW often cosponsors conferences with these organizations. For example, on May 4–6, 1979, NACAW joined with the Mexican American Women's National Association* (MANA) and the National Council of La Raza* (NCLR) in sponsoring a working meeting of thirty Hispanic women leaders in Washington, D.C. On October 23–25, 1980, NACAW held its second National Training Conference at Florida International University's Downtown Campus in Miami, Florida. Conference topics discussed were the Equal Rights Amendment, bilingual-bicultural education, the underrepresentation of Cuban Americans in United States government policy making positions, human rights, and U.S. policy toward Cuba.

NACAW publishes a bilingual newsletter, which is distributed to its members.

Sources of information on NACAW include *The Patria* (April 21, 28, 1978); *Miami Herald* (1978); *Nuestro Magazine* (April 1978); *Washington Post* (January 4, 1979); the NACAW newsletter (Summer 1980); *La Mesa Redonda* (September

1980). For purposes of this work, conversations with Dr. Perera and other Cuban American women as well as direct participation in NACAW events were utilized.

NATIONAL ASSOCIATION OF LATINO ELECTED AND APPOINTED OFFICIALS (NALEO) A primary goal of Hispanic leadership, particularly commencing in the 1970s, has been Hispanic voter education. As a response to this goal, NALEO was established in Los Angeles, Calfornia, in 1975, as a nonpartisan national organization. The Association was founded not only to devote itself to the interests and needs of the nation's Hispanic population, but also to provide a national network of Hispanic leaders that would accomplish specific goals. An important objective of the organization is a concentrated pursuit of improved health care, economic conditions, and social and educational welfare among Hispanics.

But a more fundamental goal of NALEO is to develop a comprehensive, articulate, and forceful lobbying voice in Washington, D.C., as well as in states with large numbers of Hispanics. As a way of meeting that goal, NALEO seeks to create a nationwide network of Hispanic leaders to develop a communication system about and among the diverse elements of the Hispanic community.

A chief spokesperson for this organization and the inspiration behind its creation is Edward Roybal, U.S. representative from California. Congressman Roybal has dedicated an entire lifetime to the political advancement of Hispanics, especially Mexican Americans, and was instrumental in the founding of the Congressional Hispanic Caucus* (CHC), the Mexican American Political Association* (MAPA), as well as this organization. Other leaders of NALEO have included Robert Garcia, congressman from New York, and Edward J. Avila, the organization's national director.

NALEO is supported by membership dues and sponsorships, as well as by private contributions. Its members believe that by maintaining its financial independence NALEO will be able to analyze and adopt positions on governmental policies and social issues, free of the taint of self-interest. Due to the fact that the Hispanic community faces issues that transcend party lines, intra-ethnic differences, and geographical areas, NALEO supports issues rather than candidates.

Membership in NALEO is open to all Latino elected or appointed officials and the people who support them. Additionally, anyone interested in furthering the goals of the organization may join as an associate member. There are three types of membership. Full membership requires $25 annual dues, founding members $50, and associate members $15. Sponsorship within this organization consists of individuals and organizations who are interested in furthering the goals of NALEO. A corporate sponsor contributes $500 annually, and a golden circle sponsor contributes $1,000. The structural organization consists of a president, secretary-treasurer, and national director, as well as a large body of supporters.

The projects and activities of NALEO have included the Census Watch, which was intended to ensure an accurate count of Hispanics in the 1980 census. Also, an in-depth NALEO analysis of Public Law 95-507 (*Small Business Act*) entitled "Utilization of Small Business Concerns and Small Disadvantaged Business Concerns" determined how Hispanic small businesses may be equitably included in federal procurement policies. NALEO intends to ensure the recognition by governmental agencies of the skills and abilities of Hispanic small business firms. After consultation with Hispanic educators, NALEO-identified policy positions on the reorganization of the Office of Bilingual Education and Minority Language Affairs were adopted by the Department of Education and the Hispanic community. The organization also worked to coordinate voter registration for the 1982 elections. Registration efforts focused on the importance of local school and special district elections, as well as congressional, state, and local elections. NALEO's target goal early on was 1.5 million new registered voters by November 1982.

NALEO publishes a quarterly newsletter, which keeps its readers up to date with current public policy affecting Hispanics.

The sources for NALEO's history and organizational activities are diverse. The detailed published newsletters are an important reference, as are many of the organization's publications such as the *NALEO Washington Reports, NALEO Census Watch Special Project Report* (1980), NALEO information leaflet, *NALEO Update Report* (August 1980), and *Meeting the Challenge—NALEO* (July 1980) which is a summary of NALEO's goals and objectives. Also, the widely circulated *A Guide to Hispanic Organizations* (1979) contains information on NALEO.

For purposes of this work, NALEO newsletters (April 1979; November 1979; and January–February 1980) were utilized.

NATIONAL ASSOCIATION OF PSYCHOLOGISTS FOR LA RAZA (NAPLA) The Association was founded in 1970 and is currently based in Boulder, Colorado. Formed for the purpose of developing a professional speciality of Hispanic psychology within the discipline, NAPLA is an advocate for psychological research, training, and services for Hispanics.

The Association works to interest more young Hispanics in the field. Informational programs are aimed toward this recruitment goal and as training for those already in the field. NAPLA is supported by annual membership fees and contributions. It serves as an Hispanic caucus within the American Psychological Association (APA) and is active at their annual convention.

Reference information on this organization is contained in *A Guide to Hispanic Organizations* (1979).

NATIONAL ASSOCIATION OF PUERTO RICAN DRUG ABUSE PROGRAMS (NAPRDAP) Located in Arlington, Virginia, the Association has a growing membership from various urban centers throughout the northeastern

United States, but serves programs in other cities, such as Los Angeles, Chicago, and Miami, as well. The primary purpose of this organization is networking and the exchange of information relating to the treatment, education, prevention, and rehabilitation of the Puerto Rican drug addict.

Information on this organization is contained in the archives of the Robert Kennedy Memorial in Washington, D.C.

NATIONAL ASSOCIATION OF SPANISH SPEAKING SPANISH SURNAMED NURSES (NASSSSN) Since its formation in 1974, the organization has worked to provide opportunities for Hispanics in nursing. The Association has over 250 professional nurses nationwide and in Puerto Rico. Its primary goal is to conduct research into the quality of health care in Hispanic communities. The organization publishes a quarterly newsletter. A membership association, annual dues are twenty-five dollars. Nursing students pay dues of ten dollars. Principal officers include a president, vice-president, treasurer, and secretary. The Association holds annual national conventions. Its offices are located in Seattle, Washington.

Information on this organization is contained in *A Guide to Hispanic Organizations* (1979).

NATIONAL CHICANO COUNCIL ON HIGHER EDUCATION (NCCHE) This is a membership association dedicated to improving the status of Mexican Americans in higher education. The idea for NCCHE evolved out of a May 1975 Ford Foundation–sponsored symposium on the status of Mexican Americans in higher education. Some representatives of the Mexican American academic community who participated in the meeting suggested the need for a national organization to address the needs and concerns of Mexican Americans in higher education. These same participants voted to constitute themselves as the National Chicano Council on Higher Education. NCCHE's published objectives are:

1. Examine issues affecting the status of Chicanos [*sic*] in higher education; and
2. Present position statements on matters concerning Chicanos [*sic*] in higher education; and
3. Develop programs to improve the status of Chicanos [*sic*] in higher education.

NCCHE was chartered as a nonprofit corporation in the state of California. It is governed by a board of trustees and an appointed president. Membership is open to all individuals committed to improving the higher educational opportunities of Mexican Americans both as students and faculty. Among the founders of NCCHE and early officers are Eugene Cota Robles, University of California, Santa Cruz; Tomas Rivera, former chancellor of the University of California, Riverside, and now deceased; Cecelia Burciaga, Stanford University; Rolando Hinojosa, University of Texas, Austin; Juan Gomez Quiñones, University of California, Los Angeles; Richard Griego, University of New Mexico; Luis Leal, University of California, Santa Barbara; Concepción Valadez, University of California, Los Angeles; Arturo Madrid, University of Minnesota; and Cristina Bruch, NCCHE staff.

The board of trustees sets policy and goals and develops programs. Board officers consist of a president, vice-president, secretary, and treasurer. NCCHE membership numbers forty individuals, most of whom are Mexican American academics, although some are administrators.

NCCHE has completed a number of projects, including a comprehensive study on the status of Mexican Americans in higher education. The organization commissioned Ronald Lopez of Los Angeles, and with the aid of Reynaldo Flores Macias a report was submitted to then NCCHE President Arturo Madrid for final editing. This study critically examined the participation of Mexican Americans in institutions of higher learning. Also, NCCHE joined forces with the National Chicano Research Network, now incorporated into NCCHE, to host a national invitational meeting of Mexican Americans in higher education in 1978.

The organization is most recognized for its Post Doctoral Fellowship Program. Because so few Mexican Americans hold tenured positions in institutions of higher education, NCCHE funds research projects to assist them in securing tenure. Monies for these fellowships are provided by the Ford Foundation and the Educational Testing Service. The Fellowship Program was initiated as a result of a survey of universities in the West and Southwest conducted by NCCHE staff in the spring of 1976. The survey identified fewer than 250 Mexican Americans with academic appointments at the seven major research institutions located in the states of Arizona, California, New Mexico, Texas, Utah, and Washington. Of these, 64 were tenured and 154 held tenure-track appointments. The survey also revealed that Mexican American appointments were on the decline.

In December 1976 NCCHE received a $126,000 Ford Foundation grant to support the Post Doctoral Fellowship Program. Application for the grants is open to any Mexican American academic in a tenure-track position for two to five years in a U.S. institution of higher education. Applications are screened by peer-review panels composed of six tenured Mexican American faculty, who are appointed annually to the board. The fellowships provide a modest stipend to supplement the faculty member's salary. Out of forty-two eligible applicants, fourteen awards were made during the program's first year. The Ford Foundation then decided, based on the program's first-year success, to extend the program with a followup grant of $373,500 for the 1978–80 academic years. The program continues to grant fellowships.

The 1980s represent expanded programs for NCCHE. The projects proposed for this decade are NCCHE Project Recognition, NCCHE National Information Network, and the NCCHE Center for Policy Studies and Leadership Development.

NCCHE Project Recognition proposes a program of annual awards to recognize outstanding accomplishments by Mexican American students, faculty, staff, and administrators. The Information Network would link the various sectors of the Mexican American higher education community through a national information network. This program is already functioning through publication of *La Red*, a national newsletter published under the auspices of NCCHE and for and about Mexican Americans in higher education. And finally, NCCHE's Policy Studies and Leadership Development Center proposes to be a training and education center designed to provide expert advice to policy makers as well as to promote examination of a broader range of issues affecting Mexican Americans.

Although NCCHE has been successful in facilitating advancement opportunities for Mexican American faculty under the auspices of the Ford Foundation and other funding entities, it has been less than successful in reaching out to the larger Mexican American academic community for purposes of voluntary membership. When NCCHE conducted its first study in 1976, it counted approximately 250 Mexican American academic faculty, yet eight years later it lists a membership of only 40. Whether this is indicative of the selectivity of NCCHE's leadership or merely the organization's determination that its credibility rests on its identification as a service organization rather than a membership one is not evident from the reference sources.

Reference sources for NCCHE include a brochure on the NCCHE Post Doctoral Fellowship Program available from the organization, NCCHE background sheets on the Post Doctoral Fellowship Program and organizational purpose and history.

For purposes of this work an interview was conducted with Cecilia Burciaga, a founding board member of NCCHE. Also, the completed HAVO questionnaire was utilized.

NATIONAL COALITION OF HISPANIC MENTAL HEALTH AND HUMAN SERVICES ORGANIZATIONS (COSSMHO) Formerly known as the Coalition of Spanish Speaking Mental Health Organizations, the National Coalition of Hispanic Mental Health and Human Services Organizations (COSSMHO) was founded in 1974 and is based in Washington, D.C. It is composed of a coalition of 220 local and regional organizations which seek to improve and expand services and to provide research and training for Hispanics in health and human services. COSSMHO was organized to make available a national organization and resource center through which Hispanics could assist, consult, and address health, mental health, alcohol and drug abuse, human service needs, information and expertise sharing, and the publicity, promotion, and support of each others' efforts and achievements.

COSSMHO membership is active in more than 120 cities in thirty states, the District of Columbia, and Puerto Rico. Rodolfo B. Sanchez has served as the organization's national executive director since its early beginnings. He has been assisted by a nine-member board of directors, which has included several notables in the health fields, such as the Reverend Mario Vizcaino, Ildaura Murillo-Rohde, Mario A. Anglada, J. Julian Rivera, Jose Carlos Serrato, and Nelba Chavez. John Hale serves as general counsel.

The organization identifies and conducts research and symposia studies on

Hispanic health, mental health, and human services issues in conjunction with local, state, and federal agencies as well as funding sources. It participates in the Aspira of America* (AA)–Rockefeller Fellowship Program and sponsors the Graduate Student Internship Program and the Hispanic Employment Referral Center with local, state, and federal agencies and other funding sources.

Its interest in developing a national Hispanic youth service and advocacy network has resulted in COSSMHO's National Hispanic Youth Advocacy and Action Project. One of the project's activities has been the compilation of national, annually updated directories of organizations and Hispanic individuals who provide direct services to Hispanic youth between the ages of fourteen and twenty-one. In the fall of 1978, COSSMHO sponsored the National Hispanic Conference on Families in Houston, Texas. This event focused on the strengths, contributions, and needs of Hispanic families in a changing society.

In the early 1980s, the Coalition created the National Hispanic Youth Institute to provide a nationwide focus on multiple issues affecting Hispanic youth development and to heighten youth awareness to career preparation and opportunity. The organization also conducted a series of forums in fourteen states and involving 3,600 young Hispanics. Finally, COSSMHO produced seven films with the intention of presenting Hispanic men and women as role models in the fields of medicine, dentistry, optometry, psychiatry, pharmacy, and health administration.

COSSMHO publications include the *National Directory of Hispanic Professionals in Mental Health and Human Services*, the semimonthly COSSMHO *Roadrunner*, and the bimonthly newsletter, *The COSSMHO Reporter*.

Primary reference sources utilized in this work include Rodolfo B. Sanchez, "Message to Our Members," *The COSSMHO Reporter* (May 1978); *Encyclopedia of Associations* (1979); a letter from R. B. Sanchez soliciting participation in COSSMHO's National Hispanic Youth Advocacy and Action Project; the COSSMHO letterhead; and *Nuestro Magazine* (March 1982).

NATIONAL CONFERENCE OF PUERTO RICAN WOMEN, INC. (NACOPRW) The impetus for the establishment of NACOPRW came from the recognition that Puerto Rican women often found themselves socially, economically, and politically discriminated against in general in U.S. society, both as women and as members of an ethnic minority, and within the Puerto Rican community, also, as women. A group of concerned Puerto Rican women, influenced by the women's movement and realizing the need for an organization to deal with the triple discrimination felt by Puerto Rican women, founded NACOPRW. The Conference was incorporated as a women's rights organization in February 1972 in Washington, D.C.

The primary purposes of NACOPRW are twofold. The organization aims to secure the equal rights of Puerto Rican and other Hispanic women and to effect a greater participation by these women in the socio-economic and political life in the United States.

NACOPRW is a hierarchically structured national organization. In all there are eight chapters, located in New York City, Boston, Chicago, Miami, Philadelphia, Washington, D.C., and San Juan, Puerto Rico. The national organization is headed by a board of directors composed of national officers including president, vice-president, second vice-president, treasurer, secretary, and twenty-three delegates representing the various chapters. Individual chapters elect their own officials and tailor their programs to local needs. The organization holds an annual convention in November and social and cultural activities such as fashion shows and art exhibits.

NACOPRW schedules a number of activities throughout the year. The organization holds regular workshops and conferences on women's rights and employment. NACOPRW also attempts to identify and develop leadership among Puerto Rican women. In addition, NACOPRW collaborates with other national organizations dedicated to the pursuit of equal rights.

The organization acquires operating funds through its annual dues of twelve dollars and contributions from the private sector. Corporations such as Avon, Phillip Morris, Inc., Rums of Puerto Rico, and Consolidated Edison have contributed to the activities of this organization.

Overall, NACOPRW has been an active and productive organization. Many of its members have distinguished themselves in a variety of ways. Carmen Delgado Votaw is the chairperson of the InterAmerican Commission on Women and a former president of NACOPRW. She also chaired President Carter's Commission on Women, from which she courageously resigned in protest, in response to expressed insensitivity to women's issues by the President. She was a moderator for the National Hispanic Feminist Conference held in San Jose, California, in 1980 and presided with calm and dignity over several heated sessions. Another NACOPRW former officer who has served outstandingly the Hispanic and women's communities has been Paquito Vivo. She has especially served on a number of boards and commissions dealing with women's issues and is highly respected in national feminist circles.

Information on this organization is contained in *A Guide to Hispanic Organizations* (1979). Other reference materials utilized for this work include the program of the seventh annual NACOPRW convention; the *Encyclopedia of Associations* (1979); an overview sheet printed by the organization; and several interviews with former officers of the organization including Angela Cabrera and Paquito Vivo.

NATIONAL CONGRESS FOR PUERTO RICAN RIGHTS (NCPRR) This organization was founded in 1981 as a Puerto Rican civil rights advocacy association. It is headquartered in Philadelphia, Pennsylvania. The Congress was outstanding in growth among Latino organizations during its first year of existence. It held its founding convention April 25–26 in the South Bronx, where over 550 voting delegates representing more than 100 other Puerto Rican organizations were in attendance. Juan Gonzalez, a *Philadelphia Daily News* reporter, was elected the Congress's first president. Gonzalez took a year's leave of absence from the newspaper to guide the organization through its first year of operation.

The NCPRR now has over 3,000 members with functioning chapters in New York, New Jersey, Connecticut, Pennsylvania, and Michigan and additional members in other states including Hawaii, California, and Florida.

The Congress joined the Washington, D.C., Solidarity March, a largely pro-union protest against President Reagan's policies, with 500 members strong. During that same year, it offered support to communities in the Northeast where Puerto Ricans were being victimized by police and arson fires and experiencing other challenges to their civil rights.

Because this organization was only recently formed at the time of this writing, there were few identifiable published references available. A summary of NCPRR is contained in *Nuestro Magazine* (March 1982).

NATIONAL CONGRESS OF HISPANIC AMERICAN CITIZENS (NCHAC) Founded in Washington, D.C., in 1971, NCHAC, more commonly known as El Congreso, was established to serve as a legislative, judicial, and executive advocate on behalf of the nation's Spanish-speaking communities at the state and federal levels.

The founders of the organization were a group of twelve people of Hispanic origin, with Interstate Research Associates* (IRA) spearheading the effort, who organized in Washington to express their concerns over the lack of a viable and visible lobby for the Hispanic community. There were individual representations such as lobby groups for labor, farmworkers, and education, but none dealt specifically with the Spanish-speaking community as a whole. This group recognized the void and decided to act. Chief among the founders were Paul Montemayor from Corpus Christi, Texas, the first chairperson; Polly Baca Barragan from Denver, Colorado; and Raul Yzaguirre, Rick Bela, and Sylvia Gonzales, working out of Washington, D.C., but originally from the Southwest.

In the beginning the goals of this organization focused primarily on the needs of Mexican American communities. In 1972–73 there was a reconstruction of the board of directors in order to deal with broader Hispanic issues. The organization changed from one primarily concerned with only a segment of the Hispanic population and its issues and a board made up mainly of grass-roots community-oriented individuals to a sophisticated, all-encompassing, Hispanic organization. By then the Hispanic community was seeking a unified approach to issues and a mature understanding of the political processes that reward unity and numbers.

Activities of El Congreso were many. Legislative workshops for different organizations were sponsored, as well as workshops dealing with the lobbying process. El Congreso assisted groups lobbying for bilingual education, economic development, and housing. Never before in the history of Congress were so many bills addressing Hispanic issues enacted. Thirty-three out of thirty-nine proposed bills were passed as a result of the activities of El Congreso. These bills dealt with issues such as manpower, voting rights, and bilingual education.

El Congreso was a hierarchically structured organization. Officers included a chairperson, president, vice-chairperson, treasurer, vice-chairperson secretary, and general counsel. The organization vowed to remain nonpartisan. It was founded on the principle that the Hispanic community could, and was willing, to support an organization of this kind. All operational monies were to come from membership fees and contributions, assuring the lobby's independence.

El Congreso was short-lived. It functioned actively for only eight years. The executive director for most of El Congreso's short life was Manny Fierro. Fierro, a dynamic, astute politician, can be credited with the remarkable success of the organization's lobbying efforts. Cognizant of his bargaining chips among the capital's powerful, he played them wisely. But while brilliantly attuned to Washington political dynamics, he also had a knack for alienating most of his own concerned Hispanic colleagues.

Fierro became involved in the presidential elections of 1976, seeming to favor the incumbent Ford Administration, with whom he already had solid contacts. The triumphant Carter people acknowledged the importance of El Congreso's constituency by offering its chairperson, Hank Lacayo, an advisory role to the new administration. But in reality, the Carter group did not understand or seem genuinely to believe in the validity of Hispanic issues, at least not in the beginning. The Hispanic leadership began to lose faith in El Congreso, and its monetary support declined dramatically. It should be noted here that the financial support for the organization was never really sufficient to sustain it. Fierro functioned under severe economic difficulties. The organization survived for about a year after the election and then died.

El Congreso was a necessary and mature stage in the American Hispanic experience, but it is questionable whether the community in general was ready for this kind of organization. Then too, although Fierro may have been its ideal spokesperson from the perspective of political savvy and intelligence, he lacked the leadership skills to develop allegiance and support from the entire organizational community.

It appears that the Congressional Hispanic Caucus* (CHC) has taken over most of the work of El Congreso by serving as a visible lobby for Hispanic issues in the nation's capital. But that does not deny the need for another El Congreso.

The *El Paso Times* (June 20, 1972) provides an excellent reference for this organization's activities. For purposes of this work, an oral interview with Manny Fierro was conducted, as were recollections gleaned by this author as a founder and original board member of El Congreso. Also, the El Congreso bylaws and the minutes for the meeting of March 4, 1978, were utilized.

NATIONAL COUNCIL OF LA RAZA (NCLR) The National Council of La Raza was founded in February 1968 in Phoenix, Arizona, as the Southwest

Council of La Raza, a mutual assistance association. The founders of the council recognized that the majority of Mexican Americans were not full participants in the mainstream of social, civic, and economic life of the United States. These founders included Herman Gallegos, Henry Santiestevan, and Maclovio Barraza. The first executive director was Herman Gallegos, and the first chairperson of the board was Maclovio Barraza.

Gallegos had been a social worker and civil rights activist, while the organization's guiding spirit, Maclovio Barraza, had been a national labor leader based in Arizona. Santiestevan was a prominent figure in national Democratic politics and one of the original board members of Interstate Research Associates* (IRA), a similar organization which preceded the NCLR.

The original goal of the organization was to address this mainstream exclusion of Mexican Americans. To change these conditions, the NCLR sought to provide on-site technical assistance emphasizing program development, funding, program operations, and management to Mexican American community-based organizations. NCLR has since broadened its scope to include research, public policy analysis, and advocacy at the national level to facilitate administrative and legislative decisions which benefit Hispanics. NCLR's services are available to "affiliate" neighborhood-community organizations which are nonprofit and tax-exempt.

NCLR's organizational structure consists of twenty-six board members with representative proportions from Arizona, California, Colorado, New Mexico, and Texas; an equal number of affiliate representatives; and an unlimited number of associate members made up of individuals who support NCLR's activities. The board of directors includes the executive committee board, which is responsible for control and management of the Council. Board officers are elected at their annual meeting in February and serve one-year terms. The board, which is comprised of equal representation of males and females, includes educators, elected and appointed local, state, and federal officials, labor union officials, economic development and civil rights specialists, and human service professionals. The Council has offices in Washington, D.C.; Albuquerque, New Mexico; Chicago, Illinois; Phoenix, Arizona; and San Francisco, California. Funding is provided by both federal and nonfederal organizations such as the Ford Foundation, the Office of Minority Business Enterprise, and the Rockefeller Foundation.

In 1972, around the same time that Raul Yzaguirre was named executive director, the Council's headquarters were moved to Washington, D.C. This move also coincided with the organization's increased involvement in change by way of the political and legal process. Yzaguirre was primarily responsible for the broadened scope of the organization. He had been a founder of Interstate Research Associates* (IRA), cofounder and cochair of the National Committee on Hispanic and Black Concerns, and an active member of the Americans G.I. Forum* (AGIF). Thus, he had been active in Hispanic affairs before he assumed this post.

In 1973, the organization changed its name to the National Council of La

Raza to reflect its broadened activities. These programs and activities are currently divided into the areas of technical assistance, research, public policy analysis and advocacy, and communications. Technical assistance projects include rural economic development assistance through Project AGRED (Assistance Group for Rural Economic Development), industrial development assistance to local governmental officials and community groups through Project IDEA (Industry, Development, Training, and Assistance), and planning and technical assistance grants in housing counseling and community development for the U.S. Department of Housing and Urban Development. Through its technical support program, NCLR has spawned many self-supporting programs such as the Texas-based Southwest Voters Registration Education Project.

NCLR has researched the impact of Title I Migrant Education programs nationally as well as their operational capabilities, the factors contributing to Hispanic youth employment or unemployment, and Mexican Americans' relationship to the welfare system through a symposium where experts in the field presented and discussed issue papers. The Council has provided public policy analysis beyond the usual confines of university research.

NCLR publishes a bimonthly journal, *Agenda*, which reaches the larger U.S. population as well as Hispanics. It serves as an educational as well as communications arm of the Council. NCLR communications staff also conduct training seminars in media relations skills to NCLR affiliates and other interested Hispanic community organizations.

NCLR-sponsored programs and projects are designed to assist affiliated groups. The Council has over 100 affiliates in twenty states, the District of Columbia, and Puerto Rico. The affiliates include small single-purpose organizations as well as large, multipurpose, nonprofit corporations.

NCLR's other activities include participation in many coalitions, such as Americans for Justice on the Job and Forum for Community Development Reform. The organization has produced films on Mexican Americans for National Public Television and has developed informational packages and other aids for Hispanic entrepreneurs and economic development groups. NCLR issues "Action Alerts" on pending legislation and *El Noticiero*, the official newsletter of the Council. In addition, the NCLR has helped organize a network of more than sixty national Hispanic groups for purposes of coordinated efforts under the bannerhead of the Forum of National Hispanic Organizations* (FNHO).

Because the Council is located in Washington, the organization and its leadership tend to receive an inordinate amount of attention, which moves the focus away from the affiliates. The organization was designed to act as a technical assistance agent for the many community-based organizations addressing the problems affecting the Hispanic community. Therefore, the strength of the Council is the affiliate structure, with the Council providing support to these same. A Washington-based organization cannot have the immediacy of experience that a community-based organization has, and perhaps that is why the Council has continued to open new offices in expanded geographical areas. Still, the NCLR does exhibit some identity confusion by advancing itself as a primary representative of the Hispanic community while at the same time advocating the concept of affiliate development.

An excellent reference source on the Council is the NCLR newsletter, *El Noticiero*. Also, the national journal *Agenda* gives an indication of the Council's interests and position on Hispanic affairs. The most detailed reference on this organization is its bylaws.

For purposes of this work, a personal interview was conducted with Raul Yzaguirre, executive director of NCLR. The taped meeting also covered Yzaguirre's involvement with the Forum of National Hispanic Organizations* (FNHO), and Interstate Research Associates* (IRA), but focused on the Council. Other sources included the NCLR Biennial Report (1976–77); *El Noticiero*; *National Journal* (1979); and the bylaws of the organization.

NATIONAL FARMWORKERS ASSOCIATION See UNITED FARMWORKERS OF AMERICA.

NATIONAL HISPANIC AMATEUR ATHLETIC COUNCIL, INC. (NHAAC) In 1972 the heavily Puerto Rican–populated area of East Harlem, New York City, lacked organized recreational and sports programs for Hispanic youths. A group of former athletes and athletic officials including Efrain Pirela, Freddie Rodriquez, Victor Suarez, Carlos Martinez, Oscar Alvarez, and Rafael Cora, concerned with providing a competitive athletic outlet for Hispanic young people, organized the NHAAC that same year in East Harlem.

The Council's main purpose is to promote sportsmanship, civic and family values, and education through sports competition and guidance counseling. The organization is a hierarchically structured association headed by a board of directors, which manages the NHAAC's business. The board, which is chaired by the organization's president, is composed of fourteen members. Assisting the board is a fourteen-member advisory board. Under their supervision are the standing committees concerning membership, grievances, programs, business administration, publicity, and personnel. The organization is staffed by volunteers. Membership is open to all persons who support the NHAAC's goals.

NHAAC offers a number of programs in pursuit of its goals. The majority of the organization's activities involve sports programs for boys. Among these are the Hispanic Superior Basketball League, the East Harlem Winter Basketball Tournament, and the Sports Enterprise Summer Basketball Tournament. These are conducted with the cooperation of the community school board. The organization also sponsors an annual game between a leading amateur league team from Puerto Rico and its own summer league champion. The Council also provides a summer recreation and counseling program for girls, the Sports Enterprise Softball Tournament. Too, the NHAAC operates the National Hispanic Council Guidance and Tutorial Services, designed to promote and equip youths for advanced education. The Council plans in the future to extend its programs statewide, nationally, and internationally.

NHAAC relies on professional basketball players and noted public figures, such as the Honorable Carlos Romero Barcelo, a governor of Puerto Rico, and bandleader Tito Puente, to referee games and encourage the League's participants. The organization derives its operating expenses through its annual twenty-five-dollar membership dues and contributions from other nonprofit associations and business corporations such as the F. M. Schaefer Brewing Company. The NHAAC motto is "Sports, Character, and Education." Program guides are printed for its tournaments.

References for this organization were provided by NHAAC and included the completed HAVO questionnaire, the NHAAC membership application, the program of the Fourth Annual Hispanic Superior Basketball season opener (January 17, 1976), and the organization's bylaws.

NATIONAL HISPANIC BAR ASSOCIATION (NHBA) The National Hispanic Bar Association, based in Denver, Colorado, was founded to organize Hispanic attorneys and to advance their roles in the profession. The Association has concentrated its efforts on organizing Hispanic lawyers on a national level. This has resulted in a membership growth to just under 3,000 members. It also has been working on monitoring bar exams and law school admissions relative to Hispanics. NHBA has participated in legal briefs concerning Hispanics and has made strenuous attempts to organize Hispanic judges.

The source used for this description of the Association was *Nuestro Magazine* (March 1982). Because there were few other identifiable references for this organization, historical information on the founding and the founders of NHBA is not included in this summary.

NATIONAL HISPANIC INSTITUTE OF PUBLIC POLICY (NHIPC) A nonprofit organization founded in Los Angeles, California, and Washington, D.C., in 1978, NHIPC was incorporated in 1979. The organization was formed by Carmela G. Lacayo and others to provide Hispanics with a "think tank" dealing with policy formulation for the Hispanic community. The main purpose of the Institute is to research, plan, and develop programs for improving the quality of life and strengthening motivation in the Hispanic community.

The National Hispanic Institute for Public Policy is a hierarchically structured organization governed by a board of trustees. Institute officers include Carmela G. Lacayo, president; Jack E. Christy, general counsel; and Manuel Ahuero, secretary-treasurer. The membership is composed of all elements of the Hispanic community.

The Institute purports to conduct leadership training and extensive policy analysis workshops to foster awareness in Hispanics of the issues impacting on this community. The future plans of the Institute include the publication of a newsletter and brochure. The organization seeks funding from private foundations.

The primary reference source for this organization was their completed HAVO questionnaire. Also, *A Guide to Hispanic Organizations* (1979) included a summary description of the NHIPC. Yet, although the mission of the Institute is one that would have a great impact on the Hispanic community, there is little mention of its activities in the contemporary literature. Therefore, it is doubtful that this organization is extant. Attempts to reach NHIPC's headquarters in 1984 found no listing for the organization in either the Los Angeles or Washington directories, at least under this name.

NATIONAL LATINO MEDIA COALITION (NLMC) This organization, founded in 1971, serves as an advocate and representative for national Hispanic media and telecommunications interests. The Coalition works, too, toward expanded opportunities for Hispanics in media careers. But the primary goal of the coalition is to encourage ownership of broadcast facilities among Hispanics.

The NLMC often testifies before regulating bodies on broadcasting matters and serves as an information resource for media owners working toward reforms in the industry. The organization is a membership nonprofit corporation. Dues are twenty-five dollars annually for individuals and fifty dollars for larger groups and corporations. The Coalition holds annual membership meetings.

A brief description of this organization is contained in *A Guide to Hispanic Organizations* (1979).

NATIONAL MEXICAN ARTS FESTIVAL See CANTO AL PUEBLO (SONG FOR THE PEOPLE).

NATIONAL PUERTO RICAN BUSINESS AND MARKETING ASSOCIATION (NPRBMA) A nonprofit consultancy corporation established in New York City in 1974, the organization was formed to provide minority business persons with skills and information useful for survival in the competitive metropolitan marketplace. The organization provides advice on subjects ranging from real estate to retailing. The group offers consultation on business acquisitions and expansions.

Other services offered by the NPRBMA include managerial and technical assistance and the arrangement of financing. The National Puerto Rican Business and Marketing Association also participates in cultural affairs, such as its co-sponsorship of the 1980 Hispanic World Fair at the New York Coliseum.

The NPRBM is a hierarchically structured organization. Among its leaders are Juan Vallecillo, chairman of the board; Joseph Monseriat, national director; and Manuel Alvarado, deputy director. The organization operates in both New York and Puerto Rico.

The Association operates under a grant from the Commerce Department's Office of Minority Business Enterprise. It publishes a quarterly newsletter, *BMA News*.

The NPRBMA is briefly described in *A Guide to Hispanic Organizations* (1979).

NATIONAL PUERTO RICAN COALITION (NPRC) The Coalition, based in Washington, D.C., was founded in 1980 to represent Puerto Ricans in public policy concerns. The organization encompasses most of the major national Puerto Rican associations as members as well as local groups and individuals.

The NPRC held its first national conference December 3–5, 1982, in Washington. More than 300 delegates attended the meeting, from which policy concerns were compiled. From these expressed views, position statements were refined for dissemination. In February 1982, it sponsored Project Agenda, a week-long national training program. The program was directed toward long-range planning and community development and hosted forty key Puerto Rican organizational representatives from twelve states.

Although a young organization, the Coalition has initiated several long-term projects of merit. It has established a journalism internship program in Washington, D.C., in coordination with the Hispanic Link News Service. It also began publication of a national newsletter, *NPRC Reports*, in April 1982. For continued stability, NPRC shifted its fund-raising efforts from public to private support. Finally, with input from more than 100 organizations which had participated in the December 1982 conference, the organization adopted a national Puerto Rican legislative agenda.

Because this is a young organization, references are few. There is a summary of NPRC's activities in *Nuestro Magazine* (March 1982).

NATIONAL PUERTO RICAN FORUM (NPRF) The Forum is the oldest nonprofit Puerto Rican service organization in the United States. Founded in 1957 by Antonia Pantoja and a group of Puerto Ricans, it addressed the need for a communitywide organization to promote the interests of Puerto Ricans in New York City.

The founding group was primarily concerned with developing Puerto Rican youth and in promoting educational achievement, but they were also aware of the many organizational needs of Puerto Ricans in the City. Therefore, their focus expanded to the socio-economic improvement of Puerto Ricans and other Hispanics in the United States through job training and placement, counseling, English-language and high school equivalency instruction, and advocacy.

The Forum was instrumental in the founding of Aspira of America* (AA), an education-oriented organization, and the Puerto Rican Community Development Project* (PRCDP), a citywide agency dedicated to the establishment of programs of many kinds in local Puerto Rican communities.

The NPRF is a hierarchically structured organization headed by a board of directors, which sets organizational policy and develops new programs. The national executive director, Manuel A. Bustelo, aided by the deputy director for New York operations, Fernando L. Camacho, and the deputy executive director for national operations, Iliad M. Estrada, is in charge of executing decisions taken by the board. The organization has a nationwide staff of 185 persons operating out of fifteen offices. There are six offices located throughout New York City, including the national headquarters office. Other offices are situated in Boston, Massachusetts, Chicago, Illinois, Cleveland Ohio, Hartford, Connecticut, Jersey City, New Jersey, Miami, Florida, Philadelphia, Pennsylvania, and Washington D.C. The majority of the Forum's clients are Puerto Rican and of low income.

The National Puerto Rican Forum offers a number of programs in job training, counseling, and education. The NPRF operates its Career Services and Job Placement Program in nine cities in eight states. This program provides career and job counseling and basic occupational language training. Also, program staff help to relocate Puerto Rican and Hispanic persons who qualify for clerical employment in Washington, D.C. The organization's School to Work Transition Program is conducted in four cities in three states. This program provides youths with skills in interview and test taking, resume preparation, and work ethics.

Other programs, offered only in New York, include a Puerto Rican-Hispanic Outreach and Placement Program, a Clerical, Fiscal, and Data Entry Program, an Opportunities for Bilingual Secretaries Program, and an Entry and Intermediate Office Workers Training Program. Also located in New York are the Forum's Management Services Center and Translation Bureau.

In 1979 the Forum compiled and published a statistical report on the Hispanic population in New York City and State entitled "The First Step Toward Equality." The study's purpose was to demonstrate the underemployment of Hispanics in Comprehensive Employment Training Act (CETA) positions in New York. The Forum cooperates closely with other ethnic communities in pursuing common goals.

In 1981 the Forum expanded its dialogue with the private sector, New York government, other communities of interest, and the Puerto Rican community itself in its long-term effort to help develop a realistic, positive identity for the nation's 2.1 million Puerto Ricans living on the mainland.

The NPRF has registered remarkable success rates in placing persons in jobs through its national education and training programs. For the early 1980s, it was averaging a 95 percent success rate. Also for this same period, it averaged an 88 percent success rate in placing clients in the local area. This included placement of individuals in local educational and training programs.

The NPRF, which is funded by federal, state, and local governments and by private sector monies, has as its major purpose the redress of the general impoverished socio-economic conditions of Puerto Ricans and other Hispanics via advocacy and the provision of social services.

Reference sources for the NPRF are diverse. One important resource is a Forum-produced fact sheet on Puerto Ricans on the mainland and the Forum's study *The First Step Toward Equality* (1979). Also, references to the organization's activities can be found in such contemporary works as Francesco Cordasco with Eugene Bucchioni, *The Puerto Ricans 1493–1973* (1973); *A Guide to Hispanic Organizations* (1979); and *Nuestro Magazine* (March 1982).

Summary information on NPRF is contained in the archives of the Robert Kennedy Memorial in Washington, D.C. The primary source of information for this work was the NPRF-completed HAVO questionnaire.

NEVADA ASSOCIATION OF LATIN AMERICANS (NALA) The Association, founded in 1968, performs a variety of services for Nevada's Latino population. Among these are job training, translation, legal services, assistance in obtaining U.S. citizenship, and several different kinds of counseling.

NALA, which is located in Las Vegas, sponsors day care centers for 155 chidren per day, a meal program for senior citizens, and various support services for low- and moderate-income families. The Association is a nonprofit corporation funded by federal, state, and local monies as well as by grants from private industry. The organization was also given a building by the city of Las Vegas in cooperation with the federal Department of Housing and Urban Development. The Association has officers, including a president, vice-president, and secretary-treasurer.

A summary description of the organization is contained in *A Guide to Hispanic Organizations* (1979).

NORTHWEST RURAL OPPORTUNITIES, INC. (NRO) A nonprofit services organization established in 1969 in Sunnyside, Washington, NRO was formed to meet the many needs of seasonal and migrant Hispanic workers. The organization provides services in the areas of health, referral, day care, manpower and job training, and educational support.

NRO is a hierarchically structured organization headed by a board of directors, which sets corporation goals and policy. Under the board's supervision are three directors charged with overseeing and executing organizational operations. They include an executive director, personnel director, and management director.

NRO secures its operating funds from various sources, including private foundations, the federal government, and organizational fund-raising activities.

A brief description of this organization is contained in *A Guide to Hispanic Organizations* (1979).

O

OFFICE OF THE COMMONWEALTH OF PUERTO RICO (OCPR) Although the OCPR is not a membership organization, this office has been instrumental in Puerto Rican organizational efforts. OCPR was founded in 1948 as a response to increased post-World War II migration from Puerto Rico. Governor Muñoz Marin esablished an office in New York City, supported by the government of Puerto Rico, to assist the increasing numbers of Puerto Ricans coming to the city. OCPR was founded to perform the following functions, as quoted from *The Puerto Ricans*:

1. Supervise the program of contract farmworkers brought to the mainland and expected to return to Puerto Rico at the end of a three, four, six month, or other contract period;

2. provide an employment service to Puerto Ricans;

3. identify Puerto Ricans for the purposes of establishing citizenship privileges;

4. provide a social service referral program;

5. provide educational counseling and guidance, including financial assistance information for Puerto Rican students; and,

6. provide community organization services such as the identification and utilization of local resources for Puerto Rican community advancement and development.

OCPR has also served an important public relations function by providing information on Puerto Rico and Puerto Ricans to New Yorkers, as well as information on New York to Puerto Ricans.

The OCPR assumed a vital position in the organizational efforts of Puerto Ricans in New York City. It has supported, both formally and informally, organizational activities in the city. It has provided testimony at public hearings concerning matters of interest to the Puerto Rican community. And its staff has regularly been called upon to articulate Puerto Rican needs and concerns.

OCPR has, however, suffered from an identity crisis. That it is an office of the government of Puerto Rico has caused a dilemma for Puerto Ricans wishing to establish themselves on the U.S. mainland and finding themselves represented by an arm of the government of Puerto Rico. In addition, the staffing of OCPR reflects whatever political party is in power in Puerto Rico. As a particular party is voted out of office, so OCPR undergoes administrative changes to reflect the current political administration. Although this is not unusual for government-affiliated service agencies, the fairly atypical nature of the Office as a home away from home raises ambiguities as to the OCPR's understanding of the political realities of Puerto Ricans in New York. This has, too often, given the directors of OCPR a highly visible, but controversial status in the Puerto Rican community.

One of the most visible directors of the Office was Joseph Monserrat, who served during the 1960s. He was born in Puerto Rico but as a small child came to New York, where he was raised. His tenure as director was an example of the controversial nature of the position. Articulate and astute, he could not overcome the political ambiguities of the position. He resigned from the Office in 1969 and went on to be elected president of the New York City Interim Board of Education, where he distinguished himself during a critical period for the New York City education system.

Another director to follow Monserrat in 1969 was Manuel Cassiano. Born and raised in the South Bronx, he was a very successful business executive before dedicating himself to this community service position. He left OCPR in 1970 to direct the Puerto Rican Industrial Company, popularly known in Puerto Rico as Operation Bootstrap.

After departure of Cassiano, the Office focused its efforts on job development and training. However, the importance of the office went into decline during this period. Younger, more diversely political Puerto Ricans saw less of a need for an arm of the government of Puerto Rico to address their needs, serve as a spokesperson, and provide information and reference services. They no longer felt the need for a home away from home because New York had become their home.

An important reference for the OCPR is Francesco Cordasco with Eugene Bucchoini, *The Puerto Ricans 1493–1973* (1973), from which this description of the OCPR was extracted.

ORDEN DE CABALLEROS DE HONOR, EL (ORDER OF GENTLEMEN OF HONOR) The earliest recorded date for this organization is 1910. The organization had twenty-four lodges in Texas and four in Mexico with approximately 100–250 members per lodge. The Orden was affiliated with the Masonic Lodge of Mexico. The Brownsville lodge had 300 members, while Laredo had 90, and Corpus Christi 80.

The principal goal of the organization was to upgrade the conditions of Mexicans in Texas through superior intellectual, spiritual, and ethical pursuits rather than through violence or by stepping on the rights of others. It is interesting to note these goals as reflective of a predominating spiritual, intellectual, and non-aggressive approach within the Mexican American community of the early Southwest to expressing ethnic pride and identity. In this organization, as well as others such as the Alianza Hispano Americana* (AHA), there was acknowledgment that full equality of rights could not be attained at the expense of others' rights.

The Orden modeled itself after the constitution and bylaws of the European Masonic Order, with its system of collective self-help and regulation.

The reference source for this organization is Jose Amaro Hernandez, "The Political Development of Mutual Aid Societies in the Mexican American Community: Ideals and Principles" (Ph.D. dissertation, University of California at Riverside, 1979).

ORDEN FRATERNAL HIJOS DE PUERTO RICO (FRATERNAL ORDER OF SONS OF PUERTO RICO) (OFHPR) This organization, founded in 1952, is a nonprofit fraternal corporation founded in Oakland, California, by Aurora Calderon and other local Puerto Ricans concerned with the adjustment problems of newly arrived Puerto Ricans. OFHPR is primarily a cultural and social organization welcoming and providing orientation assistance to recent immigrants. The organization is hierarchically structured and led by a board of directors charged with setting organizational goals and policy.

The primary reference for this organization is the *California Directory of Agencies and Organizations Serving Latino, Asian, and Pacific Island Communities* (1977), compiled by the office of State Senator Alex P. Garcia.

ORDEN HIJOS DE AMERICA (ORDER SONS OF AMERICA) (OHA) Organized in San Antonio, Texas, in 1921 by a small group of Mexican American community leaders, this was one of the first organizations to recognize a need for a specific organizational purpose of political power for this community. There were thirty-seven men involved in the creation of the Orden, of which the most prominent were James Tafoya, Sr., Feliciano Flores, Juan Soliz (the youngest of the group), Leo Longoria, Frank Leighton, Abran Armendarez (a baseball pitcher), Paul Coons (publisher of a Spanish-language newspaper), Vincente Roche (salesperson), and John Melchor. James Tafoya, Sr., was elected first president of the Order.

Both James Tafoya, Sr., and Feliciano Flores were very popular with the Mexican American community. Feliciano Flores had campaigned openly for the presidency of the organization and was unhappy with the outcome. He left the group with seven other members to form a rival order, the Knights of America. But the Knights disappeared almost immediately and its members were absorbed into the OHA.

The Orden restricted its membership exclusively to citizens of the United States of Mexican or Spanish extraction, either native or naturalized. The limitation of membership to American citizens marked a growing Mexican American awareness of the importance of political power to a group's goals and that political power is attained through a solid voting bloc of citizens.

The organization's awareness was articulated in their Declaration of Principles, in which the founders ask that members use their influence in all fields of social, economic, and political action in order to realize the greatest enjoyment possible of all rights and privileges and prerogatives extended by the U.S. Constitution.

The Orden, a forerunner of the Gran Liga Mexicanista de Beneficiencia y Protección* (GLMBP), was made up of a membership of white-collar and professional Mexican Americans. Their firm commitment to the ballot box as a vehicle for ensured constitutional rights eventually led to a more comprehensive posture of cultural accommodation, according to some contemporary Mexican American scholars. But this is hardly the case since it has generally been recognized that the ballot box is the most important vehicle for access to full equal rights. Regardless of the particular focal period, the group always turns back from a multitude of less accommodating gestures to the ballot box for expression.

The Orden's activities were not limited to voter registration but also involved direct political action, as demonstrated through its push in Corpus Christi, Texas, for Mexican Americans to serve on juries. There had been a history in Corpus Christi of Spanish-surnamed citizens automatically being dropped from eligible lists without ever being summoned. The Orden had taken account of Mexicans going to jail for offenses for which Anglos were given suspended sentences or let off. The Orden, therefore, wrote a letter requesting to be admitted to juries.

The OHA achieved three major accomplishments during its brief existence: the right to serve on juries; the right to sue an Anglo; and the right to use public beaches along the coast at Corpus Christi. The fact that these simple basic rights were considered milestones by Mexican Americans of that time indicates the degree of racial and ethnic prejudice that predominated in Texas.

By 1928 the Orden had successfully established seven councils, with the strongest and most politically active branches located in Corpus Christi and San Antonio. Soon a division arose over the dissatisfaction of the two more activist councils with the other slower-moving elements of the Orden. The result was the secession of the Corpus Christi and San Antonio councils and the founding of what later became the League of United Latin American Citizens* (LULAC).

For information on this organization, the reader is directed to O. Douglas Weeks, "Lulacs," *Southwestern Political and Social Science Quarterly* (December 1929), where the constitution and bylaws of the OHA are discussed; and Paul Taylor, *An American Frontier* (1939). The primary resources for this entry include Michael David Tirado, "The Mexican American's Participation in Voluntary Political Associations" (Ph.D. dissertation, Claremont Graduate School and University, 1971); and Jose Amaro Hernandez, "The Political Development of Mutual Aid Societies in the Mexican American Community: Ideals and Principles" (Ph.D. dissertation, University of California at Riverside, 1979).

P

PADRES ASOCIADOS POR DERECHOS RELIGIOSOS, EDUCATIVOS, Y SOCIALES (ASSOCIATED PRIESTS FOR RELIGIOUS, EDUCATIONAL, AND SOCIAL RIGHTS) (PADRES) PADRES was founded in 1969 in San Antonio, Texas, by Hispanic priests, mainly Mexican American, who felt that the Catholic Church was ignoring the concerns and needs of its Hispanic members, who constituted 25 percent of the church's membership.

PADRES was primarily organized to aid in the religious, educational, and social development of Hispanics. To accomplish this, PADRES provides information on Hispanics to the religious hierarchy, seeks funding for community services such as health care, child care, and education, and develops awareness programs to strengthen the communal self-image of this group. In addition, PADRES promotes bilingual-bicultural education for the Catholic education system and advocates appointing indigenous Spanish-speaking clergy for predominantly Hispanic communities.

In February 1970, PADRES held a national congress in Tucson, Arizona. The group demanded more Hispanic bishops. The apparent success of this meeting was demonstrated by the ordination, on May 5, 1970, of Father Patrick Flores of Pasadena, Texas, as auxiliary bishop of San Antonio, the first Mexican American to be appointed bishop. Soon afterward, Monsignor Gilbert Chavez was appointed auxiliary bishop of San Diego, thus opening the bishop ranks to Hispanics in California.

The membership of PADRES is divided into four categories: full membership, open to Hispanic priests with annual dues of twenty-five dollars; associate membership for Hispanic and non-Hispanic priests working with Hispanics and with annual dues of ten dollars; honorary membership for anyone who wants to support the organization with annual dues of ten dollars; and in perpetuum membership given by PADRES as an exceptional token of esteem. There were approximately 900 members listed at the time of this writing.

The board of directors, the governing body of PADRES, consists of between ten and fifteen priests, who serve for two years or until successors are qualified. The officers of the board are elected by the membership at the annual meeting, and regular meetings of the board are held quarterly. From the board of directors, an executive committee is elected whose main function is to serve as a body of consultants to the president for larger decisions which must be made between board meetings. The executive director is selected and hired by the board to coordinate the planning, execution, and implementation of PADRE's goals. The regional directors, representing eleven regions that include every state (except Hawaii) and Puerto Rico are elected by regional caucuses for two-year terms. PADRE's headquarters is located in San Antonio, Texas, where the executive director resides, while the other officers live and work in other U.S. cities.

This organization receives its funding from religious-related organizations such as the Interreligious Foundation for Community Organization, the U.S. Conference of Bishops, and the campaign for Human Development.

The Association has formed various councils relating to leadership development, legislation for migrants and farmworkers, and women in the ministry. They have also met with black groups such as the National Black Catholic Clergy Caucus to urge black and Hispanic solidarity. PADRES's publications include *Entre Nosotros*, the quarterly newsletter, and "Chicano Culture and Pastoral Theology and Border Problems," a document of the 1972 Symposium on Justice and Peace. In addition, PADRES conducts a biennial retreat seminar.

References to the activities of PADRES include the *Encyclopedia of Associations* (1979); *Entre Nosotros* newsletters; *La Luz* (May 1973); the 1975 revised PADRES constitution and bylaws; and Rodolfo Acuña, *Occupied America* (1981).

PARTIDO LA RAZA UNIDA (UNITED PEOPLE'S PARTY) (PLRU)
Formed and legally filed as a political party in 1970 in the Texas Winter Garden area of Hidalgo County, Texas, Partido La Raza Unida later the same year organized chapters in three other south Texas counties: Dimmit, Zavala, and La Salle. Also in 1970, PLRU was established in Colorado. California became the third state in which PLRU was formed. From February to July 1970, chapters were established in Berkeley, San Jose, Fresno, East Los Angeles, Long Beach, San Diego, and other California municipalities. By early 1973 there were local chapters in sixteen states of the southwestern, northwestern, and midwestern United States (Arizona, California, Colorado, Idaho, Illinois, Kansas, Michigan, Minnesota, Montana, Nebraska, New Mexico, Oregon, Texas, Washington, Wisconsin, and Wyoming).

The organizers and initial leaders of PLRU were college student activists who participated in the 1960s social-political movement. From their experience in the civil rights and antiwar struggles, these students gained useful organizational skills. Too, the founders in Texas were members of a campus organization whose goal was to organize the Mexican American community which was called MAYO (Mexican American Youth Organization*) and was later absorbed into the Movimento Estudiantil Chicanos de Aztlan* (MECHA). Among these leaders were Jose Angel Gutierrez, law student and first president of MAYO, and Mario Compean. In Colorado the main organizer of PLRU was Rodolfo "Corky" Gonzales, activist and then head of the Crusade for Justice* (CFJ). In New Mexico the organization was spearheaded by Reis Lopez Tijerina of the Alianza Federal de Pueblos Libres* (AFPL).

Social, economic, and political exploitation and institutional discrimination against Mexican Americans were a continuing reality in 1970 in the Southwest. Mexican American activists considered police harassment, high unemployment, low income, disproportionately high Mexican American prison populations, and educational discrimination to be consequences of these conditions. National candidates from both the Democratic and Republican parties had made campaign promises in the Mexican American community to seek solutions to these problems; however, little action was taken. It was from this unresponsiveness of the two-party system to the needs and concerns of Mexican Americans that PLRU was formed.

The main goal of PLRU was to help Mexican Americans gain control of those institutions that affect daily life in their communities through direct confrontation with non-Mexicans at the polls, leading to the ultimate establishment of an independent "Nation of Aztlan," a carryover from the ancient mythical nation of the Aztecs. The philosophical platform of the party was referred to as "El Plan Espiritual de Aztlan," which emphasized national goals of self-determination. A Chicano [sic] Congress, including representatives from all U.S. Mexican American communities, would be formed to govern the party and the nation.

PLRU began its work by developing local cores of grass-roots workers. These workers helped organize local chapters of PLRU, conducted political consciousness-raising teach-ins, and talked to voters in the neighborhoods about changing registration from the Democratic Party to PLRU.

PLRU was established largely in communities where Mexican Americans were the numerical majority. The local chapters sponsored candidates for mayor, city council, school board, sheriff, and controller. In 1970 Mexican Americans gained control of the city councils and school boards in Crystal City and Carrizo Springs, Texas; and in 1972, in California, PLRU candidates won city council seats in Parlier City, Huron, Reedley, Fresno, and Mendota, the mayoral office in Dinuba, and police chief in Mendota.

Following local election victories, PLRU ran candidates for some county elections in south Texas in 1970. However, most of these were disqualified on "technicalities." Later, PLRU candidates ran for state offices in Colorado and for the U.S. Congress in Texas and California but were unsuccessful.

Party conventions were held at the regional, state, and national levels, where local chapters developed platforms. The membership of PLRU included persons from various classes and occupations such as students, professionals, and working-class members. The majority of registrants have been Mexican American, although in northern California many party organizers have been non-Mexican Hispanics.

From 1970 to 1973 a number of regional and state conventions were held in Texas, Colorado, California, and New Mexico. At the 1970 regional conferences in Denver, Alamosa, Fort Collins, and Boulder, Colorado, thirty party candidates were chosen to run for local and state offices. Also, reports on the state of the party were delivered, and an official Colorado PLRU platform was adopted. This program included positions on housing, education, economic opportunities, job development, law enforcement, redistribution of wealth, and the war in Vietnam.

On September 1, 1972, PLRU held its first national convention in El Paso, Texas. This event lasted for four days and drew 3,000 participants from eighteen states. During the convention, delegates voted to establish a Congreso Nacional de La Raza Unida (La Raza Unida National Congress), whose role would be to determine social, economic, political, and educational policies for Mexican Americans in Aztlan. Jose Angel Gutierrez was elected congreso chairperson. Also, a national platform was adopted, including resolutions calling for the end of exploitation of Mexican workers and undocumented workers, community control of law enforcement agencies, bilingual-bicultural education for Mexican American children, adequate housing, and free health services.

The delegates also voted to reaffirm PLRU's stand as an independent party, denying PLRU support for candidates of other parties. Reis Lopez Tijerina and a group of delegates from New Mexico walked out of the convention protesting this decision. Cesar Chavez, whose advice and support had been sought by party organizers, was not invited to the convention because of his endorsement of the 1972 Democratic candidate for president, George McGovern.

An unintended consequence of the party's activities was that the Democratic and Republican parties nominated unprecedented numbers of Mexican American candidates to run for municipal, county, state, and national elections in the Southwest.

The particular local aims, goals, and success in registering Mexican Americans in PLRU was dependent on microenvironmental factors such as the nature of the relationship between Mexican American and Anglo populations. A number of more general factors would also seem to affect the potential success and expansion of the party. PLRU, as a party based on ethnicity, is interested in restricting membership to a numerical minority in the United States, Mexican Americans. The Mexican American population is heterogeneous, further limiting potential membership to those who agree with the PLRU goals and platform. Its progressive platform and ethnically exclusive goals have in some instances created organized Anglo reaction and dissension within the Mexican American community.

The most important source for the PLRU is Richard Santillan, *La Raza Unida* (1973), which was utilized for purposes of this work, as were the ''Texas State

La Raza Unida Platform'' (1970) and several articles and chapters from the general contemporary literature on Mexican American politics.

PENITENTES (PENITENTS) See BROTHERS OF OUR FATHER JESUS OF NAZARETH.

PERSONNEL MANAGEMENT ASSOCIATION OF AZTLAN (PMA) Formed in 1971, this organization was created to develop industrial relations policies helpful to Hispanic and other minority workers. This Association of personnel management professionals encourages scholastic attainment and awards scholarships to outstanding Hispanic business students through its education committee. PMA always works toward the placement of Hispanics in personnel management positions.

The Association is funded by annual dues of twenty-five dollars and corporate donations. PMA is concentrated in California but has made concerted efforts at expansion. It publishes a quarterly newsletter, *PMA National Newsletter*.

Although the organization is very active and has succeeded in establishing its presence nationally, there are few published references to its activities. The source for this description was *A Guide to Hispanic Organizations* (1979).

POLITICAL ASSOCIATION OF SPANISH SPEAKING ORGANIZA-TIONS (PASSO) This organization was founded in Phoenix, Arizona, following the election of John F. Kennedy to the presidency in 1960. The Viva Kennedy Campaign Clubs were the forerunners of this interstate group, although the Viva Kennedy Clubs were not actually clubs in the sense of a voluntary association but rather a loosely knit network of Kennedy supporters. In fact, the Alianza Hispano Americana* (AHA) provided a ready-made base for membership outreach for the Kennedy campaign. Also, the Alianza leadership at that time was based in Phoenix, although the actual officers were in Tucson. The president of the Alianza was Carlos McCormick, whose father-in-law, the owner of a Phoenix law practice, was Ralph Estrada. After the Kennedy election, Estrada was appointed director of operations of the Agency for International Development in Latin America. Estrada had been supreme president of the AHA until his appointment, and McCormick ascended to that position upon his departure.

It was within this political climate that an organization such as PASSO was bound to emerge for the purpose of organizing a united national political association capable of exerting political pressure at all levels of government. The organization was one of the earliest to reach out to Puerto Ricans, Cubans, and others of South American extraction. This caused considerable controversy among its Mexican American membership.

The organization experienced much organizational success in Texas. Its leadership then decided to return to Arizona to expand its membership as part of its larger goal of a national organization. But the Arizona Mexican American community was unresponsive to PASSO and its leadership. The failure to expand in Arizona seriously hampered further organizational efforts. Some contemporary Mexican American historians have attributed this failure to the nationalism, regionalism, and even localism prevalent among Hispanics. But once again the historical record refutes this. In all probability, the organizers were unable to inspire credibility among a population that had already suffered through the decline of the Alianza.

PASSO is discussed in F. Chris Garcia, *La Causa Politica: A Chicano Politics Reader* (1974); Julian Samora, *La Raza: Forgotten Americans* (1966); Michael Tirado, "The Mexican American Minority's Participation in Voluntary Political Associations" (Ph.D. dissertation, Claremont Graduate School and University, 1970).

PRIMER CONGRESO MEXICANISTA (FIRST MEXICAN CONGRESS (PCM) El Primer Congreso Mexicanista was not really a voluntary association but a coalition conference held in Laredo, Texas, September 14–22, 1911. It is included in this volume because it brought together the leading organizations of the period for the purpose of forming an umbrella coalition of organizations in the state of Texas. The history leading up to the conference paints an excellent portrait of the events that led to the formation of many of these voluntary associations.

The PCM was convened by Texas Mexicans to express and act upon a variety of social grievances brought about by the encroaching Anglo American presence and subsequent domination of Mexican Americans during the latter half of the nineteenth and early twentieth centuries. Various legal and illegal means were used to transfer Texas Mexican lands to Anglo Texans. An intensified Mexican immigration coupled with loss of economic position converted the Texas Mexican population into a cheap labor pool for the developing Anglo Texan ranching and farming interests. The Anglo Texan, with a deep sense of racial and cultural superiority, created a pattern of local, officially sanctioned segregation between the two peoples, and they were protected by nearly exclusive control of the political order and increasing economic dominance. By suppressing acts of resistance such as those of Juan Cortina and Catarino Garza and physically intimidating the Texas Mexican population as a whole, law enforcement and military authorities reflected and supported the new socio-economic order. In response to this developing climate of social oppression, Nicasio Idar and his family initiated a campaign of journalistic resistance that eventually led to the Congreso.

Born in Point Isabel, Texas, near Brownsville on December 26, 1853, Nicasio Idar moved to Laredo in 1880 after living in Corpus Christi and attending schools there. He was a journalistic and commercial printer and had also served as an assistant city marshall and a justice of the peace in Laredo. As a journalist he published *La Revista*, a Masonic review, and *La Crónica*, a weekly independent newspaper. In addition to his affiliation with the Mexican Masonry, he also belonged to the Sociedad Mutualista Benito Juarez* (SMBJ) in Laredo and was a vice-president of a Mexican and Texas Mexican fraternal lodge system known as La Orden de Caballeros de Honor* (OCH). He died on April 7, 1914, leaving a widow Jovita and eight children.

At least three children had shared not only their father's ideas but his enthusiasm and zeal in defending the rights of the Texas Mexican community. Jovita, Clemente, and Eduardo joined their father in his work as editor and publisher of *La Crónica*. The newspaper was remarkable in that it covered local and area news, Mexico, and world affairs. Eduardo covered Brownsville and the lower Rio Grande Valley as a traveling correspondent, while Jovita and Clemente served in a general capacity including considerable staff writing. *La Crónica* included invited guest writers and reprinted articles from other sources. Nicasio Idar began as its editor in the 1890s but did not become owner and publisher until 1910.

La Crónica launched an attack on the social conditions oppressing Texas Mexicans during the period 1910–11. Five issues attracted the Idars' attention and formed the social context for the Congreso: (1) deteriorating Texas Mexican economic conditions; (2) the already perceptible loss of Mexican culture and Spanish language; (3) general social discrimination; (4) the particular problem of educational discrimination; and (5) the pattern of officially tolerated lynchings of Texas Mexicans.

In 1910 an Anglo American mob burning of a Mexican national accused of having murdered an Anglo woman aroused the ire of the Idars. They bitterly attacked the burning in *La Crónica* as a barbaric act. On June 19, 1911, a fourteen-year-old boy named Antonio Gomez was asked to leave a place of business in Thorndale, Texas. When he refused, a fight ensued, and a Texan was left dead from a wound from Gomez's knife. Again, after Gomez's arrest, a mob took him from the authorities, beat him, and dragged his body around town with a buggy. Finally, Leon Cardenas Martinez was arrested and tried in July 1911 for allegedly murdering two Anglo women near Reeves, Texas. According to his lawyer, George Estes, a mob forced Martinez to confess at gunpoint. A jury member who dissented on the guilty vote was threatened, and Martinez was sentenced to death. Estes, in spite of personal threats to his life, appealed the case, and the death sentence was reduced to thirty years in prison.

La Crónica protested all of these actions. Even the *Houston Post* noted the effect of the Alamo syndrome on juries trying Mexicans. The *Post* concluded that there was very little sympathy for the "greaser" in the country. There was a general climate of racial discrimination that permeated all aspects of Texas life even in the state legislature, where State Representative J. T. Canales was called "the greaser from Brownsville" during a session of the legislature.

Discrimination particularly affected the educational process. Toward the end of 1910 and through early 1911, Clemente Idar wrote a series of exposés of the Texas public schools. Although Texas Mexicans paid school taxes, he argued, they were not permitted to participate in the educational system. The Mexican consul was called in to investigate but restricted his investigation to the largely Mexican counties of Webb, Starr, and Zapata, where he uncovered little discrimination. Idar unsuccessfully pressed the consul to visit the rest of southern and central Texas. Idar, however, continued his campaign until readers from across the state wrote *La Crónica* confirming the existence of segregation in their communities. These conditions and many others led the Idars to initiate the plans for El Primer Congreso Mexicanista.

The Idars were active members in the Orden de Caballeros de Honor* (OCH), a Texas Mexican fraternal lodge which provided the organizational model and participant resource for the Congreso. The largest groups were in Brownsville with 200 members, Corpus Christi with 80, and Laredo with 90. In January 1911 the Idars, through *La Crónica*, began calling for a convention of the various lodges, to include special guests. The convention scheduled for Laredo would take up the questions of school discrimination, the need for teaching Spanish in community-controlled schools with Mexican teachers, the Mexican consular system, ways and means to protect Mexican lives and interests in Texas, the role of the OCH, the formation of women's groups under the auspices of the OCH, the need for Texas Mexicans to acquire land and hold on to what they had, and organizing a future meeting to be known as El Primer Congreso Mexicanista.

By February 1911 the Idars had decided that it would be more practical for each OCH lodge to send a special delegation to the OCH conventions. These special delegations would then convene separately as the PCM. The reason for this change in strategy was a desire to move immediately toward resolution of Texas Mexican problems. *La Crónica* charged that Texas Mexicans could not count on change from within the Texas Anglo community, nor could they depend on Mexico for help. It urged organization, unification, and education of the Mexican masses as the only viable solutions to the problems affecting them. An open invitation to participate in the Congreso was extended to all Texas Mexican organizations, and a special invitation was extended to the Texas Mexican Masonic lodges. Further, *La Crónica* urged Texas Mexicans to organize locally in order to send delegations to the meetings.

The March 16 issue of the newspaper carried letters of support for the PCM from prominent individuals representing various groups. The most important mutual aid societies also sent support. The decision was made to hold the convention during the week of September 14–22, not only because of the historical significance of Mexican Independence Day but also because of the lower holiday train fares and the presence of large numbers of visitors in Laredo to celebrate the patriotic holiday. This tactical planning demonstrated a highly sophisticated political awareness on the part of the organizers.

On September 14, 1911, the delegates met on the second floor of a building in the town square. There were in attendance two delegates from each OCH lodge from twenty-four Texas localities. There was also an unspecified number of representatives from Masonic lodges, mutual aid societies, protective organizations, other types of social groups, special visitors such as delegations from Mexico, the press, and an unspecified number of visitors.

Nicasio Idar welcomed the participants, and the convention moved to elect a board of directors for the Congreso. The board was composed of Jose P. Reyes, president (Brownsville), Nicasio Idar, vice-president (Laredo), Lisandro Peña, secretary (Laredo), and voting members J. A. Garza (residence unknown), Isidro G. Garza (Kingsville), and Timoteo F. Gloria (Rio Grande).

The meeting itself consisted of oratorical speeches and workshops. In addition, music was presented throughout the day's activities. The Congreso opened with a boys' chorus singing patriotic songs, and a young boy reading a patriotic poem. Patriotism and Mexican nationalism permeated the Congreso.

The Congreso called for unity against the oppressor, radical working-class ideology, retention of language and culture, criminal justice, participation of women in the struggle, social and economic justice, and an end to educational discrimination.

The statewide organization with local chapters that was to emerge from the PCM was designed to provide continuous, long-range solutions to Texas Mexican problems. The objectives of this organization were essentially similar to those of the PCM. The organization was called La Gran Liga Mexicanista de Beneficencia y Protección* (GLMBP). Another organization to emerge from the PCM was the Liga Feminil Mexicanista* (LFM). But neither of these organizations appears to have survived beyond the founding year.

A detailed and important reference on the PCM is Jose Limon, "El Primer Congreso Mexicanista de 1911: A Precursor to Contemporary Chicanismo," *Aztlan* 5:1 and 2 (1974). Also, the PCM is mentioned in Jose Amaro Hernandez, "The Political Development of Mutual Aid Societies in the Mexican American Community: Ideals and Principles" (Ph.D. dissertation, University of California at Riverside, 1979); and Rodolfo Acuña, *Occupied America* (1981).

PUERTO RICAN ASSOCIATION FOR COMMUNITY AFFAIRS (PRACA)

PRACA was founded in New York City to develop leadership qualities among young Puerto Ricans, to foster a greater cultural awareness of their heritage, and to develop services for them. Formerly called the Hispanic Young Adult Association, identified sources indicate no founding date for the organization or the names of founders. Information available indicates PRACA operates a day care center and provides training and development services for organizations. The Association also runs a Puerto Rican National Training Institute.

The primary reference source for this organization was the archives of the Robert Kennedy Memorial in Washington, D.C. Attempts to secure further information from the organization were unsuccessful.

PUERTO RICAN COMMUNITY DEVELOPMENT PROJECT (PRCDP)

The PRCDP was an outgrowth of the National Puerto Rican Forum* (NPRF) and another product of the guiding spirit of Puerto Rican activist and intellectual Antonia Pantoja.

The Project, although not a voluntary organization in the formal sense, typified those community agencies during the 1960s and 1970s that took on the cohesive functions of voluntary associations through the auspices of federal, state, local, and private monies.

In 1964 the NPRF proposed a self-help project for the Puerto Rican community in New York. The basis for this proposal was the severe conditions of poverty Puerto Ricans were experiencing in the City. In 1964 they were the poorest minority group in New York.

The PRCDP was initiated as a response to economic conditions of Puerto Ricans with the following specific goals: (1) to raise family income and reduce poverty and dependence; (2) to raise the educational level; (3) to strengthen family life and cultural institutions; and (4) to strengthen Puerto Rican organizational life.

The founders of the organization advanced a unique concept in addressing the life adjustment needs of newcomers to the mainland. They suggested looking to other ethnic communities already in place to assist in the transitional process into U.S. culture and society. They reasoned that, historically, ethnic communities have provided newcomers with a sense of security by offering support of their native culture and traditions while introducing them to the cultural patterns of the new country.

The founders of PRCDP proposed an organization concerned with enhancing Puerto Rican opportunities for better education, better jobs, and higher wages. They envisioned programs designed, administered, and staffed by Puerto Ricans. Aspira of America* (AA) was an example of a project sponsored by PRCDP which eventually took on a life of its own. It was geared toward educational opportunities for Puerto Rican youth.

The organization immediately experienced internal conflict regarding long-range versus short-range goals and methods for achieving these goals. Those adhering to long-range needs reflected a more conservative and traditional approach, while the short-range goal advocates advanced a more militant stance. New York City officials, in a fashion that came to typify the majority political leadership during this period of minority protest, played on the division thereby further aggravating the split. They managed to come up with superficial excuses for not funding the Project while at the same time avoiding serious criticism.

The activists managed to capture the leadership of the organizing group and in 1965 received funding from the federal Office of Economic Opportunity. But internal political divisions continued to plague the Project, and in January 1968 fifteen top officials resigned in protest against the policies of the board of directors. The Project survived that stormy controversy, which received extensive coverage in the *New York Times*, and went on to protest the lack of support given Puerto Rican programs by the Council Against Poverty, the New York City poverty agency.

The greatest criticism of the PRCDP was that it proposed another bureaucracy, but one made up of Puerto Ricans. At least that is how it was viewed by its detractors. PRCDP created a separate board of directors for each program at the local and citywide level, suggesting maximum participation of the Puerto Rican community in decision making. Although this was a laudatory attempt at participatory governance, it made for an unwieldy and cumbersome planning and administrative process. Also, the concept of Puerto Ricans being integrated into U.S. society by way of other immigrant groups who preceded them was challenged. According to critics, the fact that Puerto Ricans arrive in New York City as U.S. citizens and are able to travel easily between the island and the mainland, combined with other forces, creates an entirely different set of circumstances.

Whether or not the Project was inadequate as an institution, its importance in the organizational development process of the Puerto Rican community cannot be denied. If it advocated Puerto Rican mainstreaming through traditional and, perhaps, conservative means, it was revolutionary in promoting the need for Puerto Ricans to assume self-confidence in designing and administering their own programs, and it spawned a number of other programs which continue to serve the interests of the Puerto Rican community not only in New York City but nationally.

The most valuable reference source for this organization is the original proposal, "The Puerto Rican Community Development Project: A Proposal for a Self-Help Project to Develop the Community by Strengthening the Family, Opening Opportunities for Youth and Making Full Use of Education" (1964). Coverage of the controversies involving the internal divisions with PRCDP can be found in the *New York Times* (January 24, 1968, and June 4, 1968).

Contemporary references that discuss the Project include Agustin Gonzales, "The Struggle to Develop Self-Help Institutions," *Social Casework* 55:2 (February 1974); and Francesco Cordasco with Eugene Bucchioni, *The Puerto Ricans 1493–1973* (1973).

PUERTO RICAN CONGRESS OF NEW JERSEY (PRCNJ) A statewide advocate for New Jersey's Puerto Rican population and other Hispanics, the Congress was founded in Atlantic City in October 1969 as an outgrowth of the first Puerto Rican Convention of New Jersey. The organization was established through the leadership of Dr. Hilda Hidalgo and Hector S. Rodriguez as a Puerto Rican institute dedicated to combatting discrimination in housing, employment, and education.

The PRCNJ plans, implements, and maintains educational, vocational, rural health, and neighborhood planning projects. Its major goals are to aid the Puerto Rican community in devising solutions to socio-economic problems particular to Puerto Ricans and to provide social services to the community. The organization seeks to secure and defend fair treatment rights for Puerto Ricans from social, economic, and political institutions in the United States.

Through seminars and training sessions, the Congress attempts to improve and increase Hispanic participation in government-funded manpower training programs. It also advises minority entrepreneurs. In 1976 the Congress established a minority business office in Perth Amboy to provide technical assistance to minority business owners and prospective owners.

The Puerto Rican Congress of New Jersey is a hierarchically structured, non-membership organization headed by a board of directors, which sets agency policy and hires the chief administrator. The board is composed of thirty-three members elected at open community conventions. The Congress received its nonprofit status in 1971 and also affiliated with the National Urban Coalition, an urban action organization that conducts local model urban programs through its coalition affiliates.

In the field of education the Congress founded the Nuevos Camino (New Paths) reading program in Jersey City in 1978. The organization also initiated an educational curricula and materials development project. The Congress joined with other organizations to lobby successfully for the New Jersey Bilingual Education Law.

The Congress established a national child abuse information dissemination project in 1980. The organization has aided in the formation of approximately thirty to thirty-five new organizations and helps to coordinate tristate (New Jersey, Pennsylvania, and Delaware) conventions. It publishes *Paso Firme* (Firm Step), a quarterly newsletter.

References utilized for this entry include the organization's completed HAVO questionnaire and *A Guide to Hispanic Organizations* (1979).

PUERTO RICAN COUNCIL MULTI SERVICE CENTER (PRCMSC) This Puerto Rican Center is located in New York City. The PRCMSC is engaged in educational, community organization, economic development, and employment outreach and referral projects. It offers language training and works closely to help improve area public schools. Tenant and block organization activities are stressed. The Council also provides job information and training opportunities announcements.

The only identifiable reference to this organization was the archives of the Robert Kennedy Memorial in Washington, D.C. The organization failed to respond to further requests for information.

PUERTO RICAN ENGINEERS AND SCIENTISTS SOCIETY, INC. (PRESS) Established in New York City, PRESS seeks to identify and represent Puerto Rican engineers and scientists. The organization also strives to provide a forum for interchange of professional and other information in the field and to make recommendations to governmental and other agencies of concern to Hispanic technical professionals. PRESS operates a precollege program and offers financial aid to Puerto Ricans aspiring to become engineers and scientists.

The only identifiable information on this organization was contained in the archives of the Robert Kennedy Memorial in Washington, D.C. The organization failed to respond to further requests for information.

PUERTO RICAN FAMILY INSTITUTE (PRFI) The Institute was founded in New York City in 1971 as a volunteer effort under the leadership of Agustin Gonzalez, a social worker. Gonzalez migrated to New York in 1952 in search of better employment opportunities. He discovered an urban city hostile to the needs of poverty families and agencies ill equipped to handle a diversity of problems within the Puerto Rican minority group. Gonzalez and his associates lobbied unsuccessfully for funding of their Institute for several years. It was not until 1964, when the War on Poverty became national policy, that new hopes for funding surfaced.

On June 12, 1965, Paul Scrivance, assistant mayor of New York, called a meeting in City Hall to announce the twenty-eight citywide community action programs to be funded by the Council Against Poverty. The first named was the PRFI. The Institute and its Program to Preserve the Integration of the Puerto Rican Migrant Family were established under the executive directorship of Agustin Gonzalez. After initial internal struggles characteristic of new, trailblazing ideas, the PRFI became one of the first mainland organizations to advance two critical goals for the Puerto Rican community.

A concern expressed by the founders of the Institute was the need for the Puerto Rican community to develop and operate their own community-based institutions. The Puerto Rican Family Institute is a grass-roots agency staffed by Puerto Ricans which provides a setting where Puerto Rican families can feel at home.

The long-term goal of the Institute is to help Puerto Ricans make a faster and more positive adjustment to New York City life by offering them both psychological and support services. The Institute's more immediate objective is to create for newly arrived Puerto Rican families the support of an extended ritual kinship system, a major feature of Puerto Rican cultures.

Agustin Gonzalez wrote about his experience in conceiving and establishing the PRFI in "The Struggle to Develop Self-Help Institutions," *Social Forces* 56:4 (June 1978). The PRFI is also highlighted in Francesco Cordasco with Eugene Bucchioni, *The Puerto Ricans 1943–1793* (1973).

PUERTO RICAN HISPANIC YOUTH COALITION, INC. (PRYC) Founded in New York City in 1968 and based in that city, the PRYC serves the Puerto Rican community by providing youth with employment services. Its membership has reached over 2,500 and its staff fifteen. There are no membership dues. Officers include an executive director, chairperson, and secretary.

There are few published references to this group. The source used for this entry was the *Directory of Spanish Speaking Community Organizations* (1970).

PUERTO RICAN LEGAL COMMITTEE (PRLC) The Committee is a nonprofit legal assistance corporation founded in Newark, New Jersey, in 1974. It was formed to deal with the issues of unlawful arrests, police brutality, and bail posting during the height of social unrest in the Puerto Rican community of

Branch Brook Park, Newark. The committee was originally constituted as the legal arm of the Hispanic Emergency Council. In 1974, with the subsiding of the Council's activities, the legal committee requested and received permission to exist as a separate entity. The organization's founders and leaders include Chali Roche, Juan Cruz, Carlos Rivera, Percy Miranda, and Ramon Rodriguez. These men share a background in legal and social services.

The aims of the PRLC are multifold. The organization seeks to provide expert legal counsel and technical information regarding legislation and the change process to the Puerto Rican and Hispanic communities. The Committee also aims to educate Puerto Rican and Hispanic students as to their constitutional rights. Further, the organization seeks to serve as a community referral agency.

The PRLC is a hierarchically structured, nonmembership organization with a constituency of over 10,000 persons. The majority of clients served by the committee are of low income, and the organization is headed by a board of directors, which sets corporation policy. Under board supervision are an executive director and several standing committees, including the programs, finances, and police committees. The PRLC controls two subsidiary corporations, the United Hispanic Federal Credit Union established in 1978 and the Mount Pleasant Community Development, Inc., formed in 1979.

The Committee sponsors a number of programs and activities which reflect the organization's goals. The corporation's main functions concern legal research, defense, class actions, and referrals on behalf of individuals, communities, and nonprofit corporations. The Committee also monitors federal and state programs to ensure compliance. In addition, the PRLC provides counseling in areas such as housing and offers technical assistance in various aspects of consumer affairs. Since 1975 the PRLC has funded a housing rehabilitation corporation and a neighborhood referral service.

The primary reference source for this organization was the PRLC-completed HAVO questionnaire. For further analysis, internal reports and evaluations as well as the organization's bylaws would provide expanded information.

PUERTO RICAN LEGAL DEFENSE AND EDUCATION FUND, INC. (PRLDEF) In 1971 a group of Puerto Rican lawyers including Lita Taracido, Casar A. Perales, Victor Marrero, and Jorge L. Batista met in New York City to discuss the feasibility of founding a Puerto Rican legal fund. It was formally established a year later as a national, nonprofit legal assistance corporation to ensure the civil rights of Puerto Ricans and other Hispanics and to promote the increase of Puerto Ricans in the legal profession. Its primary purpose is to provide legal assistance to Puerto Ricans and to challenge in the courts racially discriminatory laws and practices.

The Puerto Rican Legal Defense and Education Fund is a hierarchically structured organization headed by a twenty-two-member board of directors, which sets corporation goals and policy. Among the organization's leaders are the president and general counsel and the chairperson of the board. Under the supervision of the board are the director of education and the director of development. The majority of board and staff members are legal professionals.

Reflective of its goals, the Fund's major activities are concentrated in the areas of law reform and education. In the field of legal concerns the Fund emphasizes class action litigation in the federal courts. Such suits have led to the establishment of bilingual assistance for Spanish-speaking voters in New York City and Newark, New Jersey, and an end to discriminatory practices with regard to the hiring of Hispanics in the fire, police, and sanitation departments of New York City. The Fund initiated suit against unions and clothing manufacturers in New Jersey for underpaying laborers and the unhealthy working conditions. In the case of *Cubano* v. *Manson* the Fund supported Hispanic inmates in their suit alleging discrimination against them in employment, vocational rehabilitation programs, and counseling services in Connecticut's Somers Prison. The Fund is also involved in monitoring compliance with legal standards in several areas of the northeastern United States.

In advocating the rights of Puerto Ricans and other minorities, Fund representatives testify before public and private hearings and conduct research studies. The organization conducts research projects in the areas of education, labor, and employment as a base of support in its allegations of discrimination against Puerto Ricans. In 1978 the U.S. Department of Labor awarded the Fund a grant to research market problems and issues affecting Hispanic Americans.

In the field of educational assistance the Fund maintains a legal education and training division with offices in New York City and Newark. This division provides law students with financial and counseling assistance, writing, and test-taking skills development clinics and exposure to civil rights programs. Added to this, the Fund provides workshops and prep courses, an honors fellowship program, and summer internships for law students.

The organization is also active in encouraging young Puerto Ricans to enter the profession. The legal education division recruits potential law school candidates and holds an annual Law Day Conference providing guidance counseling.

In 1973 the Fund's total expenditures came to $129,094. By 1978 this amount had risen to $635,650. The Puerto Rican Legal Defense and Education Fund relies for support on foundations such as the Carnegie Corporation and the Ford Foundation and business corporations such as American Airlines and American Telephone and Telegraph. In addition, the organization obtains contributions from scholarship funds such as those of General Mills and the Helena Rubenstein Foundation to support its educational assistance programs.

The Fund continued to grow in the 1980s. It accomplished a successful challenge to the New York City Council's redistricting plan. The Fund determined the plan to be racially gerrymandered. It won a court decision on a vocational education program, obtaining a decree providing for the entry of limited-English-proficient Latinos into Connecticut state-run vocational programs in Bridgeport. A similar agreement was reached in Hartford as well. And in the summer of 1981, the Fund obtained a court order prohibiting the layoff of bilingual teachers in the Jersey City school system. The Fund was successful in its efforts to promote equal job opportunity within the New York Police Department (NYPD). A court victory resulted in a one-to-two quota for minority hiring in the NYPD. It also ensured a quota promotional system with the NYPD. Another major impact of the Fund includes court victories which have protected fair housing practices for Latinos in the New York area.

Information on this organization came from the Fund's completed questionnaire; the 1972 and 1978 annual reports of the Fund; *New York Times* (May 1, 6, and 8, 1979), *New York Law Journal* (May 1, 1979); *A Guide to Hispanic Organizations* (1979); and *Nuestro Magazine* (March 1982).

PUERTO RICAN MERCHANTS ASSOCIATION (PRMA) The PRMA is one of the oldest Puerto Rican organizations in New York City. The Association is a reflection of the history and culture of Puerto Rican small businesses in New York City. Puerto Rican neighborhoods, like so many other ethnic enclaves around the world, teem with colorful remnants of their native land and culture. The most obvious indicators of the Puerto Rican cultural heritage are the small businesses that cater to the needs of this diverse community and educate the surrounding population of the richness of their culture. The small *bodegas* or *colmados* (grocery stores) in every Puerto Rican neighborhood, the cozy cafes, bars, restaurants, and *botanicas* (small shops that specialize in medicinal herbs, materials for spiritualist activities, charms, religious goods, and a host of related objects), and the travel agencies urging Puerto Ricans to "travel now, pay later"; these are all typical of the small Puerto Rican businesses that make up the membership of the Association.

The principal founder of the Association was Julio Hernandez. In the late 1920s Julio's family came to New York City, where Julio was born. Caught in the depression, the family suffered from poverty but managed to send each of their children through high school. Julio Hernandez served as an officer in the Merchant Marine for ten years. He married, settled in Brooklyn, opened a grocery store, and then a restaurant. His life is representative of the lives and struggles of so many other Puerto Rican merchants seeking to establish themselves in New York. Julio Hernandez served as executive secretary of the Association for several years.

Although an exact founding date for the Association was not given in the available references, all indications are that it was founded in the mid-1950s. The Association has functioned as an important economic network for the Puerto Rican community. It has not advanced political or social activities but has significantly assisted Puerto Ricans in establishing small businesses.

This organization is discussed in Francesco Cordasco, *The Puerto Ricans 1493–1973* (1973).

PUERTO RICAN ORGANIZATION FOR WOMEN (PROW) The PROW is a nonprofit social services organization established in San Francisco by Elba

Montes. The primary purpose of this corporation is to help Puerto Rican women meet their basic needs and those of their families. This organization provides a number of services which are reflective of its goals. The group provides free meals for Puerto Rican women and maintains a food bank for emergency situations. The organization also provides housing information and assistance and direct services in health education. The Puerto Rican Organization for Women is a hierarchically structured organization headed by a board of directors, which sets organizational goals and policy. A program director assists the board in executing decisions.

Information on this organization is contained in the *California Directory of Agencies and Organizations Servicing Latino, Asian, and Pacific Island Communities* (1977), compiled by the office of California State Senator Alex P. Garcia.

PUERTO RICAN RESEARCH AND RESOURCES CENTER, INC. (PRRC)
PRRC is a national scholarly research center based in Washington, D.C. The goals of the organization include research on Puerto Rican community problems, providing services, and facilitating networking among Puerto Ricans. The Center publishes material and develops curricula on bilingual-bicultural education.

A reference source for this organization is the *Directory of Spanish Speaking Community Organizations* (1970).

PUERTO RICAN TRAVELING THEATER (PRTT) Founded in 1967 in New York City, the Theater trains students from low-income families in the theater arts. Instruction includes acting, modern dance, music, and languages. Students perform, generally outdoors, throughout New York City.

This brief description of the organization's activities is contained in the archives of the Robert Kennedy Memorial in Washington, D.C. Since many community arts groups were part of the impetus of the late 1960s and early 1970s federal thrust and many of these organizations disappeared with the change in priorities commencing with the Carter Administration and heightened during the Reagan Administration, it is possible that this organization is no longer extant. An attempt to contact PRTT was unsuccessful.

__R__

RAZA NATIONAL BAR ASSOCIATION (RNBA) A nonprofit corporation founded in 1972 in Torrance, California, RNBA was formed to help improve the status of Hispanics within the legal profession and the quality of interaction between the Hispanic community and law enforcement agents. La Raza National Bar Association works to heighten the competence of Hispanics working within the legal field and encourages members of the community to seriously consider entering the profession. The Association also works within the legislative system to protect the civil rights of Hispanics, particularly regarding treatment of Hispanics by police.

RNBA is a hierarchically structured, national organization. Among its early officers and leaders are Judge Benjamin Aranda, John Castillo, and Robert Maes. The organization's membership is comprised mainly of persons involved in the legal field: judges, attorneys, law students, and paralegal workers.

The organization secures its operating costs through donations and its thirty-five-dollar annual membership dues. RNBA publishes *La Raza News*, a quarterly newsletter.

Reference to RNBA activities is included in *A Guide to Hispanic Organizations* (1979).

RED, LA(NET) (LR) La Red is a national Colombian organization based in Los Angeles, California, designed for businessmen and other professionals. The organization members participate in roundtable discussions and various other social activities. All Colombians are welcome to attend the Wednesday gatherings at La Casita del Campo at 8 P.M. This organization is typical of the many social associations founded to provide special segments of the Hispanic community a "home away from home."

This description of La Red is contained in the archives of Professor Andre Simic, Department of Anthropology, University of Southern California.

REFORMA: NATIONAL ASSOCIATION TO PROMOTE LIBRARY SERVICES TO THE SPANISH SPEAKING (RNAPLSS) Organized in 1971 under the leadership of Arnulfo Trejo, Daniel Flores Duran, and others, the Reforma is primarily interested in promoting reading among young Hispanics. A way of pursuing this goal has been through the improvement of library and information services to Hispanic areas and including assistance in selection of books that will most benefit Hispanic readers. The organization also seeks to increase the number of Spanish-speaking librarians by acquainting more young people with the field.

The pioneering work of these individuals and this organization cannot be overestimated. Drs. Trejo and Duran, with others, established themselves within an important profession that was mistakenly neglected in the list of demands of the Chicano rights movement. Through the efforts of these people, a thrust was initiated nationwide to incorporate Spanish-speaking sections of local libraries within communities with a large Hispanic population. Also, in Oakland and San Jose, California, Latin American libraries were founded and, in the case of San Jose, formed a part of the city public library system.

The history of the early American independence movement attributes much to the education that occurs once a people organize a literary tradition, that is, establish newspapers, magazines, and other vehicles of written communication, while, at the same time, developing a reading public. This has been true of most historical movements. This organization has assured the Mexican American community of maintaining their literary tradition.

The Reforma is a nonprofit corporation with a membership of 250 librarians across the United States. RNAPLSS is supported by annual membership dues of twenty dollars for members and two dollars for students and by fund-raisers. The organization publishes a quarterly, *Reforma News*.

This organization is briefly described in *A Guide to Hispanic Organizations* (1979). An important source on the RNSSL is Dr. Trejo, who serves as editor of *Reforma News* and is on the faculty of the Graduate Library School at the University of Arizona, Tucson. The National Association of Librarians located in New York should have a file on this organization.

REPUBLICAN NATIONAL HISPANIC ASSEMBLY OF THE UNITED STATES (RNHA) The Republican National Hispanic Assembly was organized in 1975 to educate Hispanics about the American political process and to register voters. One of its principal founders was Fernando Oaxaca, a former appointee of the Nixon Administration.

RNHA serves as a reminder to politicians that ethnic groups are not to be regarded as voting blocs. The Assembly works to recruit Hispanics into the Republican Party. The organization, supported by the Republican National Committee, is concentrated in sixteen states, especially those with large Hispanic populations. The group is also represented in Maine, which is not heavily Hispanic but is traditionally Republican. This nonprofit corporation publishes a quarterly newsletter, *El Republicano* (The Republican).

Organizations such as this one have argued that Hispanics have traditionally been Democrats. As a matter of fact, they have stated, "Hispanics have been in the pocket of the Democratic Party." But the historical record shows this to be incorrect; the Republican Party tradition in the Hispanic community runs deep. But as the Hispanic community began to suffer discrimination and minority status, they moved toward the more sympathetic Democratic Party. This was especially so as this community, once made up of prosperous merchants among others, turned into an almost exclusively workers' community.

In the 1980 Republican campaign for the White House, Hispanic voters were singularly targeted. Actually, this started with the 1972 election campaign of Richard Nixon spearheaded by Alex Armendariz. For Ronald Reagan's 1984 reelection campaign, the Republican Party initiated an all-out campaign to woo Hispanic voters not only at the national level but in local campaigns also.

An important source for this organization is the Republican National Committee. Also, the organization's Washington, D.C., headquarters is recommended for detailed information. A primary reference source of wide distribution is *A Guide to Hispanic Organizations* (1979), prepared by a founder of this group, Alex Armendariz, under contract for Phillip Morris, Inc.

S

SECRETARIAT FOR HISPANIC AFFAIRS (SHA) The Secretariat was established in 1945 in San Antonio, Texas, as the Bishop's Committee for the Spanish Speaking Peoples under its chairperson, Archbishop Robert E. Lucey. This organization developed as a response to the major concerns of the social and economic problems of Mexican Americans in the Southwest and migrant farmworkers of the Midwest. In 1968 the Bishop's Committee (Secretariat) was moved to the National Conference of Catholic Bishops/United States Catholic Conference (NCCB/USCC) in Washington, D.C., to provide nationwide service. In November 1974, the Bishop's Committee, the Division for the Spanish Speaking, was elevated by the National Conference of Catholic Bishops to the Secretariat for the Spanish Speaking and, as such, became effective on January 1, 1975.

The major purpose for the formation of this organization was to assist those dioceses with a large number of Hispanics in their efforts to develop a far-reaching and effective response to their pastoral concerns. As a way of accomplishing their goals, the Secretariat for Hispanic Affairs took the role of an assistant to the NCCB and the USCC in responding to the pastoral needs of Hispanics. The Secretariat also serves as staff of the Bishops Ad Hoc Committee for Hispanic Affairs.

The goals of the Secretariat are basically to promote church unity through integration and mutual enrichment of cultures rather than through assimilation and loss of the Spanish heritage; to represent Hispanics' profound commitment to dignity, community, and social justice; to continue a ministry of liberation through advocacy, dialogue, and coordination on the local, diocesan, regional, and national levels; and to celebrate the magnificent diversity of Hispanic heritage, color, and language as well as to recognize its contribution to society.

The structural organization consists of four professional staff members. Pablo

Sedillo, Jr., is the director. Since his appointment in 1971, he has broadened the goals of the Secretariat. Initially, the primary concerns were for the social and economic betterment of Mexican Americans. Sedillo has included the pastoral priority of educating people so as to enable them in a process of faith and commitment to be builders of their own history; that is, he has added religion. Other staff include the Reverend Rank Ponce, associate director and research assistant; Sister Maria Lusia Baston, A. C. J., communications and education specialist; and Reverend Edgar Beltran, pastoral specialist. In addition, there are three full-time secretaries. Together they carry out the task of advocacy within the various structures of the Bishop's Conference, especially in that which refers to the national implementation of the Encuentro Nacional Hispano Pastoral (National Hispanic Religious Encounter). The Encuentro is a large-scale conference which brings together Hispanic bishops, priests, nuns, and lay Catholics to contribute to change in the church and society. Workshops and lectures as well as entertainment are featured, focusing on a variety of themes. For example, the Second Annual Encuentro Nacional Hispano Pastoral, which took place in Washington, D.C., in the summer of 1977, had several themes: evangelization and human rights; evangelization and integral education; evangelization and unity in pluralism.

Another task of the Secretariat is to coordinate the Hispanic apostolate at the national level, which is done by maintaining close communication and periodic meetings with six Hispanic regional offices. The task of coordination also includes maintaining open communications with Hispanic movements such as Cursillo (Religious Studies), Movimiento Familiar Cristiano (Christian Family Movement), and national Hispanic religious organizations such as Padres Asociados por Derechos Religiosos, Educativos, y Sociales* (PADRES), and Las Hermanas* (LH). The Secretariat also works with the Mexican American Cultural Center of San Antonio and the Northeast Pastoral Institute in New York.

The organization influences Hispanic communities through its activities. The Secretariat acts as an information and idea center concentrating on areas of migrant farmworker ministry, education, communications, pastoral research, information, and planning. It provides a liaison with other churches, institutions, and government and private agencies concerned with Hispanics. It maintains a small library and sponsors regional and national conferences and seminars on issues of importance to Hispanics.

The 1980s marked a turning point in ministry and service within the Hispanic community. In 1981 consciousness-raising reached a high point in the major Hispanic centers, and the Catholic Church acquired a greater sense of the potential contribution of this group. By the end of that year, two new Hispanic bishops, Alphonse Gallegos of California and Ricardo Ramirez of Texas, had been named. Vicars were being appointed and outreach programs established where there had never been a Hispanic presence before, such as in the Great Lakes area, the Northwest, Alaska, and Hawaii.

The most recognizable effort of the Secretariat, however, may have been the assistance provided in processing an estimated 100,000 Cubans who arrived that summer in the Mariel Cuban boatlift. The organization also continued to help Haitian refugees and to serve as liaison between the Immigration and Naturalization Service and the undocumented, especially in California, Illinois, New York, and Texas. Finally, a ten-issue series of reports on representative outreach efforts within the Hispanic community was completed by the National Conference of Catholic Bishops' Committee on Evangelization. They also published their first resource catalog. And Catholic publishers such as the Claretians and Liquori made available a series of publications for and by Hispanics.

Reference information on this organization's activities is contained in the Secretariat's office in Washington, D.C. These include documents published by the Secretariat. For purposes of this work, a Secretariat leaflet was utilized as well as *La Luz* 7:9 (1978); *Proceedings of the II Encuentro Nacional Hispano de Pastoral* (1978); and, *Nuestro Magazine* (March 1982).

SOCIEDAD ALBIZU CAMPOS (ALBIZU CAMPOS SOCIETY): See YOUNG LORDS PARTY.

SOCIEDAD MUTUALISTA BENITO JUAREZ (BENITO JUAREZ MUTUAL AID SOCIETY) (SMBJ) This mutual aid society first appeared in Corpus Christi, Texas, in 1879. It was composed mainly of Mexican automechanic workers and was organized into lodges resembling a workmen's union. The SMBJ, like many similar organizations of the time, provided leadership training for organizers who later helped form successful labor organizations.

This organization is briefly mentioned in Jose Amaro Hernandez, "The Political Development of Mutual Aid Societies in the Mexican American Community: Ideals and Principles" (Ph.D. dissertation, University of California at Riverside, 1979). The original reference source for Hernandez's work was Paul S. Taylor, *An American-Mexican Frontier, Nueces County, Texas* (1934).

SOCIEDAD PROGRESISTA MEXICANA (MEXICAN PROGRESSIVE SOCIETY) (SPM) This is one of the earliest and largest of the contemporary mutual aid societies founded by Mexicans in the United States. The SPM split from the Sociedad Zaragoza (SZ), first founded in 1911, and was later incorporated in California in 1929. At present, the membership of the mutual aid association numbers 9,000 persons of both sexes. Each member pays dues of $1 per month for a $500 life insurance policy and for administrative costs as well as for the local chapter benefit fund. The Sociedad consists of sixty-eight such local chapters, called *logias* (lodges), throughout the state of California, varying in size from 15 to over 300 members.

The history of the founding of the Sociedad is traced to an incident that occurred in San Bernardino, California. In 1911, a group of Mexican community leaders walking to town came upon an unattended dead man on the street. The body, that of an unknown man of Mexican descent, had lain on the street for some time. These community leaders were well aware of the conditions of deprivation and disease that existed in many of the Mexican communities of the period. In order to protect this community from the possibility of a pauper's funeral, the group organized the Zaragoza Society.

Under the Zaragoza plan, members were required to contribute a dollar each upon the death of a member to provide for a decent funeral and burial. Benefits depended on these contributions by the active membership. Whenever more than one member died in the same month, severe hardship was created for the members, resulting in inadequate resources for the families of the deceased members. Thus, a small group within the membership decided that this deficiency might be relieved by a change in procedures. This resulted in a division within the Sociedad.

The more progressive group conceived of an insurance endowment plan which would provide low-cost insurance to the membership. The majority of the members rejected this new plan, causing its proponents to break away from the original organization in 1929 and form the SPM. It was incorporated on October 16 of that same year as a nonprofit, beneficial society. The Sociedad concerned itself with the welfare of the Mexican community, particularly in its first decade of existence. During the difficult 1930s, the organization joined with other mutual benefit societies in providing assistance to the needy.

The SPM's motto is "Education, Respect, and Patriotism" and is represented by a standard with a colorful eagle and the green, white, and red of the Mexican flag. The organization uses this emblem as well as a password and meeting ritual to provide instruction in the tradition of the Masonic fraternity societies that served as models for many of the organizations of the early Hispanic Southwest. Each meeting is opened with a pledge of allegiance to both the Mexican and American flags and a tribute to those on both sides of the border who have died for the democratic cause.

The SPM admits members between the ages of eighteen and fifty. From the one-dollar monthly fee, seventy cents are allocated to the central governing board, from which sixty cents go to the insurance surplus fund and ten cents to administration. The remaining thirty cents are assigned to the local chapter subsidiary benefit fund. The local chapters then provide additional protection for a minimal cost to the membership. A unique aspect of the SPM life insurance policy is that it also covers the beneficiary. In the case of death of the beneficiary, the policyholder actually receives a stipend of $400. Also, the family of a long-time active member could receive a sizable amount of assistance from statewide donations. And in terms of human benefits, the membership offers emotional support and consolation to the grieving members.

The organization holds monthly meetings. Chapter members vote directly for all officers. Each lodge elects a delegate to a representative body called the Congreso Ejecutivo Supremo (Supreme Executive Congress), which is the legislative arm of the entire Sociedad. From this body the executive committee is elected, which is administratively responsible for the Society. Following general parliamentary organizational form, this body consists of the offices of president, first vice-president, second vice-president, first secretary, treasurer, first treasurer, marshall, sergeant-at-arms, and standard bearer. In addition, an administrative subsection, the Supreme Commission of Funds, is elected from the delegates to the Supreme Executive Congress.

The Supreme Commission of Funds consists of three members elected by the general assembly. These "trustees" are entrusted with the most prestigious positions available to the membership. The Commission administers benefit payments, savings, and auditing and reporting procedures. These trustees have been conservative in the administration of the SPM's funds. They refuse to speculate, preferring to earn fixed interest rates on their deposits. Therefore, devoid of ambitious schemes and political promotions, the leadership of the SPM has represented the interests of its members with caution and modesty, and this has largely contributed to the stability and duration of the organization. Funds are distributed among a variety of banks and savings and loans. Local chapters likewise distribute their monies to various local banks and savings and loans.

While the Sociedad is basically a fraternal association which is conservative in its activities, it has become so as relations with Anglo American culture and society have changed. From its early inception, the SPM had been involved in a variety of community improvement and help projects during the depression periods in California. However, in the present most activities are confined to social and cultural activities for members, although the Sociedad does provide funds for worthy national and international causes. Its political activities are nonexistent in the present, although individual members have been politically active in union organizing, community improvement projects, and interest group politics. By far the most frequently associated "community" activity is the distribution of stipends to Mexican American students who wish to attend institutions of higher learning. While the SPM has operated for over half a century, its membership largely represents an older, working-class cohort that is beginning to decline. Largely, the Sociedad reflects the end of the life cycle of persons who were born in Mexico and immigrated to the United States shortly before or after the Mexican Revolution of 1910. Therefore, most of their activities are congruent with the last stage of life, in which fraternity, mutuality, and interdependence are stressed. Within the next ten years this society is likely to end as its membership dies out.

An in-depth study of this organization including interviews and questionnaire data collection is contained in Jose Amaro Hernandez, "The Political Development of Mutual Aid Societies in the Mexican American Community: Ideals and Principles" (Ph.D. dissertation, University of California at Riverside, 1979). The analysis presented in Amaro Hernandez's work is scholarly and comprehensive of the forces affecting the Mexican people of the period. Another source for this entry was the SPM-completed HAVO questionnaire. The Hernandez work, however, presents the SPM as a prototype for early mutual aid societies and thus forms the basis for his work.

SOCIEDAD ZARAGOZA (ZARAGOZA SOCIETY) See SOCIEDAD PROGRESISTA MEXICANA.

SOCIETY OF FRIENDS OF PUERTO RICO (SFPR) The Society is a statewide cultural organization founded in 1956 and based in New York. The organization promotes the history and culture of Puerto Rico in the United States. Its membership totals 260, with a president overseeing the activities of the SFPR. The organization meets on a weekly basis.

The Society publishes books and a quarterly newsletter. It also sponsors exhibits of folk art and crafts through its Center for Puerto Rican Cultural Relations.

Information on this group is contained in the *Directory of Spanish Speaking Community Organizations* (1970).

SOCIETY OF HISPANIC PROFESSIONAL ENGINEERS (SHPE) The Society was founded in Los Angeles, California, in 1974 by Rodrigo Garcia, George Esquer, Fernando Nuñez, Richard Carrisoza, Alex Nidaurrazaga, and Bill Nuñez, all registered engineers. These founders, employees of city and county government in Los Angeles, recognized the lack of promotional opportunities within Los Angeles city and county government and sought to remedy this situation. They also acknowledged an underrepresentation of Hispanics in the engineering field. Their new organization would dedicate itself to the advancement of Hispanic engineering professionals and students.

SHPE works for the education, employment, and economic and social welfare of Hispanic engineering professionals and students. The Society informs the general public of technical contributions and achievements of Hispanic engineers and scientists and promotes special hiring programs for Hispanics. Membership within the organization consists of several categories that seek to encourage a broad range of participation and support for SHPE activities and include regular, associate, student, and institutional membership. Regular membership is open to anyone who holds a bachelor of science degree in engineering or science with six or more years of related experience. Regular members receive job and promotional announcements and are eligible to serve as technical consultants. Regular membership dues are twenty dollars a year.

Associate membership is open to individuals who subscribe to and support goals and objectives of SHPE but who do not qualify for regular membership. Associates have access to information on programs and activities. Dues are ten dollars for associate members. Student membership is open to any student majoring in engineering or the physical sciences. Student members are eligible for scholarships and grants and receive job announcements and summer employment information. There are no membership dues for students.

Finally, there is a category of membership open to industry, universities, and other institutions. Membership of this type entitles the participating entity to discounts on SHPE newsletter advertisements, access to university student chapters directories, and access to engineers and other technical personnel information which comprise SHPE's professional network. Dues for this category of member are $250 per year.

All members receive notices of meetings, programs, and social events as well as the national newsletter. The organization has attracted mainly members of Mexican American descent. Economically, the membership is divided into 20 percent of high income, 50 percent of middle income, and 30 percent low income. The total membership is approximately 800.

The hierarchically structured organization is headed by an Executive Advisory Council, which is composed of executive members from various industries who advise, guide, and support SHPE. The Council includes a president, newsletter editor, foundation director, Washington, D.C., representative, treasurer, first vice-president, and second vice-president. There are also committees such as Social Ways and Means, Manpower, Publicity, Professor Student Chapter, Membership, Education, Nominations, and Student Activities, with corresponding committee heads.

Among the corporations which have provided members for the Executive Advisory Council are Adolph Coors Co., Aerospace Corporation, Ameron, Hughes Aircraft Co., Amex Systems Incorporated, Atlantic Richfield Co., Bechtel Power Corporation, and Jet Propulsion Laboratory.

SHPE established a nonprofit foundation to provide scholarships to deserving students seeking careers in engineering and science. These scholarship funds are made available through individual, institutional, and corporate grants. The SHPE Foundation assures the organization of accomplishing its goal of increasing the number of Hispanic students entering engineering or other science majors by providing financial assistance to this end. SHPE works with colleges and universities in advertising the scholarships and identifying worthy students. A five-member board of directors is responsible for policies and direction of the SHPE Foundation, with Rodrigo Garcia as director.

The references for this organization are many and diverse and available from the SHPE. They include the "Society of Hispanic Professional Engineers Committee Responsibilities Report"; a review of the organization in *La Luz* 7:9 (1979); a completed HAVO questionnaire; the SHPE national newsletter, vol. 4, no. 4 (1979); SHPE's 1979–80 organizational chart; an SHPE informational leaflet; SHPE's Foundation application for scholarship; and SHPE's "Installation and Scholarship Banquet Review" (1979).

SOCIETY OF SPANISH ENGINEERS, PLANNERS AND ARCHITECTS (SSEPA) The Society was founded in 1975 for Hispanic professionals in the physical sciences. SSEPA seeks to motivate Hispanic high school students to pursue careers in physics, engineering, architecture, and related occupations.

Hispanic businesspersons and professionals participate in SSEPA's program by addressing student groups and conducting career workshops for them. The organization is a membership-supported group, with dues of twenty-five dollars per year. SSEPA is a nonprofit corporation.

The reference source for this organization is *A Guide to Hispanic Organizations* (1979).

SOUTHWEST COUNCIL OF LA RAZA See NATIONAL COUNCIL OF LA RAZA.

SOUTHWEST VOTER REGISTRATION EDUCATION PROJECT (SVREP) In 1975 a group of Mexican American community persons met in San Antonio, Texas, to discuss means of increasing the role and participation of Mexican Americans in the American democratic political process. This concern stemmed, in part, from a report commissioned by the National Council of La Raza* (NCLR), the National Council of Churches, and the United Auto Workers that revealed a relatively low participation by Mexican Americans in the political process in the southwestern states. At the same time, the Mexican American population in the United States Southwest was rapidly increasing. There was a general consensus that increasing the number of Mexican Americans registered to vote in the Southwest would be a positive first step toward improving the situation, and SVREP was formed in San Antonio that year. A number of Hispanic organizations were represented at that initial meeting. The founding members of SVREP include its executive director, William C. Velasquez, SVREP chairperson Maclovio Barraza from the National Council of La Raza* (NCLR), labor leader Arnold Flore, and attorney Armando de Leon.

SVREP has identified three main areas of activity toward achieving its goal of increasing Mexican American participation in the political process. These include the registration of Mexican American voters in the Southwest, the distribution of voter education information to minority communities, and research to counter gerrymandering attempts against minorities.

The Project is a hierarchically structured organization headed by an executive committee composed of the board of directors and organization officers. This committee sets policy and develops SVREP projects. The executive director oversees the general implementation of board decisions by the other SVREP unity directors and their staffs.

The four departments of SVREP include a research unit, which collects and analyzes data on Hispanic electoral participation, voter registration, and voting patterns. Next is a field organizing unit, which coordinates community groups for registration drives. The third department is the communications office, which provides voter education materials and disseminates research findings. Last, the legal unit initiates court cases regarding gerrymandering. This unit works closely with the Mexican American Legal Defense and Education Fund* (MALDEF).

SVREP is active in the states of Texas, New Mexico, Arizona, California, Colorado, and Utah and has about 4,000 volunteer workers. This volunteer staff is approximately 80 percent Mexican American and 20 percent native American. More than 800 community organizations have participated with SVREP at the local level.

At the time of this writing, SVREP had conducted 350 voter registration education campaigns in 125 southwestern cities, resulting in the registration of 260,000 eligible voters, and was in the midst of numerous other voter education projects in other cities in preparation for the 1984 elections. In the state of Texas the legal unit was involved in litigation to enforce the preclearance provisions of the Voting Rights Act and lawsuits to ensure equal numbers of inhabitants within each district based on the one person, one vote principle. In a similar vein SVREP also plans, in conjunction with MALDEF,* to settle, negotiate, or sue 125 political jurisdictions. SVREP was involved with other Hispanic organizations in the 1980 census drive and carefully observed redistricting efforts.

SVREP operating funds are generated largely through contributions from such private foundations as Ford, New World, Human Development, and Robert F. Kennedy Memorial and from various labor unions. SVREP has an active media section which produces *Avances*, a five-minute radio commentary, in Spanish, on events of importance to Hispanic political participation. This broadcast is currently carried on two San Antonio radio stations, and there are plans for syndication throughout the Southwest. SVREP also produces bumper stickers, tapes, posters, and newsletters.

There are a number of detailed references for this organization prepared by and distributed by SVREP. The organization's research unit has conducted many valuable studies which illustrate very well the activities of SVREP.

Sources used for this work included the SVREP-completed HAVO questionnaire, a SVREP brochure on organizational goals, a SVREP history and projects summary, *Dallas Herald Times* (May 11, 1980), and *Rocky Mountain News* (October 1, 1979), a Denver newspaper.

SPANISH AMERICAN CULTURAL CLUB (SACC) Located in New Britain, Connecticut, the Club is concerned with preserving the Hispanic heritage of its members and encouraging Hispanic arts activities. It sponsors exhibits, trips, and other cultural affairs. It also maintains a library.

This is one of many social and cultural organizations located in Hispanic communities throughout the United States. There is little published information on these organizations, although they are vibrantly active in their respective communities. The source for this brief description of the SACC is contained in the archives of the Robert F. Kennedy Memorial in Washington, D.C.

SPANISH ASSOCIATION OF THE FINGER LAKES (SAFL) Located in Geneva, New York, the Association serves the Hispanic communities of Ontario, Wayne, Seneca, and Yates counties. It provides educational, employment, cultural, and other programs for its members and the other members of the community. It publishes a monthly newsletter, *Oye Mira* (Hey Look) and also makes use of bilingual radio.

A description of this organization is contained in the archives of the Robert F. Kennedy Memorial in Washington, D.C.

SPANISH CHAMBER OF COMMERCE OF QUEENS (SCCQ) The Chamber, located in Jackson Heights, New York, is a local business development organization established to aid minority firms and funded by the Office of Minority Business Enterprise. It provides management and technical assistance to new or existing minority firms and assists them with capital acquisition, accounting, and other business services.

It is possible that this organization is now extinct. Correspondence to their most recent address was returned stamped "not forwardable." The source of this brief description was the archives of the Robert F. Kennedy Memorial in Washington, D.C.

SPANISH FORESTERS (SF) Founded in 1900 in Santa Barbara, California, the Spanish Foresters were actually a chapter of the Foresters of America, a national and international mutual aid insurance association. The original Foresters' Santa Barbara chapter shunned Mexican membership; thus, native-born Mexicans formed their own chapter. Its official name was the Junipero Serra Court No. 147, more popularly known as the Spanish Foresters.

The Spanish Foresters, the name given to them by local newspapers, were comprised of Spanish-surnamed, working-class people and a few non-Spanish-surnamed individuals from intermarried families. The organization provided sickness and death benefits to its 100–150 members. The organization and its women's auxiliary also sponsored social activities such as dances, fiestas, and barbecues for the community.

Throughout the first third of the century, the Spanish Foresters remained an important organization in the Santa Barbara Mexican community, until internal disagreement caused its demise in the early 1920s.

Information for this entry came from Albert Camarillo, *Chicanos in a Changing Society* (1979). Primary sources for Camarillo's research include the *Morning Press* (June 5, 1900); and interviews with Alfredo Dominguez, Theodore Cota, and Yldefonso Osuna. A listing of offices for both chapters of the Foresters during the early twentieth century is contained in *Morning Press* (December 3 and 5, 1901, and January 15, 1902); and *Santa Barbara City Directory* (1920).

SPANISH SPEAKING CULTURAL CLUB (SSCC) This organization is representative of several founded to conserve Hispanic culture in the Twin Cities areas of Minnesota. Minneapolis and St. Paul boast of active Hispanic communities. The University of Minnesota has offered a curriculum in Mexican American studies for a number of years. Its faculty has included some important figures in the Hispanic academic world such as Rolando Hinajosa, Arturo Madrid, and the distinguished literary critic and feminist scholar Marcela Trujillo. So although fairly isolated from the areas of highest Hispanic concentration, Hispanics are readily visible and active in these two cities. The majority of this community are individuals who traveled to Minnesota by way of the migrant stream of agricultural workers. Many decided to stay and make the Twin Cities their home.

The SSCC responds to the needs of the Hispanic community in Minneapolis and St. Paul by providing a center where members of the community can get together. It also undertakes projects to assist Spanish-origin peoples. The organization was working on the production of a film on Mexican Americans in Minnesota.

The source for this brief sketch of the SSCC's activities was the archives of the Robert F. Kennedy Memorial in Washington, D.C.

T

TRI-STATE PUERTO RICAN CONGRESS (TSPRC) The Congress is a nonprofit corporation established in 1978 as an outgrowth of the Puerto Rican Congress of New Jersey* (PRCNJ). Its main goals are to combat institutional discrimination and to promote active programs against community deterioration and juvenile crime.

The TSPRC is a hierarchically structured organization. Among its leadership are the Reverend Alfonso A. Roman, Ramon Roman, and Fanny Bermudez. There is a president, vice-president, and secretary for the Congress. TSPRC has three offices, located in Trenton, New Jersey, Philadelphia, Pennsylvania, and Wilmington, Delaware. The organization held its first convention in the summer of 1979.

The Congress's activities are centered on the creation of educational and charitable projects to aid Hispanics in Pennsylvania, Delaware, and New Jersey. The organization obtains operational funding from state and federal governments.

Because this is a young organization, reference sources are scarce. Information on TSPRC is contained in *A Guide to Hispanic Organizations* (1979).

__ U

UNIÓN PATRIÓTICA BENÉFICA MEXICANA INDEPENDIENTE (INDEPENDENT MEXICAN PATRIOTIC AND CHARITY UNION) (UPBMI)

This organization was a popular mutual aid society founded circa 1913 with chapters throughout southern California. The UPBMI did not have restrictions on membership; however, the members were predominantly foreign-born.

The primary objective of the association was to protect the interests of the Mexican population. The UPBMI also carried sickness and death benefits for its members and aided impoverished Mexican families whether or not they were active members of the organization. The UPBMI was composed mainly of working-class Mexican people.

UPBMI sponsored a variety of social functions for the community. Monthly socials such as dances and barbecues and Cinco de Mayo celebrations were regularly organized by the group. It was common for chapters to cosponsor activities. Occasionally, the UPBMI organized fund-raisers, such as one held in 1926 for flood victims of Nayarit, Mexico.

The women members of the organization formed an auxiliary known as La Unión Femenil Mexicana, established about 1926. The Unión Femenil organized cultural and social events for Spanish-speaking audiences. The two components of this organization coordinated efforts, with the women's auxiliary providing supportive services.

An important reference on this organization is Albert Camarillo, *Chicanos in a Changing Society* (1979). Camarillo has done extensive research on Mexicans in early southern California, particularly around Santa Barbara. His sources include newspaper articles, personal interviews, and other primary resources.

UNITED COUNCIL OF SPANISH SPEAKING ORGANIZATIONS (UCSSO)

In 1966 the leaders of six Richmond, California, Mexican American associations met to discuss means of combatting the effects of social and economic discrimination facing Mexican Americans in Contra Costa County. They united their organizations to form the Council as a community services agency to help address the social service needs of the county's Mexican American population. Among the organization's founders were Larry Gonzales, UCSSO president, (1966–68) and executive director (1968–70), Bill Espinosa, Paul Hernandez, and Rudolfo Viramontes.

The goals of the United Council include the improvement of the position of Mexican Americans in U.S. social and economic institutions and the defense of the civil rights of Mexican Americans. Another important UCSSO purpose is the adequate provision of social services to Contra Costa County's Mexican American community.

Since its founding UCSSO has expanded to include seven regional chapters located in the Contra Costa towns of Richmond, Oakland, Pittsburg, Martinez, Brentwood, San Pablo, and Antioch. UCSSO is a hierarchically organized association headed by a board of directors. Six delegates from each region and eight officers elected in convention sit on the board. UCSSO is also served by an executive director, and under him are an associate director and a director of administrative services. Under their supervision are the staffs of the Education, Housing, Community Services, Manpower, Comprehensive Employment Training Act (CETA) VI, Transportation, and Nutrition service units. In all, there are thirty-two member organizations with individual memberships of 10 to 120 persons. Approximately 98 percent of the members are Mexican Americans, two-thirds of low income and the other third of middle income.

The organization began in 1966 operating one program with a $16,000 budget and 5 employees. By 1978 UCSSO was overseeing thirteen service programs with a budget of $1.9 million and 120 employees. The organization has served 20,000 persons since its founding and now sees over 4,500 clients annually.

UCSSO operates a number of social service programs in the areas of education, housing, transportation, and health care. In 1967 UCSSO began a transportation service for low-income persons from home to county hospitals and clinics. In 1971 UCSSO started a program to provide affordable modern housing to low-income renters. UCSSO bought the former Blue Goose Labor Camp and converted the seventeen standing units into modern three-bedroom homes. UCSSO arranged for the former tenants to become owners through Farmer Home Administration loans. In 1974 UCSSO opened a manpower service to train unemployed youths in marketable skills. The same year the organization started a nutrition program providing hot meals to senior citizens five days a week.

In 1977 UCSSO began its major involvements in the provision of educational services to the community. That year UCSSO started a local Headstart program to provide early learning skills to preschoolers. UCSSO's Talent Search program began in 1978, offering counseling to potential Mexican American college students and assistance with admissions procedures and grant applications. The same year UCSSO initiated a Comprehensive Employment Training Act (CETA) VI project, providing job experience and staff positions to unskilled workers.

In addition to these activities, UCSSO sponsors youth dances and holds annual service awards banquets. UCSSO funding sources include United Way, the U.S. Department of Health, Education, and Welfare, Contra Costa County, the state of California, and the city of Richmond. UCSSO publishes an annual organizational report and its constitution and bylaws. Both publications are available in English and Spanish. UCSSO utilizes Aztec symbols to represent its tasks.

The primary references used in this work were provided by UCSSO and included their completed HAVO questionnaire, the UCSSO constitution and bylaws, and UCSSO annual reports (1976 and 1978).

UNITED FARMWORKERS OF AMERICA (UFW) The United Farmworkers of America was formally established as such on January 19, 1979, with Cesar Chavez as its union president. Chavez, with Dolores Huerta and Gilberto Padilla, first organized farmworkers under the National Farm Workers Association in 1962. The NFWA provided farmworkers with social and legal services, a credit union, a supplies cooperative, a bilingual newspaper, and representation before agricultural employers.

The formation of the union culminated years of struggle by workers and their leadership. In 1962 Cesar Chavez left the directorship of the Community Service Organization* (CSO) to begin organizational efforts among California's farmworkers, the most exploited sector of the working class. Organizational objectives included unionization, wage increases, and the improvement of living and working conditions through nonviolent struggle. Cesar Chavez had been greatly influenced by the nonviolent political strategies of Gandhi in India.

Chavez was born in Yuma, Arizona, in 1927, after his family had fled Mexico during the Mexican Revolution. His parents were poor migrant workers who followed the crops from Arizona to California and worked Delano's grape harvest. He never received more than an eighth-grade education and, like many others, became a full-time farmworker at age fourteen. He and his father were involved in farmworker strike activity in the late 1930s and 1940s. After military service in the Navy, Chavez married Helen Fabela in 1949 and settled in San Jose, California, where they made a living as seasonal farmworkers.

It was in San Jose where Chavez met Father Thomas McDonnell, who introduced him to community organizer Fred Ross in 1952. Ross was an exponent of Saul Alinsky's Industrial Areas Foundation, which advocated the involvement of community people in solving their problems through self-organization. The Alinsky approach was a forerunner among Mexican Americans to the later Freire organizational methodology popularized in the liberation movements of the late 1960s and early 1970s, particularly in Latin America. However, where Freire saw everyone as a potential partner in the struggle; Alinsky warned of the enemy in everyone.

Chavez was initiated by Ross into voter registration campaigns and the organization of CSO chapters throughout the state. In 1960, Chavez was appointed director of the national CSO and worked closely with Dolores Huerta, Gilbert Padilla, and Tony Orendain, all former farmworkers. In 1962 Chavez became disenchanted with the organization and resigned. He, Huerta, and Padilla decided to concentrate their organizational experience on farmworkers.

Chavez built his union through grass-roots efforts. He moved his family to Delano, California, where his brother was head of the local CSO. He went from door to door enlisting farmworkers' support, while eschewing large monetary contributions. He stressed worker involvement, including relatively high union dues of $3.50 per month.

The organization's initial followers were Mexican Americans, although Filipinos, Anglos, and blacks also comprised part of the labor force. But Chavez recognized the importance of nationalism in solidifying an organization, thus, his concentration on Mexican field hands.

By the summer of 1964 the National Farm Workers Association (NFWA) had become self-supporting, with more than fifty local organizations. And in 1965 the NFWA had some 1,700 members. Civil rights activists fresh from their victories in the South rallied to the organizing efforts of Chavez and the NFWA. Protestant groups, some Catholic priests, students, and Anglo American labor, after years of neglect, championed the union's cause. Although more a social movement than a labor union, symbolized by a red flag with a thunderbird and a banner of the Virgin of Guadalupe, the NFWA waged two small strikes in the summer of 1965 which brought higher wages and the rehiring of discharged workers.

On September 8, 1965, the Filipinos in the Agricultural Workers Organizing Committee (AWOC) struck the grape growers of the Delano area. The U.S. Labor Department had decreed, as the result of an earlier victory, that braceros would be paid $1.40 an hour. Domestic workers had been receiving twenty–thirty cents less an hour. Mexican workers joined the Filipinos in a walkout, and ten days later they received a guarantee of equivalent pay with braceros.

More important activity followed with the repeal of Public Law 78, ending the Bracero Program. The U.S. Department of Labor continued the program under another name, and this resulted in even greater discontent among Filipino farmworkers, led by Larry Itliong of the Agricultural Workers Organizing Committee (AWOC) of the American Federation of Labor–Congress of Industrial Organizations (AFL-CIO). Filipino workers receiving twenty cents less than the government established $1.40 hourly wage of the braceros walked out of the Delano grape fields. The NFWA soon joined the strike. In spite of hostile local law enforcement and grower appeals to the courts, the NFWA expanded the strike in December of 1965 to a consumer boycott.

By the spring of 1966, the NFWA had enlisted the support of national organizations and personalities. The United Auto Workers (UAW) union pledged $5,000 a month contribution, and Senator Robert Kennedy had become a loyal supporter. Boycott supporters were urged not to buy Schenley products or DiGiorgio grapes. Toward the end of the Lenten season, Chavez led strikers and supporters on a 230-mile pilgrimage to Sacramento to plea for farmworker collective bargaining rights from Governor Edmund Brown, Sr. The Teamsters refused to cross picket lines in San Francisco, and rumors of a bartenders' boycott forced seventy-five-year-old Schenley president, Lewis Solon Rosenstiel, into a settlement. Schenley signed an unprecedented contract calling for a wage of $1.75 an hour, a union hiring hall, and fringe benefits. Soon afterward, Gallo, Christian Brothers, Paul Masson, Almaden, Franzia Brothers, and Novitiate signed contracts.

The DiGiorgio Corporation was the next opponent. It was one of the largest grape growers of the central San Joaquin Valley. In April 1966 Robert DiGiorgio, its new president, announced that he would allow his workers at Sierra Vista to vote on a union. But he urged its workers to join the International Brotherhood of Teamsters (IBT), which had organized truck drivers, cannery, and packinghouse workers.

In August, Chavez's union merged with Itliong's AWOC to form the United Farmworker's Organizing Committee (UFWOC), and on the thirtieth of that same month won the election at DiGiorgio, but only after an investigation by the governor into a previously held fraudulent election. The election campaign was a bitter one, with the UFWOC redbaited by the Teamsters and the UFWOC retaliating with the distribution of excerpts from *The Enemy Within* (1960), in which Robert Kennedy scathingly indicts Jimmy Hoffa and the Teamsters.

After this victory, other growers were targeted. The first of these in 1967 was the Guimarra Vineyards Corporation, the largest producer of table grapes in the United States. Because Guimarra used other companies' labels to circumvent the boycott, it became necessary for the union to extend its boycott to all California table grapes. The boycott spread to Europe and Canada, forcing the U.S. Defense Department to take up the slack of decreasing grape sales by purchasing grapes for the troops in Vietnam. This enraged many boycott supporters, who protested the Defense Department's interference with the boycott at taxpayers' expense. In June 1970, after a costly five-year battle, the majority of growers agreed to sign three-year contracts with the union.

The UFWOC, now called the United Farmworkers, AFL-CIO (UFW), then moved into the California lettuce and strawberry fields and into the citrus groves of Florida. In that same year, 1972, the UFW claimed 55,000 members and over 200 contracts. Farmworkers now had toilets in the field, rest periods, ice water, health benefits, and a pension fund. In addition, the UFW created service centers charged with administering the Robert Kennedy Memorial health program, making work referrals, providing legal services, training union stewards, and engaging in community development work.

Battles with the Teamsters continued to plague the UFW. Although the two unions signed a "no raiding" agreement in 1967 and in 1970, the Teamsters refused to pull back, and growers refused to disqualify Teamster contracts.

Chavez refused help from professional AFL administrators, and according to one *Fresno Bee* reporter, Ron Taylor, Chavez was poor at delegating authority. The problem, though, was that the farmworkers had little experience in self-governance and Chavez patiently took the time to help them into the unfamiliar territory of self-empowerment. This was done through "ranch committees." But growers were impatient with this experiment in real democracy.

During 1971 and into 1972 the UFW built on its gains, coordinating its administration of contracts and its boycott activities. In addition, the Chavez union was used as a major catalyst for Mexican American movement activities nationwide. Within this climate of an expanded Mexican American movement, Richard Nixon ascended to the presidency and lent strong support to the efforts of the Teamsters and the growers to crush the UFW. Nixon opposed the grape boycott and sponsored a farm bill, Proposition 22, that outlawed secondary boycotts for farmworkers. This was a clear attempt to bust the union. Professional petition gatherers were hired to put Proposition 22 on the ballot. The UFW uncovered fraud in the collection of petition signatures, and then secretary of state, Edmund Jerry Brown, Jr., filed suit to take the proposition off the ballot. A grand jury investigated and indicted sponsors of the measure. On November 7, 1972, the UFW and the voters of California won.

In the meantime, Frank Fitzsimmons, IBT president, had warned the UFW to stay away from the lettuce fields. He urged an alliance between Teamsters and agribusiness along with a renegotiation of the lettuce contracts. The UFW rejected Fitzsimmons's threats, and when the first of the UFW grape contracts came up for renewal in the spring of 1973, growers abandoned the UFW and signed with the Teamsters.

The Nixon, Teamsters, and growers war against the UFW expanded with the president's reelection campaign. Teamster President Fitzsimmons was scheduled as principal speaker at the American Farm Bureau Federation Los Angeles convention on December 17, 1972, arranged by Nixon special counsel Charles Colson. Teamsters' anti-UFW tactics were unleashed with aggressive fury against UFW pickets, causing 2 deaths and more than 300 injuries, 60 by gunshot wounds; and more than 3,000 UFW pickets were jailed by hostile law officers. AFL-CIO President Meany advanced to Chavez a $1.6 million strike fund from the AFL-CIO, and additional help came from the United Auto Workers (UAW). Meany was disturbed by Chavez's unconventional behavior, while steadfastly opposing the Teamster's heavy-handed tactics. When the strike fund was exhausted at the end of 1973, the UFW had only twelve contracts and a membership of below 5,000.

After several agreements worked out between Meany and Fitzsimmons, from which Fitzsimmons consistently retreated, the tarnished image of the Teamsters forced another seemingly more permanent agreement between the two unions. However, Charles Colson, once again on behalf of Nixon, intervened and pressured the Teamsters to cancel the agreement. It looked like the UFW had finally been defeated. A corrupt contract labor system returned to the fields with union control wrestled from the farmworkers. Membership meetings and elections were unheard of in the Teamster Farmworkers Union. Teamsters negotiated an hourly wage just ten cents below that of the UFW, with a medical plan and pensions, but most benefits went to permanent workers. Growers preferred Teamster contracts, which preserved growers' control over the work force. Also, Teamsters did not object to the use of pesticides the way the UFW had. The UFW union had become a significant instrument of community change among farmworkers and the minority communities from which they came. Growers bitterly feared and resented this.

In 1975 Senator John Tunney introduced a bill to delete the words that excluded farmworkers from the original 1935 Wagner Act. Chavez continued to maintain that the National Labor Relations Act (NLRA) was ineffective. He called for a law that would be based on 1975 realities. The changing political climate in California gave Chavez that law. Edmund Jerry Brown, Jr., had been elected governor. The California legislature, in an emergency session called by the governor, passed a law in May providing for balloting within seven days after workers on a farm petitioned for union representation. A newly created Agricultural Labor Relations Board (ALRB) would supervise elections, to be held only during the season of high employment. Secondary boycotts of distributors and retailers were prohibited, although the union duly certified as winning the election could appeal to consumers to boycott certain products. Enforcement of the act began on August 28, 1975. The UFW won 17 farms within the first month. The Teamsters won 11. By November 1975, the UFW had won 167 elections, representing 24,334 workers, compared to 95 elections for the Teamsters, covering 11,802 workers.

In January 1976, electoral violations were so flagrant that the ALRB was overworked and running out of money. A bill for $3.8 million in emergency appropriations was defeated. There were widespread grower-inspired burglaries of UFW offices, which went unpublicized in the press. This gave impetus to Chavez to initiate a drive for Proposition 14, which would take the enforcement of the ALRB out of the hands of the legislators and ensure consistent application of the law. The California Farm Bureau poured millions into defeating the proposition, calling it anti-private property.

The legislature, in the meantime, funded the ALRB, while warning that passage of Proposition 14 would seriously limit their legislative powers. The proposition was overwhelmingly defeated by the voters of California. After its defeat, growers acquired more influence over the ALRB. By April 1977, however, wages had been standardized, and farmworkers in California earned $3.53 an hour with fringe benefits.

Chavez called off the boycotts of grapes and lettuce in February 1978. He concentrated his efforts from then on to winning elections and extending his union into Texas and Florida. The UFW maintains its national headquarters in Keene, California. Officers of the union include a director, secretary, and treasurer. It last reported over 20,000 members.

In 1983 and 1984 Chavez was widely criticized for his political maneuverings. He opposed visibly the election of California State Senator Art Torres and Assemblywoman Gloria Molina. He threatened publicly to mobilize his whole union machine against their candidacies. It was reported in statewide newspapers that the UFW had contributed more to political coffers than any other organization in the state of California. And these are only short summaries of the machinations the UFW has been involved in the political arena. Their most notable political battle was the attempt to seat Howard Berman as speaker of the California Assembly, from which Willie Brown emerged a compromise winner.

Several books have been written specifically on the union and Cesar Chavez. More recent publications arising from the Mexican American political movement are most useful, especially Rodolfo Acuña's *Occupied America* (1981); *Con Safos* 2:5 (1970); *Agenda* (Summer 1973); *Nuestro Magazine* (September 1979); and Armando Rendon, *Chicano Manifesto* (1971).

The union issues a publication biweekly, which provides immediate reference on its activities, called *El Malcriado* (The Rude One). Other books include Peter Mathiessen, *Sal si Puedes* (1969); Gregory Dunne, *Delano* (1967); and Ronald B. Taylor, *Chavez and the Farm Workers* (1975).

A detailed analysis of the UFW's legal and legislative battles is contained in Salvador E. Alvarez, ''The Legal and Legislative Struggle of the Farmworkers: 1965–1972,'' *El Grito* 6:2 (1972). Also, there has been extensive coverage during the entire period outlined in this UFW entry in the *Los Angeles Times* and other newspapers such as the *Arizona Republic* and the *San Francisco Chronicle*.

UNITED MEXICAN AMERICAN STUDENTS ASSOCIATION See MOVIMIENTO ESTUDIANTIL CHICANO DE AZTLAN.

UNITED NEIGHBORHOODS ORGANIZATION (UNO) This organization was founded in East Los Angeles in 1975 as a nonprofit community activist association. Residents of the East Los Angeles neighborhoods faced continuing problems in education, health, and housing, inadequate infrastructure, and discriminatory practices by insurance companies. In 1975, under the leadership of Bishop Juan Arzube and Father Pedro Villarroya (pastor of Our Lady of Talps Church), the pastors of twenty-two Catholic parishes and ten Protestant churches came together as the Interreligious Sponsoring Council to form UNO to address community problems.

Initial funding was provided by the participating churches, and a professional organizer, Saul Alinsky, was hired. UNO was modeled after San Antonio, Texas's Community Organized for Public Service* (COPS), which Alinsky also helped to establish. The primary goal of UNO is to bring neighborhood residents together in seeking solutions to community problems.

UNO is a hierarchically structured organization. Thirty-two units (or neighborhoods) comprise the federation of UNO. Each unit is headed by a five- or six-member leadership team, which meets regularly to discuss the needs of its particular neighborhood. Each unit is allotted five votes in the election of UNO officers and in policy decision making. UNO has a membership of over 5,000 individuals. The majority of the members are retired, homeowning, and church-going persons.

UNO was neither as well disciplined nor as political as COPS. Whereas in San Antonio the archdiocese gave COPS much support, in Los Angeles Cardinal Timothy Manning maintained tight control over his Hispanic clergy. But on October 7, 1979, UNO held its first annual convention, in which between 4,000 and 5,000 participated. Issues of education, housing, financial reinvestment in the East Los Angeles community, and Immigration and Naturalization Service raids on the undocumented Mexican community were discussed.

When UNO takes on an issue of community concern, the topic is first thoroughly researched and only then are public officials confronted by UNO representatives. UNO engages in a number of activities which reflect its purposes. UNO's community activism has resulted in lowered insurance rates for certain sectors of the East Los Angeles community. Before this decrease, residents paid insurance rates comparable with those of Beverly Hills. Presently, approximately 38 percent of East Los Angeles's residents save between $200 and $1,400 due to the change in insurance rates. UNO is also responsible for improved safety traffic measures and street improvements in East Los Angeles. The organization has, in addition, developed a seven-year plan for the housing renovation of 10,000 community units. UNO sought government funding for this project when it became public that Boyle Heights, the largest of the neighborhoods in East Los Angeles, had not yet received federal housing grants.

The organization's concern for the Spanish-speaking and the undocumented has resulted in the provision of Spanish-speaking operators in the Sheriff's Department and in continued health care for undocumented Mexicans. UNO also registered some 7,000 voters in East Los Angeles in 1980.

For its first two years of operation, organizational expenses were subsidized by the members of the Interreligious Sponsoring Council. Since 1977 UNO has sustained itself with membership dues. Each unit is responsible for raising funds for project costs.

Historical references to UNO can be found in such sources as Rodolfo Acuña, *Occupied America* (1981); Jose Amaro Hernandez, "The Political Development of Mutual Aid Societies in the Mexican American Community: Ideals and Principles" (Ph.D. dissertation, University of California at Riverside, 1979); *El Toro del Pueblo* 1:2 (April 1980); *Somos* 1:1 (April–May 1978); and *Directory of Community Services Organizations in Los Angeles* (1979), a publication of the University of California Institute of Industrial Relations.

UNITED STATES HISPANIC CHAMBER OF COMMERCE (USHCC)
The Hispanic Chamber of Commerce was founded in 1979 for the purpose of coordinating all state and local Hispanic chambers of commerce into a national organization. It also purports to provide resources for member business persons.

Originally located in Dallas, Texas, the USHCC's principal office is now in Kansas City, Missouri. Membership fees are $100 annually.

The Hispanic Chamber grew in 1981 from five member states to twenty. Its second annual convention and trade fair, also held in Kansas City, drew 1,000 participants and key White House officials. Members of the Chamber were invited to Mexico by President Jose Lopez Portillo for discussions with top government and commerce leaders and sought to develop international opportunities for Hispanic American commerce leaders. With the assistance of this organization, the governor of the Mexican state of Jalisco opened a trade office in Chicago in 1981.

A description of this organization is included in two primary sources. However, there is conflicting information in each, and the organization failed to respond to three mailings of the HAVO questionnaire. The most important discrepancy noted from each source is the location of the principal office. One source indicates Dallas, Texas, while the other indicates Kansas City. Perhaps the founding office was in Dallas and later it moved to Kansas City. The sources used were *A Guide to Hispanic Organizations* (1979) and *Nuestro Magazine* (March 1982).

V

VESTA CLUB, INC. (VC) The Vesta Club was formed on October 15, 1953, in Phoenix, Arizona, at a dinner attended by local Mexican American residents concerned with the improvement of the Spanish-speaking community. The founding members were graduates of Arizona State University, the University of Arizona, and Northern Arizona University and were predominately businesspersons, professionals, and civic leaders. Among Vesta's past presidents are Dr. Eugene A. Marin, director of financial aid at Arizona State University; Tony Vicente, auditor of the city of Phoenix; Dr. Ray Pisano, optometrist and vice-mayor of Phoenix; Bennie Gonzalez, architect; Ben Picone, employment manager with AiResearch; and Ralph A. Cordova, certified public accountant.

The major aims of Vesta Club are to increase understanding between Mexican Americans and others and to raise the moral, social, and cultural standards of Mexican Americans. Further, Vesta Club seeks to assist community youths in attaining the highest possible education. In these stated goals, the Vesta Club resembles earlier Hispanic associations.

Vesta Club is a hierarchically structured organization. It is governed by a nine-member board of directors composed of Vesta officers and one member at large. The board oversees the execution of its decisions by ten standing committees: scholarship, nominations, elections, public relations, program, audit, Fiesta de Amigos, membership, debutante ball, and planning and development. Vesta Club membership is restricted to persons who are college or university graduates and who are employed in business or in the professions. The organization has a membership of 599, most of whom are Mexican American, although there is a sizable minority of Anglos. In 1974, a Vesta Club branch was established in Yuma, Arizona.

Vesta Club's major program involves the awarding of scholarships to outstanding Spanish-speaking graduates of Arizona high schools. This activity reflects its motto, "Progress Through Education." In 1954 Vesta Club awarded one scholarship in the amount of $800. By 1974 Vesta Club had received a $40,000 Federal Scholarship Grant from the Office of Economic Opportunity to be matched by private funds and to be awarded to needy students. Vesta Club operates a scholarship bank with twenty institutional and business corporation members. Members of this bank include American Express, Glendale Community College, First Federal Savings and Loan, League of United Latin American Citizens* (LULAC) No. 361, and the Tucson League of Mexican American Women. In 1974 Vesta Club awarded scholarships to 120 students, with awards ranging from $35 to $1,200.

Vesta Club also engages in a number of other social and cultural activities. Each year the club hosts one or two banquets called Fiesta de Amigos (Party of Friends). Featured guests have included Miss America, Vonda Kay Van Dyke, and the Ballet de Mexico of Mexico City. Vesta Club annually conducts a debutante ball, or Quinceanera (Coming Out Party) in spring. Too, Vesta Club presents plays in Spanish and sponsors a lecture series. Vesta Club also arranges bus excursions for members to Guaymas, Navajoa, Ciudad Juarez, and other locales in Mexico for recreation and cultural enhancement. Blocks of tickets are purchased by the Club for its members to sporting events such as Arizona State University vs. University of Arizona football games.

The organization obtains operating expenses from several sources, including donations from business and industry, contributions from foundations, wills, and bequests, and fund-raising activities. The name "Vesta" was adopted from the Roman goddess of hearth and fire.

References to the activities of this organization were provided by the organization and included the Vesta Club twenty-fifth anniversary booklet and the Vesta Club scholarship bank brochure (n.d.)

VIKKI CARR SCHOLARSHIP FOUNDATION (VCSF) In the 1960s a young Mexican American vocal artist conquered the popular music world with her powerful but sensitive renditions of hit music. Vikki Carr experienced the usual difficulties for those attempting to break into the mainstream pop music world. She sang in local clubs and the Las Vegas circuit, always encouraged to success by her ever-present parents. Vikki Carr never forgot her roots, and in 1970 she founded the Scholarship Fund in Los Angeles, California, in recognition of the economic obstacles confronting many Mexican American youths who attend or plan to attend college. Further impetus for the establishment of this Fund came from a survey by the College Entrance Examinations Board, "Access to Colleges for Mexican Americans in the Southwest," which revealed that there were relatively low numbers of Mexican Americans in American colleges and that financial aid funds available were inadequate.

The goals of the VCSF are to help increase the number of Mexican Americans in higher educational institutions and to give public recognition to Mexican American academic achievers. The main foundation effort in pursuing these goals is the provision of financial assistance to eligible college students from low-income families. The Foundation is run by a board of directors and two administrative assistants. The board's main tasks center around the process of selecting scholarship awardees, reviewing applications, and interviewing finalists. The board consists of chairperson Vikki Carr, professional entertainer; VCSF President Bil Avila; Dr. Manuel Guerra, educator; Dr. Julian Nava, educator; Dr. Armando Morales, psychologist; and two student scholarship awardees. Assisting with Foundation matters are the VCSF general manager and administrator and the VCSF accountant.

The first VCSF scholarships were awarded in 1970. Since that time, more than 100 undergraduate scholarships have been distributed, ranging in value from $250 to $1,500. In addition, VCSF has awarded three Cardona Fellowships to graduates, an award named for Carr's father. In the first seven years of operation the Fund has expended more than $100,000.

VCSF requires that recipients of undergraduate awards be California residents and between the ages of seventeen and twenty-two. Criteria used in screening applicants include financial need, motivation, educational and career goals, scholastic achievement, and community involvement. Each year the board reviews more than 1,000 applications. Of the original seventy-seven awardees (forty-one male, thirty-six female), four are now working in the field of law, four in social work, four in education, three in health, two in agriculture, one in medicine, one in psychology, one in finance, and one in entertainment.

Foundation funds are derived from several sources. The bulk of the money is raised by Vikki Carr in benefit performances and lectures, through her 1971 milk commercials, and from the proceeds from the sales of her souvenir books at concerts. Additional contributions come from her fan club and from business corporations such as ARCO and Carnation.

The primary reference for this organization was their completed HAVO questionnaire and a foundation history and background bulletin printed by the VCSF (n.d.).

VIVA KENNEDY CAMPAIGN CLUBS See POLITICAL ASSOCIATION OF SPANISH SPEAKING ORGANIZATIONS.

W

WESTERN REGIONAL PUERTO RICAN COUNCIL (WRPRC) This organization, also known as Concilio Regional de Organizaciones Puertoriqueños del Oeste, the Spanish name for the same, is a nonprofit corporation founded in San Jose, California, by Jorge Piniero and other concerned Puerto Ricans. The primary goal of the organization is to identify and define the socio-economic needs of the Puerto Rican community. Once these needs are identified, the Council advocates before private and government institutions on behalf of the community and provides services and activities to help meet those needs. The WRPRC is a hierarchically structured organization headed by a board of directors, which sets organizational goals and policy.

Information on this organization is available in the *California Directory of Agencies and Organizations Serving Latino, Asian, and Pacific Island Communities* (1977), compiled by the office of State Senator Alex P. Garcia. An interview was conducted with Jorge Piniero for purposes of this work, but neither information nor formal organizing documents were readily made available on the activities of the WRPRC.

YOUNG LORDS ORGANIZATION (YLO) An organization of Puerto Rican streetwise activists, the Young Lords was formed in Chicago in the late 1960s. The Lords emerged from the neighborhoods where they were raised, borrowing some impetus from the Black Panthers but essentially evolving their own style. Originally a street gang, the Lords, under the leadership of Jose (Cha Cha) Jimenez, shifted emphasis to political issues and organizational alliances. After their political conversion, the YLO targeted Chicago's political machines and governmental agencies as enemies of the community. They used political weapons such as strikes, boycotts, and sit-ins to push their cause.

In the fall of 1968 the YLO took over the Armitage Street Methodist Church, renamed it the People's Church, made it their headquarters, and began a day care program. In the spring of 1969, the YLO led hundreds of Puerto Ricans to an empty lot desigated to be a $1,000-membership private tennis courts and transformed that into a children's park.

The YLO was a national organization until 1970, when it split with the New York branch. After that, the YLO focused on Chicago politicians and their fight against an urban renewal plan that proposed West Lincoln Park as an inner city suburb for middle-income whites. YLO activity can best be described under the heading of general community welfare. Their projects in Chicago resulted in improved children's parks, free health clinics, and better housing.

The sincerity of these young people, a quality that arose from daily confrontations with the harsh realities of life in poor urban neighborhoods, deserves much admiration and credit. Although streetwise and tough, they were possessed of the nobility of purpose of the early altruistic, southwestern Hispanic organizations. The later politically ambitious organizations of the 1970s left these young people disillusioned and indifferent.

An excellent reference for this organization is Michael Abramson, *Palante!*

Young Lords Party (1971). Also some information on the YLO can be found in Clifford A. Hauberg, *Puerto Rico and the Puerto Ricans* (1974).

YOUNG LORDS PARTY (YLP) This organization was formed as the result of a June 1970 political split within the Young Lords Organization* (YLO). The New York Young Lords became the Young Lords Party. Although the YLP espoused goals similar to those of the YLO and focused on the immediate needs of the Puerto Rican community such as housing, education, and health care, a difference of opinion surfaced as to organizational tactics and priorities, and this resulted in a schism.

The New York chapter evolved out of a political organization called the Sociedad Albizu Campos, most of whose members had either graduated from or dropped out of college in or around New York. Members of the New York chapter were more sophisticated politically and better educated than their Chicago counterparts, and this led to a more theoretical approach to organizing goals and purposes and, perhaps, to a less altruistic, less innocent approach.

The YLP, like the YLO, nevertheless concentrated on community action. In July 1969 they constructed a garbage barricade of El Barrio (Spanish Harlem), to protest their inability to obtain brooms from the Sanitation Department to clean East 110th Street. And on December 29, 1969, in order to initiate a free breakfast for children campaign, they staged an eleven-day occupation of the First Methodist Church on Lexington Avenue. They also renamed the building the People's Church and succeeded in establishing a communal enclave offering free breakfasts, free clothing and health services, a day care center, a liberation school, community dinners, films, and ideological celebrations.

Young Lords Party membership was comprised mainly of children of poor migrants, raised in urban ghettos, and with English as their first language. Their official thirteen-point program and platform as published in their newspaper, *Palante*, outlines their basic goals. The YLP platform called for self-determination and liberation, not only for Puerto Ricans but for all Latinos and Third World people.

The Young Lords were not strictly a Puerto Rican party but a socialist movement that arose from within the poor Puerto Rican working class on the mainland. The thrust of most protest groups in Puerto Rico is nationalistic and strongly defensive of traditional Puerto Rican culture. The YLP was more ideological than nationalistic, but the organization did call for education in the Spanish and Creole language and culture.

Reference sources for this organization include Michael Abramson, *Palante! Young Lords Party* (1971); and Clifford A. Hauberg, *Puerto Rico and the Puerto Ricans* (1974).

Listing of Identified Hispanic Organizations Sent HAVO Questionnaires

This appendix contains a list of Hispanic organizations identified for purposes of this work. Each of these organizations was sent a HAVO mail questionnaire and a request for further information such as organizational bylaws and constitution. Each association that failed to respond to the first mailing was sent a second, and finally third mailing. The organizations are listed by state. Organizations included in the text are marked with an asterisk.

ARIZONA

Arizona Mexican American Chamber of Commerce*
Chicano Alliance Drug Abuse Programs
Chicanos por la Causa, Inc.*
Guadalupe Organization, Inc.
National Chicano Institute
Mexican American Liberation Committee
Mexican American Student Organization
Southwest Council of La Raza*
Valle del Sol, Inc.
Xicanindio Coalition

CALIFORNIA

American Association of Spanish-Speaking Certified Public Accountants*
Asociación Nacional de Grupos Folkloricos*
Asociación Nacional pro Personas Mayores*
Association of Latin American Women
Association of Mexican American Educators*
Association of Puerto Rican Professionals
Barrio Assistance
Bishop's Committee for the Spanish Speaking Peoples*
Busy Bees

CAFE de California, Inc.*
California Coalition of Hispanic Organizations*
California Democratic Chicano/Hispanic Caucus
California Rural Legal Assistance, Inc.
Campesinos Unidos, Inc.
Carnales Unidos Reformando Adictos, Inc.
Casa Raza
Causa, La
Centro Chileño Lautaro*
Centro Cultural de Costariqueñas
Centro Cultural de la Gente
Chicana Coalition*
Chicana Nurses Association
Chicana Service Action Center, Inc.*
Chicanas
Chicano Athletic Association
Chicano Coalition
Chicano Coalition of Workers
Chicano Correctional Workers Association
Chicano Federation
Chicano Press Association
Chicanos Club
Chicano Social Scientists' Association
Circulo Para Chiapas
Clinica de la Raza
Club Acaponetense
Club Civico Social Puertoriqueño
Club Guadalajara
Club Panama
Club Puertoriqueño de San Francisco, Inc.
Club Social y Cultural Mexicano
Coalición de Boricuas, Inc.*
Comision Femenil Mexicana Nacional, Inc.*
Compañeros del Barrio, Inc.
Concilio de Fresno, Inc.
Concilio de Mujeres
Concilio de Orange County
Concilio de Organizaciones Puertoriqueñas
Concilio de Sacramento
Concilio Mexicano de Chico
Confederación de Uniones de Campesinos y Obreros Mexicanos del Estado de California*
Council of Chicano Organizations
Council of Mexican American Affairs
Council for the Spanish Speaking of Stockton
Cuban Chamber of Commerce of Los Angeles
Damas de la Caridad
East Bay Spanish Speaking Citizens Foundation
East Los Angeles Community Union*

EMPLEO ~~por unidad~~

Federal Employees of Latin American Descent
Hermanas*
Hispanic American Coalition for Economic Revitalization
Hispanic American Democrats
Hispanic Postal Employees and Friends*
Institute of Puerto Rican Unity, Inc.*
Jobs in Action for Latin Americans
Latin American Club, Inc.
Latin American Club of Union City
Latin American Professional Women's Association
Latin American Teachers' Association
Latin Businessmen's Association
Latino Peace Officers Association
Latinos Unidos de Newark Association
Los Angeles County Chicano Employees Association
Luna
Mexican American Business and Professional Men's Scholarship Association
Mexican American Community Programs Foundation
Mexican American Community Services Agency*
Mexican American Concilio of Yolo County
Mexican American Correctional Association
Mexican American Council on Alcoholism
Mexican American Documentation and Educational Research Institute
Mexican American Educational Association
Mexican American Engineering Society*
Mexican American Golf Association of California
Mexican American Grocer's Association
Mexican American Industrial Opportunity Council
Mexican American Legal Defense and Education Fund*
Mexican American Manpower Agency
Mexican American Opportunities Center
Mexican American Opportunity Foundation
Mexican American Political Association*
Mexican American Service Center
Mission Language and Vocational School, Inc.
Mexican Manpower Development Association
Movimiento Estudiantil Chicano de Aztlan*
Mujeres en Cambio
National Association for the Betterment of Mexican Americans
National Chicana Foundation
National Chicana Welfare Rights Organization
National Chicano Council on Higher Education*
National Concilio of America
National Hispanic Chamber of Commerce*
National Hispanic Institute of Public Policy*
National Hispanic Scholarship Fund
National Institute of Spanish Speaking Women

National Mexican American Hispanic Chamber of Commerce
National Spanish Speaking Coalition on Domestic Affairs
National Spanish Speaking Commission on Alcoholism
Orden Fraternal Hijos de Puerto Rico*
Organization for the Legal Advancement of Raza
Unidad Puertoriqueña Inc.
Personnel Management Association of Aztlan*
Public Service Satellite Consortium
Puerto Rican Civic Association
Puerto Rican Resource Center
Raza en Acción Local
Raza Centro Legal
Raza Health Alliance
Raza National Bar Association*
Raza National Law Students Clearing House
Raza National Lawyers Association
Raza Olympia
Raza for the Prevention of Child Abuse and Neglect
Raza Tennis Association
Reforma National Spanish Speaking Librarians*
Ruiz Productions, Inc.
Sacramento Concilio, Inc.
San Francisco Puerto Rican Social Club
Society of Hispanic Professional Engineers*
Spanish Speaking Unity Council
Teatro de la Esperanza
Union de Trabajadores del Valle Imperial
United Council of Spanish Speaking Organizations of Contra Costa County
United Farmworkers of America*
United Latins for Justice
Venceremos
Vikki Carr Scholarship Foundation*
Western Regional Puerto Rican Council*
West Los Angeles Community Service Organization

COLORADO

Alianza Hispano Americana
Cameo Club
Chicano OXME
Chicanos Unidos for Action
Comisión Honorífica de Nortre América
Congress of Hispanic Educators
Fondo San Isidro
Latin Chamber of Commerce*
Mexican American Service Agency
Mujeres de LULAC
National Association for Chicano Studies*

National Association of Psychologists for La Raza*
Northwest Centro de Amistad
Our Lady of Guadalupe Society
Padrinos
Pueblo Action, Inc.
Pueblo Congress of Hispano Educators
Southern Colorado Charro Association
Zaragoza Hall

CONNECTICUT

Casa de Puerto Rico*
Connecticut Hispanic Artists and Cultural Organizations
Institute for the Hispanic Family
Junta for Progressive Action
Puerto Rican Business Association
Sociedad Portoriqueña de New Britain
Spanish American Center
Spanish American Coalition of Connecticut
Spanish American Cultural Club

FLORIDA

Acción Community Service Center
Asociación los Viejos Útiles*
Camara de Comercio Latina de los Estados Unidos*
Centro Hispano Catolico
Clinica Borinquen
Colegio Nacional de Abogados de Cuba en Exilio
College of Architects of Cuba in Exile Association*
Commission on the Spanish Speaking Populace of Florida
Community Habilitation Center
Confederación de Profesionales Cubanos
Crusada Spanish Publications
Cuban American Service Agency
Cuban Confederation in Exile
Cuban Dental Association in Exile*
Cuban Medical Association in Exile*
Cuban Municipalities in Exile
Cuban National Planning Council*
Cuban Nurses Association in Exile
Cuban Refugee Assistance Program
Cuban Refugee Emergency Center
Cuban Representation of Exiles
Cuban Women's Club*
Encuentro
Latin Affairs Division of Miami Dade County
Latin Builders Association, Inc.

Latin Chamber of Commerce*
Little Havana Activities Center*
National Hispanic Assembly of Florida
SABER, Inc.
Spanish American League Against Discrimination
Spanish Economic Development Corporation
Physician's Association of Clinics, Hospitals and Annex Medical Branch of the Cuban
  Confederation of Professionals in Exile
Puerto Rican Opportunity Center

GEORGIA

Latin American Association*

ILLINOIS

Casa Aztlan
Centro de Formación Politica
Hispanic American Committee for Professional Development
Illinois Federation of Hispanic Chambers of Commerce
Latin American Construction Contractors
Latin American Task Force
Latino Institute*
Latinos Unlimited
Mexican American Chamber of Commerce
Mexican American Chamber of Commerce and Industry of Chicago
Mexican American Council on Education
Midwest Institute of Puerto Rican Studies and Culture
Midwest Latino Council on Higher Education*
Mujeres Latinas en Accion
Spanish Action Committee of Chicago
Spanish Coalition for Jobs
State of Illinois Spanish Speaking Peoples Study Commission

INDIANA

Centro de Estudios Chicanos y Investigaciónes Sociales
Cuban Association, Inc.
Latin American Family Education
Mexican American Studies
Mexican Mutualist Society
Midwest Council of La Raza
Puerto Rican Benefit Society

KENTUCKY

Midwest Cuban Federation*

MARYLAND

American Association of Teachers of Spanish and Portuguese
Association of Cuban American Government Employees
Asociación Hispanamericana de Anne Arundel
Asociación Internacional de Hispanistas
Circulo Cubano
Club Argentino
Club Puerto Rico
Hora Hispana
Maryland Governor's Commission on Hispanic Affairs
Incorporated Mexican American Government Employees*
Parada de Banderas

MASSACHUSETTS

Alianza Hispana*
Council for Opportunity in Graduate Management Education
Inquilinos Boricuas en Acción*
National Latino Media Coalition*
Organización Estudiantil Boricua
Spanish American Center of Holyoke
Spanish American Center of Lowell
Spanish and American Union

MICHIGAN

Association of Chicanos for College Admission
Committee on Puerto Rican Affairs
Hispanic Republicans of Michigan, Inc.
Hispanic Women's Society
Hispanos Organized to Promote Entrepreneurs, Inc.*
Latin American Businessmen's Association
Latin American Community Association
Latin American Council for Western Michigan
Latin American International Steelworkers
Latin Americans for Social and Economic Development
Latin Americans United for Political Action
Latino Welfare Rights Organization
Michigan Spanish Speaking Democrats
National Chicano Research Network
Project Latino
Raza Advisory Committee to the Michigan State Board of Education
Renacimiento, Inc.
Spanish American Scholarship Committee
Spanish Speaking Information Center of Flint
State of Michigan Commission on Spanish Speaking Affairs

MINNESOTA

Mexican American Cultural and Educational Center
Spanish Speaking Cultural Club
State of Minnesota Spanish Speaking Affairs Council

MISSOURI

Hispanic Chamber of Commerce of Missouri
Mexican American Organization for Progress

NEBRASKA

Nebraska Mexican American Commission

NEVADA

Centro de Información Latino Americano*
Las Vegas Family Abuse Center, Inc.
Nevada Association of Latin Americans*
Nevada Latin Chamber of Commerce

NEW JERSEY

Commission for Puerto Rican Civil Rights
Community Organization for Puerto Rican Affairs
Cuban American Institute
Multi-Lingual Center
Puerto Rican Congress of New Jersey*
Puerto Rican Legal Committee*
Puerto Rican Youth Action, Inc.
Spanish Business Association
Tri-State Puerto Rican Congress*

NEW MEXICO

Albuquerque Hispano Chamber of Commerce
American G.I. Forum Auxiliary*
Association to Help Our Race Advance
National Chicana Institute

NEW YORK

Acción Presbiteriana Hispana, Inc.
American Association of Spanish Speaking People
American Council for Emigres in the Professions
American Spanish Committee
Arwak Consulting Corporation
Aspira of America, Inc.*

Association of Hispanic Arts, Inc.*
Center for Cuban Studies*
Center for Puerto Rican Studies*
Centro de Orientación Dominicano
Charas, Inc.
Coalition of Puerto Rican Women, Inc.*
Comité Estado 51, Puerto Rico*
Congress of Organizations of Puerto Rican Hometowns*
Council of Puerto Rican and Hispanic Organizations of the Lower East Side, Inc.
Council of Puerto Rican and Spanish American Organizations
Cuba Resource Center
Experimental and Bilingual Institute
Federación de Mujeres Cubanas
Grand Council of Hispanic Societies in Public Service
Hispanic American Family Civic Cultural Association
Hispanic American Ministries Commission
Hispanic American Veterans Association
Hispanic Businessmen's Association, Inc.
Hispanic Institute in the United States*
Institute of Contemporary Hispanic Arts
Interamerican College of Physicians and Surgeons
Ladies Committee for Puerto Rican Culture, Inc.
Latin Exchange
Liga de Acción Hispana
Metropolitan Spanish Merchants Co-op*
Mexican Chamber of Commerce of the United States*
Museo del Barrio
National Association for Bilingual Education*
National Association of Hispanic Civil Rights
National Association for Puerto Rican Civil Rights*
National Conference of Puerto Rican Women, Inc.*
National Congress of Puerto Rican Veterans
National Council of Hispanic Rights
National Council of Puerto Rican Volunteers
National Hispanic Amateur Athletic Council, Inc.*
National Puerto Rican Business and Marketing Association, Inc.*
National Puerto Rican Development and Training Institute, Inc.
National Puerto Rican Forum*
National Spanish Speaking Management Association
Puerto Rican Affirmation
Puerto Rican Association for Community Affairs*
Puerto Rican Bar Association of New York
Puerto Rican Center for the Arts
Puerto Rican Civil Service Employees Association
Puerto Rican College Graduates Association
Puerto Rican Community Council of East Harlem
Puerto Rican Community Development Project*
Puerto Rican Council Multi Service Center*

Puerto Rican Economic Development Council
Puerto Rican Engineers and Scientists Society, Inc.*
Puerto Rican Family Institute*
Puerto Rican Guidance Center
Puerto Rican Inter-Agency Council
Puerto Rican Leadership Alliance
Puerto Rican Legal Committee*
Puerto Rican Legal Defense and Education Fund, Inc.*
Puerto Rican Media Action and Education Council
Puerto Rican Solidarity Committee
Puerto Rican Sports Council
Puerto Rican Traveling Theater*
Puerto Rican Voters League
Realidades, Inc.
Society of Friends of Puerto Rico*
Society of Spanish Engineers, Planners and Architects*
Spanish American Feminists
Spanish Association of the Finger Lakes*
Spanish Chamber of Commerce of Queens*
United Puerto Rican and Spanish Organizations of Bay Ridge
United States Spanish Merchants Association

OHIO

Council of Spanish Speaking Organizations
Ladies Society Saint Rosa of Lima
Raza Unida de Ohio

OKLAHOMA

Asociación Liberación de Mexicanos Americanos

OREGON

Aguila, Inc.
Chicano Cultural Center
Oregon State Chicano Concilio

PENNSYLVANIA

Acción Puertoriqueña de Filadelfia
Congreso de Latinos Unidos, Inc.
Council of Spanish Speaking Organizations
Governor's Council on Opportunity for the Spanish Speaking
Latin American Congress of Pennsylvania
Ramos Antonini Development Center
Spanish Merchants Association of Philadelphia, Inc.
Taller Puertoriqueño, Inc.

TEXAS

Canto al Pueblo*
Centro Studies Program
Chicana Research and Learning Center
Chicano Alliance
Chicano Faculty Association
Chicano Legal Defense Fund
Chicano Teachers of English
Chicano Training Center
Chicano Studies Program
Chicanos Unidos de Central Texas
Club Sembradores de Amistad de Houston
Commission for Mexican American Affairs
Contratistas Unidos de Valle
Federation for the Advancement of the Mexican American
Hispanic American Institute
Hispanic Organization of Women
Federation for the Advancement of the Mexican American
Involvement of Mexican Americans in Gainful Endeavors
Juarez Lincoln University
League of United Latin American Citizens*
Mexican American Affairs
Mexican American Bar Association of El Paso
Mexican American Business and Professional Women's Club
Mexican American Business and Professional Women's Clubs of San Antonio
Mexican American Center for Economic Development
Mexican American Chamber of Commerce of Austin
Mexican American Chamber of Commerce Contractors Association
Mexican American Chamber of Commerce, Inc., of Forth Worth
Mexican American Chamber of Commerce of Corpus Christi
Mexican American Chamber of Commerce of Travis County
Mexican American Contractors Association
Mexican American Council for Economic Progress
Mexican American Cultural Center
Mexican American Democrats of Texas
Mexican American Economic Council
Mexican American Republicans of Texas
Mexican American Research Center
Mexican American Resources
Mexican American School Board Members Association
Mexican American Unity Council*
Mexican American Youth Organization
Movimiento Estudiantil Chicano de Aztlan*
Movimiento Familiar Cristiano
Mujeres pro Raza Unida
National Trabajadores de la Raza
Organización Chicano de Aztlan

Padres Asociados por Derechos Religiosos, Educativos, y Sociales*
Partido La Raza Unida*
Professional Organization of Mexican Americans in Communications
Political Action Spanish Organization
Puerto Rican Bar Association, Inc.
Raza Unida Women of Texas
Rio Grande Federation of Health Centers, Inc.
San Antonio Area Council of Spanish Speaking Program Coordinators
San Antonio Mexican Chamber of Commerce
SER–Jobs for Progress, Inc.
Southwest Voter Registration Education Project*
Spanish Toastmasters Clubs
Texas Association of Mexican American Chambers of Commerce
Texas Farmworkers Union Support Committee
Texas Institute for Educational Development
United States Hispanic Chamber of Commerce*

UTAH

Chicanas Unidas

VIRGINIA

Fairfax Community Action Program Spanish Outreach Program
Institute for the Study of Hispanic American Life and History
National Association of Puerto Rican Drug Abuse Programs
National Mexican American Anti-Defamation Committee
Puerto Rican American Women's League

WASHINGTON

Active Mexicanos
National Association of Spanish Speaking Spanish Surnamed Nurses*
Northwest Chicano Health Task Force
Northwest Rural Opportunities, Inc.*

WISCONSIN

Centro Hispano
Latin American Union for Civil Rights Foundation
Organización Hispana Americana
Spanish Centers of Racine, Kenosha, and Walworth, Inc.
United Migrant Opportunity Services, Inc.

WYOMING

Club Amistad

WASHINGTON, D.C.

Ayuda, Inc.
Chicana Caucus of the National Women's Political Caucus
Chicana Forum*
Círculo de Puerto Rico, Inc.*
Club Hispano de Prensa*
Concilio Nacional de Estudios Chicanos
Congreso Nacional de Asuntos Colegiales*
Congressional Hispanic Caucus*
Council of Hispanic Agencies
Cuban National Planning Council*
Educational Organization for United Latin Americans, Inc.
Forum of National Hispanic Organizations*
Greater Washington Ibero-American Chamber of Commerce*
Grupo de Artistas Latino Americanos*
Hispanic Counselors Caucus of the American Personnel and Guidance Association
Hispanic Organization of Professionals and Executives*
Labor Council for Latin American Advancement
Latin American Manufacturers Association*
Latin Committee for Civic Action
LULAC National Educational Service Centers, Inc.
Mexican American Women's National Association*
National Advisory Committee on Education of Spanish and Mexican Americans
National Alliance of Spanish Speaking People for Equality
National Association of Cuban American Women, Inc.*
National Association of Farmworkers Organizations———
National Association of Latino Elected and Appointed Officials*
National Association of Spanish Broadcasters
National Coalition of Cuban Americans
National Coalition of Hispanic Mental Health and Human Services Organizations*
National Concilio for Chicano Studies
National Council of La Raza*
National District of Columbia Council of Spanish Speaking Coordinators
National Economic Development Association
National Hispanic Cultural Commission
National Hispanic Housing Coalition, Inc.
National Hispanic Institute of Public Policy*
National Institute for Chicana Women
National Organization for Mexican American Services
National Spanish Speaking Housing Development Corporation
Puerto Rican Research and Resource Center, Inc.*
Puerto Rican Youth Public Policy Institute
Raza Association of Spanish Surnamed Americans
Republican National Hispanic Assembly of the United States*
Spanish American League Against Discrimination
Spanish Catholic Center
Unidad Hispana
Universidad Boricua
Secretariat for Hispanic Affairs*

Chronology

The listing that follows is a historical chronology for the three major Hispanic groups—Mexican Americans, Puerto Ricans, and Cuban Americans—as well as a listing of the founding dates for the organizations included in this volume. In this way, voluntary association activity can be compared with the historical context in which particular types of organizations were created. For instance, the political movement years of the 1960s and 1970s are heavily represented by issue-oriented and problem-solving agencies, while the earlier years represent periods of fraternity and mutual aid.

1200

Oldest known Indian settlement in the United States in Oraibi, Arizona, by the Hopi.

1492

Columbus reaches northern Cuba.

1493

Columbus discovers Puerto Rico.

16th century to 1898

Cuba is colonized by Spain.

1508

Ponce de León establishes the island of San Juan Bautista, naming its northern coast harbor Puerto Rico.

1539

Marcos de Niza, a Franciscan priest, is the first European known to have entered Arizona.

1610

Governor Pedro de Peralta establishes Santa Fe, New Mexico.

1769

Father Sera establishes the first California mission at San Diego.

1775

Francisco Garces, a friar, probably is the first white man to enter Nevada.

1776

Tucson, Arizona, is founded.

1794

Brothers of Our Father Jesus of Nazareth.

1820

The steam engine is introduced in Cuba as part of sugar production and expansion of the structure of production.

1824

Mexico becomes a republic and adopts its first constitution.

1824–92

Juan Cortina, military and political leader.

1828–85

Carlos Esparza, philosopher.

1830–67

Padre Antonio Martinez provides leadership in New Mexico.

1836

Texas declares its independence from Mexico.

1837

Railways are introduced in Cuba, completing large-scale sugar production capacity.

1841

New Mexicans defeat an invasion of Anglo Texans.

1842

On March 9, in what is now Newhall, near Los Angeles, Francisco Lopez discovers gold.

1846

On May 13, the United States declares war on Mexico.

1848

On February 2, the Treaty of Guadalupe Hidalgo is signed ending the Mexican American War. Mexico loses one-third of its territory to the United States.

1848–51

Narcisco Lopez attempts to liberate Cuba from Spain.

1848–76

Juan Cortina forms his La Raza Unida Party and organizes a movement.

1850s

In Nevada, Ignacio Parades establishes Mexican American settlements.

1853

The United States tries to purchase Cuba from Spain for $130 million.

1855

California establishes the "Greaser Act" against Mexican Americans.

1858

On July 13, in Brownsville, Texas, Juan Cortina shoots a city marshal for pistol whipping a Mexican American. This incident launches the Cortinista movement into warfare against the Texas Rangers.

1861–65

American Civil War.

1865

On May 12, General Santos Benavides defeats federal forces at Palmio Hill, near Brownsville, Texas. He wins the last battle of the Civil War.

1868

El Grito de Yara calls for Cuban independence and begins ten years of guerrilla warfare in which such notables as Antonio Maceo and Maximo Gomez participate.

1875

On January 23, in San Jose, California, Judge David Belden sentences Tiburcio Vasquez to death.

1876–92

Juan Cortina's exile in Mexico.

1877

Club Unión

1879

Sociedad Mutualista Benito Juarez

1886

Spain emancipates the slaves in Cuba.

1888–1905

Teresa Urrea carries out her evangelical mission to fight Diaz and give hope to the Mexican people.

1890s

Guante Negro Mutualista

1894

Alianza Hispano Americana.

1895

The Cuban War of Independence begins, with the government-in-exile headed by Tomas Estrada Palma and aided by Jose Martí, poet and journalist, who is killed in battle.

1898

The U.S.S. *Maine* blows up in Havana harbor.
The Spanish American War, followed by the Treaty of Paris on December 10, and U.S. annexation of Puerto Rico.

1900

The Foraker Act establishes the first civil government in Puerto Rico.
Spanish Foresters

1901

The Platt Amendment, which gives the United States the right to intervene in Cuba, is incorporated into the Cuban Constitution at U.S. insistence.

1902–06

Tomas Estrada Palma serves as first president of Cuba.

1907

On August 23, Ricardo Flores Magon and other members of the Mexican Liberal Party are arrested and beaten in Los Angeles.

1910

Leñadores del Mundo.
On November 20, Francisco Madero crosses from Texas into Mexico and starts the revolution that ends the Porfirio Diaz regime.
The mainland Puerto Rican population reaches 1,1513.
Orden de Caballeros de Honor

1911

On January 28, Ricardo Flores Magón captures Mexicali and controls the border region for six months.
Agrupación Protectiva Mexicana
Gran Liga Mexicanista de Beneficiencia y Protección

Liga Femenil Mexicanista
Primer Congreso Mexicanista

1913

Unión Patriótica Benéfica Mexicana Independiente

1914

Liga Protectora Mexicana

1914–18

World War I.

1916

Pancho Villa raids Columbus, New Mexico.

1917

On January 19, Germany's Zimmerman Note asks Mexico to join World War I to regain its lost land from the United States.
On June 27, in Bisbee, Arizona, 1,186 copper miners protest against labor abuses. They are raided out of the region by vigilantes and deported.
The Jones Act grants U.S. citizenship to Puerto Ricans and provides for popular election of both houses of the legislature and a resident commissioner.
Club Mexicano Independencia

1920

Hispanic Institute in the United States
Lázaro Cárdenas Society

1921

Liga Protectora Mexicana
Mexican Chamber of Commerce of the United States
Orden Hijos de America

1922

On November 21, Ricardo Flores Magón dies in the federal prison in Leavenworth, Kansas.

1925–33

The regime and tyranny of Gerardo Machado in Cuba.

1928

Confederación de Uniones Obreras Mexicanas.
League of United Latin American Citizens

1929

Sociedad Progresista Mexicana

1930

Five thousand farmworkers strike in the Imperial Valley, southern California.
The mainland Puerto Rican population reaches 53,000.
Depression causes reverse migration to Puerto Rico.

1932

On November 18, the *Los Angeles Times* reports that 11,000 local Mexican Americans have been forceably deported (500,000 deportees and repatriates left between 1930 and 1934, of which 150,000 were U.S. born or naturalized).

1933

Asociación de Jornaleros

1934

Abrogation of the Platt Amendment and the rise of Fulgencio Batista in Cuba through the "Sergeants' Revolt."

1934–59

Batista rules Cuba directly or indirectly and enriches himself.

1935

Frente Popular Mexicano

1938

Mexican Congress

1940–45

World War II cuts practically all movement between Puerto Rico and the United States.

1943

On June 9, servicemen attack Mexican American youths in San Diego, California, as "Zootsuit Riots" develop.

1945

With the end of World War II, great migration begins from Puerto Rico.
Secretariat for Hispanic Affairs

1947

Congress amends Act of 1917 granting Puerto Ricans the right to elect their own governor.
Community Service Organizations

1947–48

Laws enacted regulating recruitment of Puerto Rican farm laborers to the mainland.

1948

Luís Muñoz Marín inaugurates a program of economic development in Puerto Rico.
American G.I. Forum
Office of the Commonwealth of Puerto Rico

1949

Luís Muñoz Marín is elected first governor of Puerto Rico by popular vote.
Asociación Nacional México Americana

1950s

Movement from Puerto Rico to the mainland increases. The Puerto Rican Forum is
    founded to promote interests of Puerto Ricans in New York City.

1952

On July 25, Constitution Day, the Free Associated State of Puerto Rico is established,
    providing commonwealth status to Puerto Rico.

1953

On July 26, Fidel Castro and his followers attack Moncada Barracks in Cuba.
Council of Mexican American Affairs
Vesta Club, Inc.

1955

Azteca Club

mid-1950s

Puerto Rican Merchants Association

1956

Eighty-two men led by Fidel Castro land on Cuba to overthrow Batista.
Society of Friends of Puerto Rico

1957

Círculo de Puerto Rico, Inc.
National Puerto Rican Forum

1958

Congress of Organizations of Puerto Rican Hometowns
Mexican American Political Association

1959

On July 26, Batista flees Cuba. On January 1, Castro's guerrillas march into Havana.

1959–62

The first stage of Cuban migration to the United States begins in January 1959 and ends
    in October 1962 with the cancelation of commercial flights.

1960

American Puerto Rican Action League
Grand Council of Hispanic Societies in Public Service
Political Association of Spanish Speaking Organizations

1961

On January 3, the United States breaks diplomatic relations with Cuba.
The Bay of Pigs invasion and defeat.
Aspira of America, Inc.
College of Architects of Cuba in Exile Association

1962

On September 30, in Fresno, California, César Chavez establishes the National Farm
    Workers Association, later to become the United Farmworkers of America.
On June 28, the Migration and Refugee Assistance Act, Public Law 87-510, authorizes
    funds for the Cuban Refugee Program.

1962–65

The second stage of Cuban migration to the United States occurs between October 1962
    and December 1965, largely through unconventional means.

1963

A commission on the status of Puerto Rico is appointed by the U.S. Congress.
Alianza Federal de Pueblos Libres

1964

Latin American Research and Service Agency
Mexican American Community Services Agency
Puerto Rican Community Development Project

1965

The Civil Rights Act rules out literacy tests for Puerto Rican voter registration in New
    York City. The Puerto Rican Community Development Program is funded by the Office
    of Economic Opportunity in New York.
Association for Puerto Rican-Hispanic Culture, Inc.
Association of Mexican American Educators
Camara de Comercio Latina de los Estados Unidos
Latin Chamber of Commerce

1965–73

The third stage of Cuban migration to the United States occurs between October 1965
    and April 1973 on commercial flights.

1966

Report submitted by the Commission on the Status of Puerto Rico to the U.S. Congress
    calls for a plebiscite on the issue of civil status.
Crusade for Justice
Houston Cuban Association
Movimiento Estudiantil Chicano de Aztlan
United Council of Spanish Speaking Organizations

1967

In July, a plebiscite chooses the Free Associated State of Puerto Rico. *Down These Mean Streets* by Piri Thomas is published.
There is a riot in New York's "El Barrio."
Casa de Puerto Rico, Inc.
Metropolitan Spanish Merchants Co-op
Mexican American Legal Defense and Education Fund
Mexican American Unity Council
Midwest Cuban Federation
Puerto Rican Traveling Theater

1968

The Popular Party splits into two parties, causing Luis Ferre and the New Party, which are committed to Puerto Rican statehood, to win the elections. The Young Lords, a militant Puerto Rican youth group in New York City, is formed.
Arizona Mexican American Chamber of Commerce
East Los Angeles Community Union
Inquilinos Boricuas en Acción
Interstate Research Associates
Liceo Cubano
National Council of La Raza
Nevada Association of Latin Americans
Puerto Rican Hispanic Youth Coalition, Inc.
Young Lords Organization

1969

A citizens voter registration campaign in the city of New York registers blacks and Puerto Ricans.
Alianza Hispana
Chicanos por la Causa, Inc.
Northwest Rural Opportunities, Inc.
Padres Asociados por Derechos Religiosos, Educativos, y Sociales
Puerto Rican Congress of New Jersey

1970

On August 29, in Los Angeles, the National Chicano Moratorium demonstrates against the Vietnam War. A riot ensues when police attack the demonstrators. Journalist Ruben Salazar is killed by a deputy sheriff.
Herman Badillo is elected the first Puerto Rican U.S. congressman.
Association for the Advancement of Mexican Americans
Comisión Femenil Mexicana Nacional
Communities Organized for Public Service
Confederación de Profesionales Cubanos
Hermanas
National Association of Psychologists for La Raza
Partido La Raza Unida
Vikki Carr Scholarship Foundation
Young Lords Party

1971   *1969 First Women's International Women's Conference*

On July 26, Reies Lopez Tijerina is freed from Springfield Prison in New Mexico after
  serving three years for fighting government use of land grants.
Asociación Los Viejos Utiles
Congreso Nacional de Asuntos Colegiales
Cuban Liceum of Detroit
Incorporated Mexican American Government Employees
Institute of Puerto Rican Unity
National Congress of Hispanic American Citizens
National Latino Media Coalition
Personnel Management Association of Aztlan
Puerto Rican Family Institute
Puerto Rican Legal Defense and Education Fund, Inc.
Reforma National Association to Promote Library Services to the Spanish Speaking

Chicano moratorium San fron 1969

1972

American Association of Spanish Speaking Certified Public Accountants
Center for Cuban Studies
Centro de Servicios para Hispanos
Chicana Service Action Center, Inc.
Cuban National Planning Council
Latin American Association
National Association for Chicano Studies
National Association of Cuban American Women
National Conference of Puerto Rican Women, Inc.
National Hispanic Amateur Athletic Council, Inc.
Raza National Bar Association

1973

Latin American Manufacturers Association
Little Havana Activities Center

1974

On September 28, California Governor Ronald Reagan vetoes a bill, stopping farm
  laborers from receiving unemployment compensation. Governor Reagan also vetoes a
  bill that would have prevented further child labor violations.
Asociación Nacional de Grupos Folkloricos
Latino Institute
Mexican American Business and Professional Women's Club
Mexican American Engineering Society
Mexican American Women's National Association
National Association of Spanish Speaking Spanish Surnamed Nurses
National Coalition of Hispanic Mental Health and Human Services Organizations
National Puerto Rican Business and Marketing Association
Puerto Rican Legal Committee
Society of Hispanic Professional Engineers

1975

Raul Castro becomes the first Mexican American governor of Arizona since statehood was granted in 1912.
Jerry Apodaca is elected the first Mexican American governor of New Mexico since 1918.
Asociación Nacional pro Persones Mayores
Association of Hispanic Arts, Inc.
CAFE de California, Inc.
Centro de Información Latino Americano
Forum of National Hispanic Organizations
National Association for Bilingual Education
National Association of Latino Elected and Appointed Officials
National Chicano Council on Higher Education
Republican National Hispanic Assembly of the United States
Society of Spanish Engineers, Planners and Architects
Southwest Voter Registration Education Project
United Neighborhoods Organizations

1976

The Cuban Refugee Program is phased out.
Chicana Forum
Chicano Alliance of Drug Abuse Programs
Congressional Hispanic Caucus
Grupo de Artistas Latino Americanos
Latin American Chamber of Commerce of Nevada, Inc.
Mexican American Women's Political Caucus

1977

Association of Chicana-Latina Nurses
California Coalition of Hispanic Organizations
Canto al Pueblo
Congreso de Latinos Unidos
Federation of Hispanic Organizations of the Baltimore Metropolitan Area, Inc.
Greater Washington Ibero-American Chamber of Commerce

1977–79

Carmen Delgado Votaw, a Puerto Rican feminist, serves as President Carter's appointee to cochair the National Commission on Women. She resigns along with cochair Bella Abzug in protest over Carter's stands on women's issues.

1978

Hispanic Higher Education Coalition
Kansas State University Mexican American Alumni Association
National Hispanic Institute of Public Policy
Tri-State Puerto Rican Congress

1979

Cuban exile relations with Cuba are established.
Chicana Coalition
Círculo de Cultura Cubano, Inc.
Club Hispano de Prensa
Hispanic Postal Employees and Friends
Instituto Internacional de Cooperación y Solidaridad Cubana, Inc.
United States Hispanic Chamber of Commerce

1980

Over 2,000 Hispanic women gather in San Jose, California, for the First National Hispanic
    Feminist Conference, where the predominantly Mexican American participants unite
    with other Hispanics to propose a feminist agenda for the future.
The Mariel exodus from Cuba.
Comité Estado 51, Puerto Rico
Hispanic Health Council
Midwest Latino Council on Higher Education
National Puerto Rican Coalition

1981

Richard Rodriquez's critically acclaimed *Hunger of Memory* angers the Mexican American
    community by advocating assimilation strategies for minorities. Psychologically pain-
    ful, the book is widely reviewed by both Anglo and Mexican American critics in such
    public forums as the *New York Times Book Review*, but with insightfully divergent
    perspectives from each group.
National Congress for Puerto Rican Rights

1982

Acción '80's

1983

Hispanic Professional Action Committee

1984

The Simpson-Mazzoli Immigration Reform Bill passes the House of Representatives, to
    the consternation of Hispanics, reflecting a rising tide of anti-immigration sentiment
    generated by President Reagan's articulated need for "controlling the borders."

The following are organizations included in this volume for which the reference literature
gives no founding date.

Center for Puerto Rican Studies
Centro Chileno Lautaro
Club Arpa
Coalición de Boricuas, Inc.
Coalition of Federal Hispanic Employee Organizations
Coalition of Puerto Rican Women

Colonia Holguinera
Cuban Association, Inc.
Cuban Dental Association in Exile
Cuban Medical Association in Exile
Cuban Women's Club
Hispanic Organization of Professionals and Executives
Hispanics Organized to Promote Entrepreneurs, Inc.
National Association for Puerto Rican Civil Rights
National Association of Puerto Rican Drug Abuse Programs
National Hispanic Bar Association
Orden Fraternal Hijos de Puerto Rico
Puerto Rican Association for Community Affairs
Puerto Rican Council Multi Service Center
Puerto Rican Engineers and Scientists Society, Inc.
Puerto Rican Organization for Women
Puerto Rican Research and Resources Center, Inc.
Red, La
Spanish American Cultural Club
Spanish Association of the Finger Lakes
Spanish Chamber of Commerce of Queens
Spanish Speaking Cultural Club
Western Regional Puerto Rican Council

Organization Functions

This section suggests the types of voluntary associations historically developed among Hispanic communities. In some cases, the category represents the only function of the organization; in others, the specialization indicates only one—but an important one—organizational activity or commitment. In cases where there are overlapping functions, the organization is listed under more than one category.

The categories listed in this volume were devised by me for purposes of this work, although they do parallel those found in similar works. But because of the uniqueness of this first effort, it was necessary to identify categories in keeping with the historical and functional evolution of Hispanic voluntary associations. In an attempt to categorize all of the organizations included in this volume, some associations may be narrowly defined categorically whereas their true function may be broader than indicated here. Also, in the case of the earlier fraternal and mutual aid societies, most were Masonic lodges or affiliates. A separate category is not listed in this section under Masonry because it was felt that the Masonic-influenced altruism of these early organizations led them to initiate other first-priority functions.

ADVOCACY

Acción '80's
Alianza Federal de Pueblos Libres
American G.I. Forum
Casa de Puerto Rico, Inc.
Center for Cuban Studies
Chicana Coalition
Comité Estado 51, Puerto Rico
Communities Organized for Public Service
Crusade for Justice
Gran Liga Mexicanista de Beneficiencia y Protección
Guante Negro Mutualista
Hispanic Professional Action Committee
Lázaro Cárdenas Society

League of United Latin American Citizens
Mexican American Women's National Association
Mexican Congress
National Association of Cuban American Women
National Conference of Puerto Rican Women, Inc.
National Congress for Puerto Rican Rights
National Council of La Raza
Office of the Commonwealth of Puerto Rico
Puerto Rican Congress of New Jersey
Tri-State Puerto Rican Congress
United Neighborhoods Organization
Western Regional Puerto Rican Council
Young Lords Organization
Young Lords Party

AGING

Asociación Los Viejos Útiles
Asociación Nacional pro Personas Mayores

ARTS AND CULTURAL

Asociación Nacional de Grupos Folkloricos
Association for Puerto Rican-Hispanic Culture, Inc.
Association of Hispanic Arts, Inc.
Canto al Pueblo
Grupo de Artistas Latino Americanos
Puerto Rican Traveling Theater
Society of Friends of Puerto Rico

ATHLETIC

National Hispanic Amateur Athletic Council, Inc.

BUSINESS

Arizona Mexican American Chamber of Commerce
Camara de Comercio Latina de los Estados Unidos
Chicana Forum
Greater Washington Ibero-American Chamber of Commerce
Hispano Organized to Promote Entrepreneurs, Inc.
Latin American Chamber of Commerce of Nevada, Inc.
Latin American Manufacturers Association
Latin Chamber of Commerce
Metropolitan Spanish Merchants Co-op
- Mexican Chamber of Commerce of the United States
National Puerto Rican Business and Marketing Association
Puerto Rican Merchants Association

Spanish Chamber of Commerce of Queens
United States Hispanic Chamber of Commerce

CIVIC

CAFE de California, Inc.
Coalition of Federal Hispanic Employee Organizations
Hispanic Postal Employees and Friends
Incorporated Mexican American Government Employees
Leñadores del Mundo

COALITION

California Coalition of Hispanic Organizations
Coalition of Federal Hispanic Employee Organizations
Council of Mexican American Affairs
Federation of Hispanic Organizations of the Baltimore Metropolitan Area, Inc.
Forum of National Hispanic Organizations
Grand Council of Hispanic Societies in Public Service
Hispanic Higher Education Coalition
Mexican Congress
Midwest Cuban Federation
National Council of La Raza
National Puerto Rican Coalition
Primer Congreso Mexicanista

COMMUNITY SERVICE

Alianza Hispana
American Puerto Rican Action League
Centro de Información Latino Americano
Centro de Servicios para Hispanos
Chicana Service Action Center, Inc.
Chicanos por la Causa, Inc.
Coalición de Boricuas, Inc.
Comisión Femenil Mexicana Nacional
Community Service Organization
Congreso de Latinos Unidos
Congress of Organizations of Puerto Rican Hometowns
Crusade for Justice
Cuban National Planning Council
East Los Angeles Community Union
Institute of Puerto Rican Unity
Interstate Research Associates
Latin American Association
Latin American Research and Service Agency
Little Havana Activities Center
Mexican American Community Services Agency

Mexican American Unity Council
National Association for Puerto Rican Civil Rights
National Puerto Rican Forum
Nevada Association of Latin Americans
Office of the Commonwealth of Puerto Rico
Puerto Rican Association for Community Affairs
Puerto Rican Community Development Project
Puerto Rican Council Multi Service Center
Puerto Rican Family Institute
Spanish Association of the Finger Lakes
Spanish Speaking Cultural Club
Tri-State Puerto Rican Congress
United Council of Spanish Speaking Organizations

EDUCATION

Aspira of America, Inc.
Association of Mexican American Educators
Center for Puerto Rican Studies
Círculo de Cultura Cubano, Inc.
Club Unión
Congreso Nacional de Asuntos Colegiales
Hispanic Higher Education Coalition
Hispanic Institute in the United States
Kansas State University Mexican American Alumni Association
Liga Femenil Mexicanista
Midwest Latino Council on Higher Education
Movimiento Estudiantil Chicano de Aztlan
National Association for Bilingual Education
National Association for Chicano Studies
National Chicano Council on Higher Education
Vesta Club, Inc.
Vikki Carr Scholarship Foundation

FRATERNAL

Alianza Hispano Americano
Brothers of Our Father Jesus of Nazareth
Círculo de Puerto Rico, Inc.
Leñadores del Mundo
Orden de Caballeros de Honor
Orden Hijos de America

HEALTH

Association of Chicana-Latina Nurses
Chicano Alliance of Drug Abuse Programs
Hispanic Health Council
National Association of Psychologists for La Raza

National Association of Puerto Rican Drug Abuse Programs
National Association of Spanish Speaking Spanish Surnamed Nurses
National Coalition of Hispanic Mental Health and Human Services Organizations

LABOR

Asociación de Jornaleros
Asociación Nacional México Americana
Confederación de Uniones Obreras Mexicanos
Frente Popular Mexicano
Liga Protectora Mexicana
United Farmworkers of America

LEGAL

Mexican American Legal Defense and Education Fund
National Hispanic Bar Association
Puerto Rican Legal Committee
Purto Rican Legal Defense and Education Fund, Inc.
Raza National Bar Association

LOBBY

Congressional Hispanic Caucus
National Association of Latino Elected and Appointed Officials
National Congress of Hispanic American Citizens

MEDIA

Club Hispano de Prensa
National Latino Media Coalition

MIGRANT

Northwest Rural Opportunities, Inc.

MUTUAL AID

Agrupación Protectiva Mexicana
Alianza Hispano Americana
Azteca Club
Brothers of Our Father Jesus of Nazareth
Club Mexicano Independencia
Lázaro Cárdenas Society
Sociedad Mutualista Benito Juarez
Sociedad Progresista Mexicana
Spanish Foresters
Unión Patriótica Benéfica Mexicana Independiente

POLITICAL ACTION

Mexican American Political Association
Partido La Raza Unida
Political Association of Spanish Speaking Organizations
Republican National Hispanic Assembly of the United States
Southwest Voter Registration Education Project
Young Lords Party

PROFESSIONAL

American Association of Spanish-Speaking Certified Public Accountants
College of Architects of Cuba in Exile Association
Confederación de Profesionales Cubanos
Cuban Dental Association in Exile
Cuban Medical Association in Exile
Hispanic Organization of Professionals and Executives
Mexican American Business and Professional Women's Club
Mexican American Engineering Society
Personnel Management Association of Aztlan
Puerto Rican Engineers and Scientists Society, Inc.
Reforma National Association to Promote Library Services to the Spanish Speaking
Society of Hispanic Professional Engineers
Society of Spanish Engineers, Planners and Architects

REFUGEE ASSISTANCE

Instituto Internacional de Cooperación y Solidaridad Cubana, Inc.
Liga Protectora Latina

RELIGIOUS

Centro de Servicios para Hispanos
Hermanas
Padres Asociados por Derechos Religiosos, Educativos, y Sociales
Secretariat for Hispanic Affairs
United Neighborhoods Organization

RESEARCH

Casa de Puerto Rico, Inc.
Interstate Research Associates
Latin American Research and Service Agency
Latino Institute
National Hispanic Institute of Public Policy
Puerto Rican Research and Resources Center, Inc.

SOCIAL

Centro Chileño Lautaro
Club Arpa

Colonia Holguinera
Cuban Association, Inc.
Cuban Liceum of Detroit
Houston Cuban Association
Liceo Cubano
Orden Fraternal Hijos de Puerto Rico
Spanish American Cultural Club

TENANTS RIGHTS

Inquilinos Boricuas en Acción
Puerto Rican Council Multi Service Center

YOUTH

Association for the Advancement of Mexican Americans
Puerto Rican Hispanic Youth Coalition, Inc.

VETERANS

American G.I. Forum

WOMEN

Chicana Coalition
Chicana Service Action Center, Inc.
Coalition of Puerto Rican Women
Comisión Femenil Mexicana Nacional
Cuban Women's Club
Liga Femenil Mexicanista
Mexican American Business and Professional Women's Club
Mexican American Women's National Association
Mexican American Women's Political Caucus
National Association of Cuban American Women
National Conference of Puerto Rican Women, Inc.
Puerto Rican Organization for Women

Index

About the Author

SYLVIA ALICIA GONZALES is an Educational Consultant in Tucson, Arizona. She is the author of *Que Tal Anthology* and *La Chicana Piensa* and has contributed articles and chapters to *Nuestro, Comparative Perspectives of Third World Women, Frontiers, The Chicano Literary World 1974, The Chicanos as We See Ourselves,* and *Women's Studies: An Interdisciplinary Collection.*